D0011493

THE ONE WHO IS TO COME

The One Who Is to Come

by

Joseph A. Fitzmyer, S.J.

WILLIAM B. EERDMANS PUBLISHING COMPANY
GRAND RAPIDS, MICHIGAN / CAMBRIDGE, U.K.

© 2007 Joseph A. Fitzmyer, S.J.

All rights reserved

Published 2007 by
Wm. B. Eerdmans Publishing Co.
2140 Oak Industrial Drive N.E., Grand Rapids, Michigan 49505 /
P.O. Box 163, Cambridge CB3 9PU U.K.

Library of Congress Cataloging-in-Publication Data

Fitzmyer, Joseph A.
    The One who is to come / by Joseph A. Fitzmyer.
        p.   cm.
    Includes indexes.
    ISBN 978-0-8028-4013-4 (pbk.: alk. paper)
    1. Messiah — Prophecies. 2. Bible. O.T. — Criticism, interpretation, etc.
    3. Messiah — Biblical teaching. 4. Messiah — Judaism.   I. Title.

    BT235.F58   2007
    232′.12 — dc22

                                        2006034541

www.eerdmans.com

Contents

CONTENTS

Preface

The title of this book is taken from the question that John the Baptist's disciples ask of Jesus of Nazareth, "Are you the one who is to come?" (Matt 11:3; Luke 7:19), and resembles the title of the English version of a book written by the Norwegian scholar Sigmund Mowinckel, *He That Cometh.*[1] I imitate the title of Mowinckel's book because of the great influence his book has had in recent decades in the study of messianism and because of much that I have learned from it. The reader will also notice how my discussion at times parallels that of Mowinckel or summarizes his treatment.

In borrowing the title, I also hope to offer a corrective to the use of the word "Messiah" and "messianic" in Mowinckel's book, especially for a number of Old Testament passages that Mowinckel has treated. At times Mowinckel was critical of other scholars (e.g., Gressmann, Sellin) because, though they acknowledged that some psalms or other Old Testament passages spoke of a Davidic king with mythical or superhuman traits, they did not recognize that those passages were not dealing with "an *eschatological* figure." Mowinckel himself admits at the outset that "'Messiah', 'the Anointed One', as a title or technical term for the king of the final age, does not even occur in the Old Testament,"[2] but then he goes on to use it in a broader sense at times, which creates a difficulty. In doing so, Mowinckel

---

1. *Han som kommer* (Copenhagen: C. E. G. Gad, 1951); in English, *He That Cometh,* trans. G. W. Anderson (Nashville: Abingdon, 1956; repr. BRS. Grand Rapids: Wm. B. Eerdmans, 2005).

2. Mowinckel, *He That Cometh,* 4.

claims to be adopting "early Church" usage, but he then anachronistically reads back into certain Old Testament passages Christian "messianic" meanings. Thus, he fails to respect the history of ideas and the proper delineation of how the notion of a promised Coming One, even an Anointed One, gradually developed into that of a Messiah as an expected anointed "king of the final age." As a result, the terms "Messiah," "messianic," and "messianism" have been given a rubber-band comprehension, so that even "the Servant of the Lord" and "the Son of Man" are said to be "messianic" figures in pre-Christian Judaism.[3] Many other writers in recent times, especially Christian writers, have done the same.

There have been, however, a number of writers who also have criticized this way of reading the Old Testament and its so-called messianic prophecies or messianic expectations. Even the first part of Mowinckel's book is critical of this way of reading it. To this mode of critical interpretation I intend to add the discussion in this book.

Let it be said at the outset that I have no difficulty in imitating "early Church" usage and in seeing Jesus of Nazareth as "the Son of Man," "the Servant of the Lord," and even as "the suffering Messiah," because New Testament writers have predicated all these titles of him, sometimes distinctively and sometimes in conjunction with others, so that they all become titles of him who is for Christians "the Messiah." Hence, in Christian usage, "Son of Man," "Son of God," and "Servant of the Lord" can be called messianic titles. The problem, however, is whether such titles were used in a "messianic" sense in *pre-Christian Judaism,* in the Old Testament or in other pre-Christian Jewish writings.

Moreover, I reckon with the Old Testament as part of the Christian canon and recognize that that canonical relationship is important for Christian interpretation. Moreover, since there is at least one passage in the writings of that testament that reveals the emergence of messianism within its ambit, it becomes the prelude for the fact that the New Testament predicates that title of Jesus of Nazareth. One has to respect, however, the historical development within the Old Testament itself and not anachronistically use the later term to describe passages that may only be

---

3. Mowinckel discusses these titles on pp. 187-257 and 346-450. Of the first title he says that "these prophecies were not intended to be Messianic, but . . . Jesus gave them decisive importance for the concept of the Messiah" (p. 187). That, however, is to use a later adoption of the title and derive from it a "decisive importance for the concept of Messiah," which has not yet emerged.

building toward such an emergence. One cannot foist a later Christian meaning on a passage that was supposed to have a distinctive religious sense in guiding the Jewish people of old.[4]

A Christian interpreter of the Old Testament should be able to agree with a contemporary Jewish interpreter of the Hebrew Scriptures on the literal meaning of a given passage, even one mentioning *māšîăḥ*, or one related to such a concept, before the Christian invokes his or her canonical meaning. After all, the extent of the writings that the Jewish interpreter regards as the written word of God is identical with the Old Testament that the Christian interpreter seeks to expound.[5] For the Christian canonical sense of the Old Testament is a "plus," a sense added to the literal meaning of the Old Testament. That meaning may be a "closed" meaning for the Jewish interpreter, but it remains "open" for the Christian interpreter, who has to reckon with the literal meaning in its historical formulation and take into account all the aspects that it may have that allow it to be "open" to the subsequent Christian interpretation.

My intention, then, is to review the data brought forth by Mowinckel and others in order to put them into what I regard as the proper historical perspective so that one can see how the biblical tradition about a Coming One gradually developed in pre-Christian Judaism and fed into the Jewish tradition about a coming "Messiah." Once messianism in the true sense emerged in that tradition, it also fed into the early Church's tradition about Jesus of Nazareth as God's Messiah, or "Jesus Christ." This is, then, an attempt to respect properly the history of ideas and to reckon with the late emergence of the concept of Messiah in pre-Christian Judaism.

In this regard, new data have also contributed to the discussion of developing messianism because of the discovery of the Dead Sea Scrolls. Only a small portion of such data would have been available to Mowinckel, whose book was published in 1951, before the discovery of Qumran Caves

4. For this reason, I would not agree with the approach of writers who speak of "the christology of the Old Testament" (e.g., H. Cazelles, *Le Messie de la Bible: Christologie de l'Ancien Testament.* Collection 'Jésus et Jésus-Christ' 7 [Paris: Desclée, 1978]; A. J. Maas, *Christ in Type and Prophecy,* 2 vols. [New York: Benziger Bros., 1893-96]; D. J. Reimer, "Old Testament Christology," in *King and Messiah in Israel and the Ancient Near East: Proceedings of the Oxford Old Testament Seminar,* ed. J. Day. JSOTSup 270 [Sheffield: Sheffield Academic, 1998] 380-400).

5 Prescinding, obviously, from the difference of Protestant, Orthodox, and Roman Catholic canons.

2-11.[6] Many are the articles and books that have been devoted to Qumran messianism, which is an important stage in our knowledge about this historical development in Judaism.

Lastly, I have to record here my gratitude to those who have assisted me during the research and writing of this book. I am indebted above all to James P. M. Walsh, S.J., who read an earlier form of this book and commented on many aspects of its discussion. If this discussion has any merit, no little part of it has come from his comments. I am also indebted to J. Leon Hooper, S.J., director of the Woodstock Theological Library, housed at Georgetown University, and to members of his staff for the help graciously given to me as I made use of the library's resources. Finally, I owe a debt of thanks to Allen C. Myers and other members of the Wm. B. Eerdmans publishing staff who brought my manuscript into book form.

Joseph A. Fitzmyer, S.J.
Professor Emeritus, Biblical Studies
Catholic University of America
Resident at the Jesuit Community,
Georgetown University
Washington, DC 20057-1200

6. Neither the author's preface to the English version (1954) nor the translator's preface makes any mention of changes in the text of the book because of this discovery. There are, however, references to a few Qumran texts, which became known in the early 1950s (see pp. 201, 289, 301, 356, 417, 464).

Abbreviations

General Abbreviations

AB	Anchor Bible
ABD	*Anchor Bible Dictionary.* Ed. D. N. Freedman. 6 vols. New York: Doubleday, 1992
ABRL	Anchor Bible Reference Library
ACEBTSup	Amsterdamse cahiers voor exegese van de Bijbel en zijn traditie Supplement
AGJU	Arbeiten zur Geschichte des antiken Judentums und des Urchristentums
AnBib	Analecta biblica
ANET	*Ancient Near Eastern Texts Relating to the Old Testament.* Ed. J. B. Pritchard. Princeton: Princeton University Press, 1950
Ant.	Josephus, *Antiquities of the Jews*
AOT	*The Apocryphal Old Testament.* Ed. H. F. D. Sparks. Oxford: Clarendon, 1984
APOT	*The Apocrypha and Pseudepigrapha of the Old Testament in English.* Ed. R. H. Charles. 2 vols. Oxford: Clarendon, 1913
ASE	*Annali di storia dell'esegesi*
ATA	Alttestamentliche Abhandlungen
ATR	*Anglican Theological Review*
AuOr	*Aula orientalis*
b.	*Babylonian Talmud* (followed by name of the tractate)
BAR	*Biblical Archaeology Review*
BBB	Bonner biblische Beiträge
BBR	*Bulletin for Biblical Research*

BETL	Bibliotheca ephemeridum theologicarum lovaniensium
BFCT	Beiträge zur Förderung christlicher Theologie
Bib	*Biblica*
BJRL	*Bulletin of the John Rylands Library*
BK	*Bibel und Kirche*
BKAT	Biblischer Kommentar, Altes Testament
BN	*Biblische Notizen*
BRev	*Bible Review*
BRS	Biblical Resource Series
BSac	*Bibliotheca Sacra*
BWANT	Beiträge sur Wissenschaft vom Alten und Neuen Testament
BZ	*Biblische Zeitschrift*
BZAW	Beihefte zur *ZAW*
CahRB	Cahiers de la *RB*
CahT	Cahiers théologiques
CBET	Contributions to Biblical Exegesis and Theology
CBQ	*Catholic Biblical Quarterly*
CBQMS	Catholic Biblical Quarterly Monograph Series
ConBOT	Coniectanea biblica: Old Testament Series
CSEL	Corpus scriptorum ecclesiasticorum latinorum
DJD	Discoveries in the Judaean Desert
DSD	*Dead Sea Discoveries*
EBib	Etudes bibliques
EDSS	*Encyclopedia of the Dead Sea Scrolls.* Ed. L. H. Schiffman and J. C. VanderKam. 2 vols. Oxford: Oxford University Press, 2000
EncJud	*Encyclopaedia Judaica,* 16 vols. New York: Macmillan and Jerusalem: Keter, 1971-72
ErIsr	*Eretz-Israel*
ESBNT	Fitzmyer, J. A. *Essays on the Semitic Background of the New Testament,* London: Chapman, 1971; repr., Missoula: Scholars, 1974. See *SBNT*
EvT	*Evangelische Theologie*
ExpTim	*Expository Times*
FAT	Forschungen zum Alten Testament
Frg	*Fragmentary Targum* (= *Targum Yerushalmi II*)
FRLANT	Forschungen zur Religion und Literatur des Alten und Neuen Testaments
GCS	Griechische christliche Schriftsteller
GHB	Joüon, P. *Grammaire de l'hébreu biblique,* 2nd ed. Rome: Pontifical Biblical Institute, 1947
HALOT	Koehler, L., W. Baumgartner, and J. J. Stamm. *The Hebrew and*

	Aramaic Lexicon of the Old Testament. 5 vols. Leiden: Brill, 1994-2000
HAR	*Hebrew Annual Review*
HAT	Handbuch zum Alten Testament
Herm	Hermeneia
HS	*Hebrew Studies*
HSM	Harvard Semitic Monographs
HTR	*Harvard Theological Review*
HUCA	*Hebrew Union College Annual*
IDB	*Interpreter's Dictionary of the Bible.* Ed. G. A. Buttrick. 4 vols. Nashville: Abingdon, 1962
IEJ	Israel Exploration Journal
j.	*Jerusalem Talmud* (followed by name of the tractate)
JBC	*The Jerome Biblical Commentary.* Ed. R. E. Brown, J. A. Fitzmyer, and R. E. Murphy. Englewood Cliffs: Prentice-Hall, 1968
JBL	*Journal of Biblical Literature*
JBT	*Jahrbuch für biblische Theologie*
JJS	*Journal of Jewish Studies*
JNSL	*Journal of the Northwest Semitic Languages*
JQR	*Jewish Quarterly Review*
JRR	*Journal from the Radical Reformation*
JSJ	*Journal for the Study of Judaism in the Persian, Hellenistic and Roman Periods*
JSOT	*Journal for the Study of the Old Testament*
JSOTSup	Supplements to the *JSOT*
JSPSup	Journal for the Study of the Pseudepigrapha Supplement
JSQ	*Jewish Studies Quarterly*
JTS	*Journal of Theological Studies*
J.W.	Josephus, *Jewish War*
KBL	Koehler, L., and W. Baumgartner. *Lexicon in Veteris Testamenti Libros.* 2 vols. 2nd ed. Leiden: Brill, 1958
LCL	Loeb Classical Library
LD	Lectio divina
LQ	*Lutheran Quarterly*
LXX	Septuagint
m.	Mishnah (followed by name of the tractate)
Mowinckel, *He That Cometh*	Mowinckel, Sigmund. *He That Cometh.* 1956; repr. BRS. Grand Rapids: Wm. B. Eerdmans, 2005
MT	Masoretic Text
Mur	Murabbaʿat
NAB	New American Bible

NCBC	New Century Bible Commentary
Neof	*Targum Neofiti 1*
NICOT	New International Commentary on the Old Testament
NIV	New International Version
NJV	New Jewish Version
NovT	*Novum Testamentum*
NRSV	New Revised Standard Version
NTS	*New Testament Studies*
OBO	Orbis biblicus et orientalis
Onq	*Targum Onqelos*
OT	Old Testament
OTL	Old Testament Library
OTP	*The Old Testament Pseudepigrapha*. Ed. J. H. Charlesworth. 2 vols. Garden City: Doubleday, 1983-85
OtSt	Oudtestamentische Studiën
PsJ	*Targum Pseudo-Jonathan (= Targum Yerushalmi I)*
PTSDSSP	The Princeton Theological Seminary Dead Sea Scrolls Project. Ed. J. H. Charlesworth et al. 10 vols. Tübingen: Mohr Siebeck; Louisville: Westminster John Knox, 1994–
PVTG	Pseudepigrapha Veteris Testamenti graece
RB	*Revue biblique*
RechBib	Recherches bibliques
RevQ	*Revue de Qumran*
RHPR	*Revue d'histoire et de philosophie religieuses*
RivB	*Rivista biblica*
RSR	*Recherches de science religieuse*
RSV	Revised Standard Version
RTP	*Revue de Théologie et de Philosophie*
RTR	*Reformed Theological Review*
SANT	Studien zum Alten und Neuen Testament
SB	Sources bibliques
SBLEJIL	Society of Biblical Literature, Early Judaism and Its Literature
SBLMS	Society of Biblical Literature, Monograph Series
SBLSCS	Society of Biblical Literature, Septuagint and Cognate Studies
SBNT	Fitzmyer, J. A. *The Semitic Background of the New Testament: Combined Edition of Essays on the Semitic Background of the New Testament and A Wandering Aramean: Collected Aramaic Essays*. BRS. Grand Rapids: Wm. B. Eerdmans and Livonia: Dove, 1997. See *ESBNT* and *WA*
SDSSRL	Studies in the Dead Sea Scrolls and Related Literature
Sem	*Semitica*

SJOT	*Scandinavian Journal of the Old Testament*
SJT	*Scottish Journal of Theology*
SNTSU	*Studien zum Neuen Testament und seiner Umwelt*
SSN	Studia semitica neerlandica
STDJ	Studies on the Texts of the Desert of Judah
StPB	Studia post-biblica
Str-B	Strack, H. L., and P. Billerbeck. *Kommentar zum Neuen Testament aus Talmud und Midrasch.* 6 vols. in 7. Munich: C. H. Beck, 1922-1961
SUNT	Studien zur Umwelt des Neuen Testaments
SVTG	Septuaginta: Vetus Testamentum Graecum auctoritate Academiae Scientiarum Gottingensis editum
SVTP	Studia in Veteris Testamenti Pseudepigrapha
t.	*Tosephta* (followed by name of the tractate)
TBC	Torch Bible Commentaries
TDNT	*Theological Dictionary of the New Testament.* Ed. G. Kittel and G. Friedrich. 10 vols. Grand Rapids: Wm. B. Eerdmans, 1964-1976
TDOT	*Theological Dictionary of the Old Testament.* Ed. G. J. Botterweck, H. Ringgren, and H.-J. Fabry. 17 vols. Grand Rapids: Wm. B. Eerdmans, 1974–
TGl	*Theologie und Glaube*
TICP	Travaux de l'Institut Catholique de Paris
TOTC	Tyndale Old Testament Commentaries
TRE	*Theologische Realenzyklopädie.* Ed. G. Krause and G. Müller. 35 vols. Berlin: de Gruyter, 1977-2003
TS	*Theological Studies*
TSK	*Theologische Studien und Kritiken*
TynBul	*Tyndale Bulletin*
TZ	*Theologische Zeitschrift*
VT	*Vetus Testamentum*
VTSup	Supplements to *VT*
WA	Fitzmyer, J. A. *A Wandering Aramean: Collected Aramaic Essays.* SBLMS 25. Missoula: Scholars, 1979. See also *SBNT*
WUNT	Wissenschaftliche Untersuchungen zum Neuen Testament
WW	*Word & World*
YOSR	Yale Oriental Series. Researches
ZAW	*Zeitschrift für die alttestamentliche Wissenschaft*
ZNW	*Zeitschrift für die neutestamentliche Wissenschaft*

Dead Sea Scrolls Abbreviations

1QM	Milḥamah (War Scroll) from Qumran Cave 1
1QS	Serek hay-Yaḥad (Rule of the Community) from Qumran Cave 1
1QSa	Appendix A of 1QS (Rule of the Congregation) (1Q28a)
1QSb	Appendix B of 1QS (Collection of Blessings) (1Q28b)
4QapMos	Apocryphal Moses Text from Qumran Cave 4 (4Q375-77)
4QapPent	Apocryphal Pentateuch from Qumran Cave 4
4QBer^b —	Copy 2 of Berakot (Blessings) from Qumran Cave 4 (4Q287)
4QD^{a-g}	Copies 1-7 of CD from Qumran Cave 4 (4Q266-72)
4QFlor	Florilegium from Qumran Cave 4 (4Q174)
4QM^{a-e}	Milḥamah (War Scroll) from Qumran Cave 4 (4Q491-95)
4QparaKings	Paraphrase of Kings from Qumran Cave 4 (4Q382)
4QPBless	Patriarchal Blessings from Qumran Cave 4 (now = 4QpGen^a)
4QpGen	Pesher of Genesis from Qumran Cave 4
4QpIsa^{a-e}	Pesher of Isaiah from Qumran Cave 4 (4Q161-65)
4QpPs	Pesher of the Psalter from Qumran Cave 4 (4Q173)
4QPrEnosh	Prayer of Enosh from Qumran Cave 4 (4Q369)
4QS^{a-j}	Copies 1-10 of Serek hay-Yaḥad of Qumran Cave 4 (4Q255-64)
4QSefM	Sepher Milḥamah from Qumran Cave 4 (related to 1QM, 4QM)
4QTestim	Testimonia from Qumran Cave 4 (4Q175)
6QD	Copy of CD from Qumran Cave 6 (6Q15)
11Melch	Melchizedek Text from Qumran Cave 11
CD	Damascus Document from the Cairo Genizah
p	Pesher (Commentary)
pap	papyrus

CHAPTER 1

The Term "Messiah"

The term "Messiah" is used so commonly in the English language that few people ever reflect on its meaning or its origin. It is used by both Jews and Christians, but not always in the same sense. For Christians, it refers to a figure from the past, to Jesus of Nazareth, whom they normally call Jesus Christ, i.e., Jesus the Messiah or the Anointed One. For them, Jesus has already come and has fulfilled the messianic expectations that were part of the belief of the Jewish people in his day. For many religious Jews of today, there is a belief in a Messiah still to come, although this may be understood in a variety of ways. A commonly-used English dictionary defines "Messiah" as "the expected king and deliverer of the Jews."[1]

"Messiah" comes into English and other modern languages from the Greek μεσσίας (John 1:41; 4:25), as the double s in the English term reveals. Μεσσίας is a grecized form of Aramaic משיחא (mĕšîḥā'), which is related to the Hebrew המשיח (ham-māšîăḥ), "the Messiah." The term expresses a notion that emerged in Palestinian Judaism in pre-Christian centuries and denoted an eschatological figure, an *anointed* human agent of God, who was to be sent by Him as a deliverer and was awaited in the end time.

In the days of Jesus of Nazareth, Jews in Judea were awaiting the coming of such an anointed agent, a Messiah. The Matthean and the Lukan Gospels depict the imprisoned Jew, John the Baptist, sending messengers to Jesus and asking, "Are you the 'One who is to come' (σὺ εἶ ὁ ἐρχόμενος) or

---

1. *Webster's Ninth New Collegiate Dictionary* (Springfield, MA: Merriam-Webster, 1987) 745.

are we to look for someone else?" (Matt 11:3; Luke 7:19). The "One who is to come" is a title of an awaited figure derived from the LXX of Mal 3:1, ἰδοὺ ἔρχεται, "Look! He is coming!" which is said of the Lord's "messenger." It is a matter of debate among interpreters whether the "One who is to come" in Malachi means directly the Messiah, but John the evangelist depicts the Samaritan woman who converses with Jesus as aware of the Jewish belief that Μεσσίας ἔρχεται, using the same verb, "the Messiah is coming" (John 4:25). As we shall see, the expectation of an anointed agent of God was alive in ancient Judea in the days of Jesus and his disciples.

Luke portrays the Apostle Peter preaching to Jews gathered in Jerusalem for their Feast of Assembly (i.e., *Asartha*, as Josephus calls it[2]), or Pentecost, the first feast celebrated fifty days after Passover. It was during Passover that Jesus was put to death. To the assembled Jews Peter proclaims, "Let all the house of Israel know for sure, then, that God has made him both Lord and Messiah (Κύριον καὶ Χριστόν), this Jesus whom you crucified" (Acts 2:36). That was the nucleus of the early Christian preaching or *kērygma*. It meant for Peter and his fellow Jewish Christians that Jesus was indeed the anointed agent sent by God for the good of His people. The implications of that sending are spelled out in the rest of the New Testament, the Gospels and Epistles that Christians have inherited from those of his early followers, which we shall have occasion to discuss further in due course.

Because "Messiah" already denoted in pre-Christian Palestinian Judaism an *eschatological* agent to be sent by God in the end time, Mowinckel has rightly emphasized that "it is, therefore, a misuse of the words 'Messiah' and 'Messianic' to apply them, for instance, to those ideas which were associated in Israel or in the ancient east with kings who were actually reigning, even if . . . these ideas were expressed in exalted and mythical terms."[3] "An eschatology without a Messiah is conceivable, but

---

2. *Ant.* 3.10.6 §252, "the fiftieth (day), which Jews call Asartha." The Greek name *asartha* represents Aram. ʿᾰṣartāʾ, related to Heb. ʿᾰṣeret, "solemn assembly." Cf. *J.W.* 6.5.3 §299. Josephus does not explain why Jews would assemble on this feast.

3. *He That Cometh*, 3. Later Mowinckel explains, ". . . the Messiah is a political and eschatological figure, and as such an object of hope for the future, there is obviously a connexion between this figure and the future hope as a whole. The Messiah is simply the king in this national and religious future kingdom, which will one day be established by the miraculous intervention of Yahweh. . . . It means that the Messianic faith is by its very nature linked with Israel's hope of restoration" (p. 155).

not a Messiah apart from a future hope."[4] Mowinckel criticized F. Delitzsch and F. Buhl for the misuse of the term in the titles of books they published,[5] for employing "Messianic expectations" when they really meant "eschatological expectations." He further noted that "the Messiah as a concrete eschatological figure, the king of the final age, the founder of the glorious kingdom, is far less prominent in the Old Testament than in the New."[6]

Furthermore, a Jewish scholar noted for his interpretation of the Hebrew Scriptures and of ancient Near Eastern texts, H. L. Ginsberg, once described the "Messiah" in a noteworthy way:

> a charismatically endowed descendant of David who the Jews of the Roman period believed would be raised up by God to break the yoke of the heathen and to reign over a restored kingdom of Israel to which all the Jews of the Exile would return. This is a strictly postbiblical concept. Even Haggai and Zechariah, who expected the Davidic kingdom to be renewed with a specific individual, Zerubbabel, at its head, thought of him only as a feature of the new age, not as the author or even agent of its establishment. One can, therefore, only speak of the biblical prehistory of messianism.[7]

It is important to take notice of such an explanation by a prominent Jewish scholar. Although I hope to show that the concept of Messiah certainly emerged in Palestinian Judaism well before "the Roman period," Ginsberg's view at least agrees with that of Mowinckel about the future and eschatological character of the "Messiah," even though he differs from him in speaking only of "the biblical prehistory of messianism." Because the Roman period is usually considered to begin with Pompey's taking of Jerusalem in 63 b.c.,[8] that is a date far too late for the emergence of the

---

4. *He That Cometh*, 8.

5. See F. Delitzsch, *Messianic Prophecies in Historical Succession* (New York: Scribner's, 1891; German original, 1890); F. Buhl, *De messianske Forjaettelser i det gamle Testament* (Copenhagen: Gyldendal, 1894).

6. *He That Cometh*, 3-4.

7. See "Messiah," *EncJud* 11:1407. Cf. D. Flusser, "Messiah, Second Temple Period," *EncJud* 11:1408-10.

8. See Josephus, *Ant.* 14.4.3 §66: "When the city was taken in the third month [of the siege], on the Fast Day [Day of Atonement], in the 179th Olympiad, in the consulship of Gaius Antonius and Marcus Tullius Cicero . . . ." That would be 63 b.c.

concept. Ginsberg's view, however, alerts us to the realistic way in which the various passages of the Old Testament that have been considered to be "messianic prophecies" or "messianic expectations" have to be read and understood, because of the many times that the Hebrew word מָשִׁיחַ occurs in the Old Testament.

It is important, however, to note this meaning of the terms "Messiah" and "messianic," since in the rest of my discussion it will be used in this strict and narrow sense, of an awaited or future anointed agent of God. I emphasize this narrow meaning because there have been and are many attempts to use "Messiah" and "messianic" in a broad sense, which enables one to use diverse promises of a coming or eschatological salvation, redemption, or deliverance of people in the Old Testament as part of its messianic teaching.[9]

The broad sense is found at times even in the writings of other Jewish scholars. For instance, Joseph Klausner, whose book *The Messianic Idea in Israel* has been a widely used classic in the study of this topic, distinguishes between what he calls "the vague *Messianic expectation* and the more explicit *belief in the Messiah*."[10] He defines the messianic expectation as:

> *The prophetic hope for the end of this age, in which there will be political freedom, moral perfection, and earthly bliss for the people Israel in its own land, and also for the entire human race.*

He then defines belief in the Messiah as:

9. Many authors in modern times have used "messianic" in this broad sense: e.g., G. van Groningen, *Messianic Revelation in the Old Testament* (Grand Rapids: Baker, 1990) 21 (with explicit rejection of Mowinckel's "narrow" view); H. Lockyer, *All the Messianic Prophecies of the Bible* (Grand Rapids: Zondervan, 1973); C. A. Briggs, *Messianic Prophecy: The Prediction of the Fulfilment Redemption through the Messiah: A Critical Study of the Messianic Passages of the Old Testament in the Order of Their Development* (New York: Scribner's, 1886; repr. Peabody: Hendrickson, 1988); A. Bentzen, *King and Messiah* (London: Lutterworth, 1955); I. Engnell, "The 'Ebed Yahweh Songs and the Suffering Messiah in 'Deutero-Isaiah,'" *BJRL* 31 (1948) 54-93, esp. 57, 90 n. 1; M. Hengel, "The Effective History of Isaiah 53 in the Pre-Christian Period," in *The Suffering Servant: Isaiah 53 in Jewish and Christian Sources*, ed. B. Janowski and P. Stuhlmacher (Grand Rapids: Wm. B. Eerdmans, 2004) 75-146, esp. 100-1, 103, 136.

10. See J. Klausner, *The Messianic Idea in Israel: From Its Beginning to the Completion of the Mishnah* (New York: Macmillan, 1955; London: Allen and Unwin, 1956) 9 (his emphasis).

> *The prophetic hope for the end of this age, in which a strong Redeemer, by his power and his spirit, will bring complete redemption, political and spiritual, to the people Israel, and along with this, earthly bliss and moral perfection to the entire human race.*[11]

In such definitions, however, one notes the disappearance of an "anointed agent of God" (for which a "strong Redeemer" is substituted) and the extension of the Messiah's role from a national to a universalistic scope that will affect "the entire human race."

Broader still is the definition given by R. J. Z. Werblowsky:

> The term messianism, derived from the Hebrew word *mashiaḥ* ('anointed') and denoting the Jewish religious concept of a person with a special mission from God, is used in a broad and at times very loose sense to refer to beliefs or theories regarding an eschatological (concerning the last times) improvement of the state of man or the world, and a final consummation of history.[12]

In giving such a broad and loose meaning to "messianism," Werblowsky has severed it from its roots in an awaited anointed human figure sent by God for the deliverance of His people and transferred it to theories about an eventual improvement of the state of humanity, and even to the "final consummation of history." He then illustrates that state by descriptions of so-called messianic movements, religious or secular, in primitive religions, Islam and Zoroastrianism, Hinduism, Buddhism (along with their successes and failures). Why such ideologies and movements, which are so far removed from the prime analogate of the Judeo-Christian tradition, are called "messianism," and even by a Jewish writer, is far from clear.

The same has to be said of T. L. Thompson, who maintains that the Messiah epithet is not uniquely Jewish, but functions within the symbol system of the ancient Near Eastern royal ideology.[13] There are also many

---

11. Klausner, *The Messianic Idea in Israel*, 9 (his emphasis).

12. "Messiah and Messianic Movements," *The New Encyclopaedia Britannica* (Chicago: Encyclopaedia Britannica, 1976), Macropaedia 11:1017.

13. See T. L. Thompson, "The Messiah Epithet in the Hebrew Bible," *SJOT* 15 (2001) 57-82 (writing against the Princeton Symposium's definition). His view of messianism reduces it, in effect, to the "wide-spread ancient Near Eastern myth of the ideal king" known from both Egyptian and cuneiform literature (p. 61) — another rubber-band concept, which fails to see anything specific in "anointing."

subterfuges used by writers who want to avoid the obvious meaning of the term; for instance, "the function of a messiah" (with lower-case *m*) and "the title Messiah" (with capital *M*): "the former denotes a figure of the king and his dynastic rule, and thus refers to many successive figures; the latter, by contrast, presumes a once-for-all figure coming either at the end of time, or heralding it."[14]

All of this reveals, however, how in modern discussions "messianism" or "the messianic idea" has become "a rubber-band concept" that is made to embrace far more than "Messiah" was ever meant to denote when it first emerged and gradually developed in Palestinian Judaism in pre-Christian times. Part of the problem is that this extension began with interpreters of the Hebrew Scriptures or the Old Testament, and the title of Klausner's book, *The Messianic Idea in Israel: From Its Beginning to the Completion of the Mishnah*, shows how the extension has been carried out, even when he discusses many of the same passages that Mowinckel and others handle more critically in a different sense.[15]

This extension is often made by Christian writers, who may begin with the correct understanding of Jesus of Nazareth as the Messiah but, in using hindsight, impose, perhaps subconsciously, on various passages of their Old Testament a meaning that has developed only with the emergence of Christianity and its way of reading the Hebrew Scriptures. To cite but one example, there is the vague definition of "messiah" proposed by John Collins: "an agent of God in the end-time who is said somewhere in the literature to be anointed, but who is not necessarily called 'messiah' in every passage."[16] That

14. See S. E. Gillingham, "The Messiah in the Psalms: A Question of Reception History and the Psalter," in J. Day, *King and Messiah in Israel and the Ancient Near East*, 209-37, esp. 211.

15. Other writers who have complained about the misuse of "Messiah" and "messianic": J. Becker, *Messianic Expectation in the Old Testament* (Philadelphia: Fortress, 1980) 11-13; J. Coppens, *Le messianisme royal: Ses origines, son développement, son accomplissement*. LD 54 (Paris: Éditions du Cerf, 1968) 11-15; C. W. Emmet, "Messiah," *Hastings Encyclopaedia of Religion and Ethics* (Edinburgh: T. & T. Clark, 1916) 8:570-81, esp. 570; C. Klick, "Are You He Who Is to Come?" *LQ* 24 (1972) 51-65; S. H. Levey, *The Messiah: An Aramaic Interpretation: The Messianic Exegesis of the Targum* (Cincinnati: Hebrew Union College, 1974) xviii-xix (but then he falls into the same usage on p. xx, where he says the Hebrew text of Ezekiel has "messianic intentions"); J. J. M. Roberts, "The Old Testament's Contribution to Messianic Expectations," in *The Messiah: Developments in Earliest Judaism and Christianity*, ed. J. H. Charlesworth et al. (Minneapolis: Fortress, 1987) 39-51.

16. J. J. Collins, "'He Shall Not Judge by What His Eyes See': Messianic Authority in the Dead Sea Scrolls," *DSD* 2 (1995) 145-64, esp. 146.

"somewhere in the literature" is not precise enough and again permits the extension that makes one uneasy, since it shows no respect for the history of ideas. For the question is rather: When did the idea of "an agent of God in the end-time," who is anointed, emerge in Judaism, and how did it emerge?

To put the matter another way, it is often said, *Novum Testamentum in Vetere latet, Vetus in Novo patet!* (The New Testament lies hidden in the Old, and the Old is opened up in the New!). This, however, is a good Christian principle of interpretation, but even as such it cannot be applied naively, because the question remains, *Quomodo latet et quomodo patet?* (How is it hidden and how is it opened up?).

My concern, then, will be to let the Old Testament use of משיח and its teaching about the continuing Davidic dynasty reveal their developing senses, from the preexilic period to the exilic and postexilic periods of Palestinian Jewish history, so that the reader can see how in the course of time the concept of a Messiah as an awaited or future anointed agent of God (in the narrow sense) gradually emerged in Israel, then how it was used in postbiblical Jewish writings in pre-Christian times, then how it was taken over by the early Christians who wrote the Christian Scriptures, and then how it continued to develop in Jewish writings after the New Testament. In doing this, I shall discuss briefly many of the Old Testament passages that have been drawn into the discussion of the "messianic idea" in order to establish for them what I regard as the proper sense that they have, when they are not slanted by Christian "messianic" hindsight.

CHAPTER 2

The Use of מָשִׁיחַ in the Old Testament

Because the title "Messiah" developed in pre-Christian Judaism out of the use of מָשִׁיחַ *(māšîaḥ)* in the Old Testament, one has to trace the Old Testament usage of that word. It is important to realize at the outset that the idea of מָשִׁיחַ as an awaited or future anointed agent of God in the end time developed only gradually in Old Testament times. In fact, "Messiah" as such is a relatively late development.

מָשִׁיחַ is a *qatīl*-type Hebrew noun, really a passive participle meaning "anointed."[1] The anointing of an agent may seem strange today, but that was a mode of designating persons for a role or function in the society in which they lived in ancient Israel. The custom of anointing a king was apparently inherited from a Hittite or Canaanite practice and was used for kings in Israel for many centuries.[2] The king of Israel was not sworn in as he began his reign, but was crowned sometimes, and at his enthronement his head was anointed, usually with scented olive oil as an unguent (see

---

1. The passive participle in Hebrew is usually a *qatūl*-type (קָטוּל, *qātûl*), but some are formed like the adjectival *qatīl*-class; thus *'āsîr*, "prisoner" (lit., "bound"); *pāqîd*, "deputy" (lit., "appointed"); *nāzîr*, "Nazirite" (lit., "consecrated"); *nāgîd* (lit., "one [placed] in front"), "leader, prince." So too מָשִׁיחַ; cf. Joüon, *GHB* §88Eb.

2. See H. Gressmann, *Der Messias.* FRLANT 43 (Göttingen: Vandenhoeck & Ruprecht, 1929) 5; E. Kutsch, *Salbung als Rechtsakt im Alten Testament und im Alten Orient.* BZAW 87 (Berlin: de Gruyter, 1963) 36-39, 52-63; cf. S. Mowinckel, *He That Cometh,* 5; J. Becker, *Messianic Expectation in the Old Testament* (Philadelphia: Fortress, 1980) 42-43. Jotham's fable, which may reflect premonarchic times, tells of trees that went to anoint a king over them (Judg 9:8-15).

1 Sam 10:1). He was thereby made holy, i.e., set apart from the rest of the people as a theocratic vassal; and he represented them before Yahweh, their God.[3] So it came about that the verbal adjective מָשִׁיחַ, "anointed," was substantivized and became a title, "Anointed One," most frequently applied to a king. As מְשִׁיחַ יהוה, "the LORD's Anointed One," his regal appellative declared his relation to Yahweh, the God of Israel.

One has to distinguish, however, the use of the noun מָשִׁיחַ (māšîăḥ), "anointed one," from that of the verb מָשַׁח, "smear, anoint."[4] The verb מָשַׁח (māšaḥ) occurs sixty-nine times in the MT of the Old Testament. Almost half of the instances have to do with the anointing of Aaron and his sons,[5] priests,[6] the altar,[7] or cultic objects,[8] thus consecrating them to the awesome service of Yahweh in the Temple. The other half of the instances of the verb are found in passages that mention the anointing of historical kings of Israel or Judah: Saul,[9] David,[10] Solomon,[11] Jehu,[12] Joash,[13] Jehoahaz.[14] In 1 Kgs 19:15-16, Elijah is told to anoint Hazael as king of Syria and Shaphat of Abelmeholah as the prophet to succeed him; so the rite was not restricted, even in the Old Testament, to an Israelite king. Such instances of the verb for the anointing of kings are found apart from the use of the title מָשִׁיחַ, and in 1 Sam 10:1 the anointed king's title is given as נָגִיד (nāgîd), "prince."[15] Moreover, there is never an instance of the verb denoting the anointing of a "Messiah" in the narrow sense, i.e., of an awaited or future agent of God. So the uses of the verb have little to do with this discussion.[16]

---

3. See further P. K. McCarter, Jr., 1 Samuel. AB 8 (Garden City: Doubleday, 1980) 178. Cf. H. Ringgren, "König und Messias," ZAW 64 (1952) 120-47.

4. See H. Weinel, "מָשַׁח und seine Derivate," ZAW 18 (1898) 1-82.

5. E.g., Exod 28:41; 29:7, 29; 30:30.

6. Lev 16:32; Num 3:3; 35:25.

7. E.g., Exod 29:36; 40:10; Num 7:1, 10.

8. E.g., a pillar (Gen 31:13); the tent of meeting (Exod 30:26); the tabernacle (Exod 40:9); the holy of holies (Dan 9:24).

9. E.g., 1 Sam 9:16; 10:1; 15:1, 17.

10. E.g., 1 Sam 16:3, 12, 13; 2 Sam 2:4, 7; 3:39.

11. E.g., 1 Kgs 1:34, 39, 45.

12. 1 Kgs 19:16; 2 Kgs 9:3, 6, 12; 2 Chr 22:7.

13. 2 Kgs 11:12; 2 Chr 23:11.

14. 2 Kgs 23:30.

15. Lit. "(someone) set in front of (the people)."

16. The same has to be said also about other nouns formed from the same root, either mišḥāh, "anointing" (e.g., Exod 37:29; Lev 21:12) or mošḥāh, "anointing" (Exod 29:29; 40:15).

Important, however, is the use of the noun מָשִׁיחַ itself, which occurs thirty-nine times in the MT of the Old Testament.[17] Once it may refer to Saul's shield as an anointed object, or perhaps to Saul himself (2 Sam 1:21); the text is unclear, and its meaning is debated by commentators.[18] Moreover, in two instances interpreters question whether the term is used of the people of Israel as a whole or of their (unnamed) reigning king: Hab 3:13; Ps 28:8.[19] Otherwise, in the vast majority of its occurrences, מָשִׁיחַ refers to a reigning king (usually of Israel), contemporary or past. Its basic denotation is that such a ruler is or has been regarded as an anointed agent of God designated for the guidance or deliverance of those who are at that time His people. As "the Anointed of the LORD," he was the king of Yahweh's people, of Israel, and in time the title took on political meaning, which would persist even when מָשִׁיחַ came to denote "Messiah" in the narrow sense as an eschatological figure for Judaism of a later time.

In the beginning the Hebrews lived as a theocratic people who were governed by Judges (שֹׁפְטִים, šōphĕṭîm, Judg 2:16), or even by a ruler or prince (נָגִיד, nāgîd) with centralized authority. Yet Gideon refused to establish a hereditary kingship, when the people of Israel asked him to do so (Judg 8:22-23). In time, however, the kingship emerged in imitation of neighboring peoples (1 Sam 8:5, 19-20; 9:16; 10:1), and after Saul it became a Davidic monopoly, a dynasty that ruled over "the house of Judah" (2 Sam 2:4), eventually over Israel as well (5:1-3), and even over Ammon (12:30). Thus there arose an ideal kingship in ancient Israel, in which the king is clearly "the LORD's Anointed One."[20] When, however, Jeroboam severed Israel from Judah and set up golden calves in Bethel and Dan for worship, this was regarded as "a sin" (1 Kgs 12:28-32), because he established high places in Israel with priests and a cult in opposition to those of Jerusalem in Judah. Thereafter the Davidic dynasty ruled only in Judah and at times even functioned also as priests (2 Sam 8:18; 1 Kgs 3:4; Psalm 110).

17. Or forty times, when one includes Sir 46:19.

18. Perhaps the real passive participle (מָשׁוּחַ, māšûaḥ) should be read there instead.

19. Mowinckel regards the interpretation that it means the Israelite people to be "based on erroneous exegesis"; He That Cometh, 7.

20. See Mowinckel, He That Cometh, 21-95. But Mowinckel goes too far when, following others, he says that "in the official Israelite conception of the king . . . , he is a superhuman, divine being" (his emphasis). He cites Ps 45:7 and claims that the king is there addressed as אֱלֹהִים ('ĕlōhîm, "God") and as אָדוֹן ('ādôn, "Lord") in Ps 110:1; Jer 22:18, etc. That, however, is to give a fundamentalistic interpretation to disputed passages.

Eventually, especially when the monarchy was no more because of the deportation of kings of Judah to Babylon, משיח was applied to the High Priest of the time. He was the "anointed priest" in a special sense, the heir of the kings. There are also two instances where the title may be attributed to either prophets or patriarchs, but the interpretation is disputed.[21] The breakdown of occurrences is as follows:

(1) *Kings*
(a) A king in a generic sense or an unnamed king of the Davidic dynasty: 1 Sam 2:10, 35; 16:6; Ps 2:2; 20:7; 84:10; possibly 28:8 (see above).
(b) Saul: called משיח יהוה, "Yahweh's Anointed One," in 1 Sam 24:7, 11(Eng. 6,10); 26:9, 11, 16, 23; 2 Sam 1:14, 16; cf. 1 Sam 12:3, 5.[22]
(c) David (as a historical king): 2 Sam 19:22(Eng. 21); 22:51; 23:1; Ps 18:51(50); 89:39, 52(38,51); 132:10, 17 (in some of the last-mentioned instances משיח is also extended to descendants of David on his throne, or to a "Davidic king").
(d) Solomon (with David?): 2 Chr 6:42.
(e) Zedekiah: Lam 4:20 (cf. 2 Kgs 25:4-6).
(f) Cyrus, king of Persia: Isa 45:1.

(2) *Priests*
הכהן המשיח, "the anointed priest": Lev 4:3, 5, 16; 6:15[23]

(3) *Prophets/Patriarchs*
1 Chr 16:22; Ps 105:15

(4) **Dan 9:25, 26** (to be discussed in chapter 5)

What should be noted about these occurrences, first of all, is the books in which they occur. There is no reference to a king as משיח in the Pentateuch in any sense, either to a reigning king or an awaited one.[24] Nor

21. Some commentators appeal to Isa 61:1 ("the Lord has anointed me") to support the prophetic meaning.

22. This is echoed in Sir 46:19.

23. Here the term is used as an adjective, not a title, as the prefixed article in המשיח shows.

24. This is undoubtedly the reason for the failure of the Samaritans, who recognized only the Pentateuch as their Scriptures, to believe in a coming Messiah. Instead, they spoke

is the term used of a historical king of Israel in any of the major prophets. Zedekiah of Judah is usually understood as the "LORD's Anointed" in Lam 4:20, but in the Hebrew Scriptures that book is grouped not with the Prophets but with the Writings. Moreover, it is striking that Cyrus, the founder of the Achaemenid dynasty and king of Persia, is the only one called משיחו, "His Anointed One," in the entire book of Isaiah (45:1). He is thus honored in Israel's Scriptures because he allowed the Jews to return from Babylonian Captivity to their homeland, Judah.

Second, some of these passages, where משיח is used of David or of his descendants, celebrate the king's historic accession to the throne. The title "Anointed One" is given thus to a reigning king. Even if in one or other of these passages the sense of the verb is future and might refer to a future king, it is rather the everlasting character of the Davidic dynasty that is being noted. משיח never means "Messiah" in the narrow sense in any of the passages listed above in 1a-f, where it has to be translated merely as "Anointed One."[25]

Third, as Mowinckel has noted,[26] one has to distinguish the preexilic age, when the monarchy was at its height, from the postexilic age, when Judah became a Persian and later a Hellenistic province (יהוד, Yĕhûd, or 'Ιουδαία), with Jerusalem as its capital, and when the hope for the restoration of the monarchy or the Davidic dynasty grew. Out of such a hope there likewise developed the expectation of a Messiah in the narrow sense, but only after several centuries. Certain Old Testament texts of preexilic

---

of hat-Tāhēb (Hebrew) or Tāhĕbā' (Aramaic), "the Returning One," an active participial form (Memar Marqah 2:9; 4:11, 12), a development in Samaritan teaching of "the prophet like Moses" (Deut 18:15, 18). The name Tāhĕbāh is said sometimes to mean "Restorer," but that is more an interpretation than a translation.

See J. Macdonald, Memar Marqah: The Teaching of Marqah, 2 vols. BZAW 84 (Berlin: Töpelmann, 1963) 1:44, 108, 110-11. Cf. A. Merx, Der Messias oder Ta'eb der Samaritaner: Nach bisher unbekannten Quellen. BZAW 17 (Giessen: Töpelmann, 1909) 34-45; J. Macdonald, The Theology of the Samaritans (Philadelphia: Westminster, 1964) 17 n. 3, 362-71; J. A. Montgomery, The Samaritans: The Earliest Jewish Sect: Their History, Theology and Literature (Philadelphia: J. C. Winston, 1907; repr. New York: Ktav, 1968) 239-51; R. J. Coggins, Samaritans and Jews: The Origins of Samaritanism Reconsidered (Atlanta: John Knox, 1975) 146.

25. S. H. Levey (The Messiah [Cincinnati: Hebrew Union College, 1974] 145) lists the following passages as "not Messianic," even though targums render the Hebrew title in Aramaic as משיחא: 1 Sam 2:35; 12:3, 5; 16:6; 24:7, 11; 26:9, 11, 16, 23; 2 Sam 1:14, 16; 22:51; Isa 45:1; Hab 3:13; Pss 2:2; 18:51; 20:7; 28:8; 84:10; 89:29 (sic, but read 39); 132:10; 2 Chr 6:42.

26. He That Cometh, 10.

provenience, however, have been considered at times to be expressions of "messianic faith" or "the messianic idea," but that is an abuse of the term "messianic," because the preexilic period was still the time of the flourishing monarchy and the phrase "Yahweh's Anointed One" always refers to the historical and then reigning king(s), especially those of the Davidic dynasty. Moreover, although all the kings from Solomon on may well have been anointed at their accession to the throne, not all of them are given the title מָשִׁיח יהוה in such preexilic writings; and no one can say for sure why some were so designated and others not. Even such good kings as Hezekiah (lauded in 2 Kgs 18:5) or Josiah (in 2 Kgs 23:25) are not known in the Bible as "Yahweh's Anointed One."

Fourth, some of the passages listed above call for comment, because there are at times problems in the details. We begin with preexilic references.

(1) The first instance (1 Sam 2:10) actually refers to the time in Israel when there was not yet a king ruling over Israel. Hannah, who had been childless, has begged Yahweh for a son, whom she promises to dedicate to His service and finally gives birth to Samuel. When she returns to Shiloh to dedicate Samuel to Yahweh's service, she utters a prayer of triumph and thanksgiving, saying, "Against them [the enemies of Israel] may He thunder from heaven; may the LORD judge the ends of the earth. May He give strength to His king and lift up the horn of His Anointed One." Thus Hannah acknowledges Yahweh as the judge of all things and deliverer of the oppressed. She concludes her prayer that He will stand by Israel's ruler. The "king" has to be understood either generically as one of the ruling Judges or, more likely, as one of the coming kings, possibly Saul or David, considered as an ideal ruler. מְשִׁיחוֹ, "His Anointed," stands in parallelism to "His king" (unnamed), who is to sit on the throne of Israel and will enjoy the support of Yahweh, just as Hannah did in her barrenness. מָשִׁיח is, then, part of the normal court style, glorifying a soon-to-be-reigning king of Israel as the ideal anointed agent of God.[27] *Pace* É. P. Dhorme, Hannah's

---

27. The first part of 1 Samuel is usually regarded as composed from a "Late Source" (dating from the latter days of the monarchy) in contrast to the "Early Source" used in ch. 26 to the end of 2 Samuel (dating from the time of Solomon). Moreover, the final editing of the books of Samuel seems to have occurred in the postexilic period. So some of the formulation of Hannah's prayer (e.g., the use of "king") may reflect a later period, when David's dynasty was well established and there was already a king in Israel. See R. P. Knierim, "The Messianic Concept in the First Book of Samuel," in *Jesus and the Historian: Written in Honor*

prayer is not a "messianic psalm," which sings the praise "of the Messiah."[28] Such an interpretation of it is eisegetical, because the religious sense of Hannah's prayer is clear from its context, even if the formulation of v. 10 may use a term from a later age.

(2) In 1 Sam 2:35, at the end of the passage that recounts the condemnation of the house of Eli, the author introduces God saying that Eli's two sons, Hophni and Phinehas, will die on the same day because of their conduct (see 1 Sam 2:34), as a sign to the people of Israel. Then God is quoted saying, "I will raise up for myself a faithful priest, who shall act according to what is in my heart and on my mind; and I will build him a sure house, and he shall go in and out before my Anointed One forever." The "faithful priest" becomes Zadok (2 Sam 8:17; 15:24; 1 Kgs 1:8; 2:35), and the "sure house" is the Zadokite priestly line after him (Ezek 44:15). The "Anointed One" may be Saul or David, and the priestly service that is to continue "forever" will assist the dynasty that is to spring from David. Although the verse supposes that the kingship has been established and promises a lasting dynasty of anointed kings, it does not even hint at a "Messiah" in the narrow sense. Many anointed heirs will mount the Davidic throne, and many Zadokite priests will serve them, before משיח as "Messiah" emerges in history.

(3) In 1 Sam 16:6, where Samuel is sent to anoint a king from among the sons of Jesse, the prophet at first thinks it is Eliab, who stands before him: "Surely, His anointed is now before the LORD" (אך נגד יהוה משיחו); but the LORD rejects him despite his stature (resembling that of Saul in 9:2; 10:23). The account ends with Samuel anointing rather young David in the presence of his brothers (וימשח אתו), but the title משיח is not used of David there (16:13). Clearly there is no "messianic" nuance to the term in v. 6.

(4) In 1 Sam 24:7-11(Eng. 6-10) the phrase משיח יהוה is applied to Saul, the first king of Israel, three times, as David swears that he would never raise his hand against him: "The LORD forbid that I should do such a thing to my sovereign, the LORD's Anointed, to lift my hand against him, for he is the LORD's Anointed" (v. 7[6]; cf. v. 11[10]). In 1 Sam 26:9-23, the

---

of Ernest Cadman Colwell, ed. F. T. Trotter (Philadelphia: Westminster, 1968) 20-51; D. Jobling, *1 Samuel.* Berit Olam (Collegeville: Liturgical, 1998) 133, 166-69, but beware of what he calls "the contradiction between the closing words in 2:10 and the general tendency of the rest of the song" (p. 167).

28. É. P. Dhorme, *Les livres de Samuel.* EBib (Paris: Gabalda, 1910) 29, 32. Dhorme is right, however, in rejecting M. Löhr's interpretation that "the Messiah represents the community."

same phrase is applied again to Saul four times (vv. 9, 11, 16, 23) in another form of the story, derived from an earlier source. Similarly in 2 Sam 1:14, 16. The use of the phrase in these passages about Saul implies the inviolable character of the king of Israel; "being anointed, he is tabu and sacrosanct" and "it is sacrilege and a capital offence to lay hands on him."[29] The phrase, however, is clearly devoid of any "messianic" connotation.

(5) In 1 Samuel 12:3-5, in the course of the prophet's farewell address to all Israel, Samuel maintains that he has always walked uprightly before the people and calls upon "the LORD and His Anointed One" to bear witness to what he claims. The Anointed One is not named, but in this context it cannot refer to anyone but Saul, whom Samuel and all the people have just made king over Israel in Gilgal (11:15–12:2).[30]

(6) In 2 Sam 19:22(Eng. 21), David, as king over Israel, answers the query of Abishai, "Should not Shimei be put to death for this, that he has cursed the LORD's Anointed?" (את־משיח יהוה). In reply, David, the anointed king, says to Shimei, "You shall not die," and he makes his promise on oath.[31] Clearly the term has no "messianic" connotation here.

(7) In 2 Sam 22:51, and also in Ps 18:50-51(Eng. 49-50), a lengthy thanksgiving psalm is recorded, in which a king is grateful for his victory in battle.[32] It probably was composed in a cultic setting, but was inserted in 2 Samuel as a summary of David's gratitude for the victories of his warrior-activity. The psalm has two main parts: (a) vv. 2-20, which depict the king's victory as a rescue from the peril of raging waters because of Yahweh's theophanic aid; and (b) vv. 29-51, which describe the king as a conqueror of distant lands again because of Yahweh's aid. In between these parts are vv. 21-28, which express the king's fidelity and Yahweh's justice and graciousness. It all ends with a paean of praise:

> For this reason will I extol you among the nations, O LORD, and sing
> praise to your name, the One who gives to His king great triumphs and

---

29. Mowinckel, *He That Cometh*, 65.

30. The phrase is echoed in the Praise of Famous Men in Sir 46:19 at the end of the encomium of Samuel: העיד ייי ומשיחו, "he called Yahweh and His Anointed to testify"; LXX: ἐπεμαρτύρατο ἔναντι κυρίου καὶ χριστοῦ αὐτοῦ, "he called on (them) to witness before the Lord and His Anointed."

31. See P. K. McCarter, Jr., *II Samuel*. AB 9 (Garden City: Doubleday, 1984) 420-21.

32. See G. Schmuttermayr, *Psalm 18 und 2 Samuel 22: Studien zu einem Doppeltext*. SANT 15 (Munich: Kösel, 1971).

shows loving kindness to His Anointed, to David and his descendants forever.

Here מְשִׁיחוֹ stands in parallelism to מַלְכּוֹ, "His king." Although the term directly refers to David, who is thanking God for the recent deliverance "from the hand of all his enemies and from the hand of Saul" (2 Sam 22:1), the thanksgiving (especially in Psalm 18) could be uttered by any successor on David's throne after a military victory. That is implied in the extension, "and his descendants forever," which is a sort of afterthought, tagged on at the end of the reason for the thanks.[33] The emphasis, however, is put on the everlasting dynasty of David that is about to emerge, and there is not yet a hint of anything "messianic," even in Psalm 18, because "there is no suggestion that the psalmist looked forward to any once-for-all-time coming figure."[34]

(8) In 2 Sam 23:1, מָשִׁיח is used of the historical King David. "These are the last words of David: 'The utterance of David, son of Jesse, the utterance of the man God raised up, the Anointed of the God of Jacob (מְשִׁיח יַעֲקֹב אֱלֹהֵי), the favorite of the sons of Israel.'"[35] As did Balaam in Num 24:3, King David begins by giving his name and titles but does not call himself a "Messiah," as is generally recognized in the versions.

In the foregoing seventeen Old Testament passages (§ 1-8), which refer to preexilic times (despite an occasional later formulation), the use of מָשִׁיח has always been applied to a king reigning in the undivided monarchy of Israel. In none of them is the religious literal meaning even hinting at a "Messiah" or a "messianic expectation" — despite the way that some of them are interpreted at times by commentators.

In some Old Testament passages of postexilic times one can see the same usage persisting:

(9) It is found once in 2 Chr 6:42 and applied to King Solomon, who

33. In fact, it has often been considered a secondary addition, but it may reflect "the ancient (Solomonic) promise of kingship to David underlying II Samuel 7"; McCarter, *II Samuel,* 472. Dhorme (*Livres de Samuel,* 432) omits the last phrase as a secondary addition and asserts that מְשִׁיחוֹ refers to "the ideal Messiah who is to rule over the entire universe," without giving any evidence for such an interpretation.

34. S. E. Gillingham, "The Messiah in the Psalms," in *King and Messiah in Israel and the Ancient Near East.* JSOTSup 270 (Sheffield: Sheffield Academic, 1998) 214.

35. In 4QSamᵃ (4Q51) 155-58:24 (DJD 17:181), הקים על is read instead of הקם על of the MT, usually translated, "raised on high." The LXX agrees with the Qumran reading: ὃν ἀνέστησεν κύριος, "whom the Lord raised up."

is depicted consecrating the Temple and ending his prayer of dedication thus: "O LORD God, do not reject the plea of Your Anointed Ones; but recall the (deeds of) kindness to David Your servant."[36] Here a specific historical descendant of David uses the term of himself (and probably of David, because the form is plural, משיחיך), but not in any "messianic" sense, no more than in Ps 132:8-10, which is reflected here. (See §19 below.) Contrast the ending of Solomon's dedicatory prayer in 1 Kgs 8:56-61, which summons the people of Israel rather to observance of the Law.

(10) Another instance is found in Lam 4:20, "The LORD's Anointed, our breath of life,[37] was caught in their traps, of whom we used to say, 'We shall live in his shadow among the nations.'" This is undoubtedly an allusion to King Zedekiah, who at the end of the Davidic monarchy was captured by Nebuchadnezzar and carried off to Babylon (cf. 2 Kgs 25:4-6), and so the people have lost their independence and the source of their power. Since the verse refers in the past tense to an event already taken place, there is no future connotation or reference to a Messiah, even in "we shall live in his shadow."

(11) In Isa 45:1-3, Deutero-Isaiah records the charge given by God to Cyrus, the founder of the Achaemenid dynasty and king of Persia, and the one who allowed the Jews to return from Babylonian Captivity to their homeland, "Thus says the LORD to His Anointed, to Cyrus (למשיחו לכורש), whose 'right hand I have grasped, subduing nations before him; I ungird the loins of kings, opening doors before him and gates that may not be barred.' 'I will go before you and level the mountains . . . that you may know that it is I, the LORD, the God of Israel, who call you by your name.'" Even though he is not a king of Israel, he is accorded by the prophet the august name of an anointed agent of the LORD, because he allowed the Jews to return to worship Yahweh, their God, in the Temple to be rebuilt.[38] Still

---

36. The Hebrew is unclear; לחסדי דויד could also mean "the gracious deeds/loyalty of David."

37. Lit., "the breath of our nostrils," the image is derived from Egyptian mythology about the god Amon-Re (see Stele of Amen-hotep III's Building Inscription, *ANET,* 376). Recall the symbolism of breath in creation; see W. Wifall, "The Breath of His Nostrils: Gen 2:7b," *CBQ* 36 (1974) 237-40.

38. As J. J. Collins notes, Cyrus is not one who restores the Davidic kingship, but rather "an agent of deliverance for the Jewish people"; *The Scepter and the Star: The Messiahs of the Dead Sea Scrolls and Other Ancient Literature.* ABRL (New York: Doubleday, 1996) 31. The interpretation of the title as applied to Cyrus is quite contested, whether it is original or

more important in these verses (1-8), in which God speaks directly to Cyrus, is the emphasis given to the effect of Cyrus's action on other peoples of the world who will come thereby to recognize that "the God of Israel" (45:3) is the only God: "I am the LORD, and there is no other" (45:6c). This instance of משיח is noteworthy in Deutero-Isaiah because it is the only place where the title appears, and not only in Deutero-Isaiah, but in the whole book of Isaiah. This solitary instance must be deliberate, and it instructs us not to read "messianic" nuances into Isaiah 1–39.

(12) Similarly from the postexilic period, when the Davidic monarchy flourished no more, משיח is predicated of the High Priest, who functions in the Temple of Jerusalem: "If the anointed priest sins, bringing guilt on the people, let him offer to the LORD a young bull without blemish as a sin offering to the LORD" (Lev 4:3; cf. also 4:5, 16).

(13) Leviticus also prescribes how Aaron and his sons are to offer a cereal offering on the day of their anointing (6:12); then it continues, "The anointed priest who succeeds him from among the sons of Aaron shall do it (too) — this is an ordinance for all time — it shall be burned entirely for the LORD" (Lev 6:15).[39]

(14) The only place in the Old Testament where משיח may be applied to prophets is found in 1 Chr 16:22, which is identical with Ps 105:15: "Touch not My anointed ones, do no harm to My prophets!" The poetic parallelism of משיחי and נביאי suggests the identity, but the context of vv. 12-15 in Psalm 105 speaks of patriarchs, who may be regarded as "prophets," as Abraham himself is called in Gen 20:7 (כי נביא הוא, "for he is a prophet"). Although a prophet is said to be anointed in 1 Kgs 19:16; Isa 61:1, the meaning of these passages is controverted, and משיח may not yet be a title for a prophet.[40]

---

a later gloss and in what sense it is to be understood, if taken as original; see L. S. Fried, "Cyrus the Messiah? The Historical Background to Isaiah 45:1," *HTR* 95 (2002) 373-93; "Cyrus the Messiah," *BRev* 19/5 (2003) 24-31, 44. Cf. H. G. M. Williamson, "The Messianic Texts in Isaiah 1–39," in J. Day, *King and Messiah in Israel and the Ancient Near East*, 239.

39. See D. Fleming, "The Biblical Tradition of Anointing Priests," *JBL* 117 (1998) 401-14. Fleming rightly stresses the antiquity of this tradition, which undoubtedly existed along with the anointing of kings.

40. See the commentators on these passages. Cf. J. Giblet, "Prophétisme et attente d'un messie prophète dans l'Ancien Testament," in *L'Attente du Messie*, ed. L. Cerfaux. RechBib 1 (Bruges: Desclée de Brouwer, 1958) 85-129. The use of the title for prophets will show up in Qumran texts; see below, pp. 99-100.

In the Psalter there are a number of royal psalms (2, 18, 20, 21, 45, 72, 89, 101, 110, 132, 144:1-11), in which God is praised by a king or God's blessing is invoked on an unnamed king sitting on the Davidic throne. None of these psalms names a specific king, but some of them celebrate or commemorate a king's enthronement, express thanks in view of a recent victory, or utter a prayer for success in a coming battle. In some of them מָשִׁיחַ appears, but not in all of them; it is absent in Psalms 21, 45, 72, 101, 110, 144:1-11, even when in one or other of these psalms the verb מָשַׁח (*māšaḥ*) occurs. (These will be discussed in the next chapter.) There are also other psalms, which are not "royal," in which מָשִׁיחַ does occur (28, 84, 105; see below).

The dating of the Psalms is problematic; some of them seem to be very old, but it is not always easy to discern their proper place in time. With that caution, we treat them here together, beginning with the royal psalms that use מָשִׁיחַ.[41]

(15) In Psalm 2, an early preexilic liturgical composition probably written for the enthronement of some historical king, the psalmist sings, "Kings of the earth set themselves up, and rulers conspire together against the LORD and against His Anointed One (מְשִׁיחוֹ). . . . 'I have installed My king on Zion, My holy hill.' I will recount the decree of the LORD: He said to me, 'You are My son; this day I have begotten you'" (2:2, 6-7).

Although subject peoples may dare to rebel or withdraw their allegiance at the coming of a new king, the psalmist recalls God's promise about the king's guaranteed and lasting reign, for the king not only has been enthroned by God, but also been adopted by God as His son. He thus stands in a closer relation to God than anyone else. This is an echo of the Oracle of Nathan in 2 Sam 7:14, "I will be his father, and he shall be My son," which is clearly a divine promise not only about the immediate king being enthroned, but also about the enduring character of the Davidic dynasty. It is also a good instance of the concept of sacral kingship in the preexilic period, and also of the king's eschatological destiny.[42] Although

---

41. See Mowinckel, *He That Cometh,* 11-12; D. Starling, "The Messianic Hope in the Psalms," *RTR* 58 (1999) 121-34; G. von Rad, "Erwägungen zu den Königspsalmen," *ZAW* 58 (1940-41) 216-22.

42. See Mowinckel, *He That Cometh,* 67; Becker, *Messianic Expectation in the Old Testament,* 43; A. Maillot and A. Lelièvre, *Les Psaumes* (Geneva: Éditions Labor et Fides, 1961), 1:30-32. Cf. C. Rösel, *Die messianische Redaktion des Psalters: Studien zur Entstehung und Theologie der Sammlung Psalm 2–89.* Calwer theologische Monographien, ser. A19 (Stuttgart: Calwer, 1999) 99-105, 218-22 (a carefully nuanced interpretation).

THE ONE WHO IS TO COME

מְשִׁיחוֹ occurs here along with מַלְכִּי, "my king," and with the idea of adoptive sonship, there is not even a hint of a "messianic" connotation of the term or of a remote future, when a Messiah might appear. Not even v. 8, which has a future sense and says, "I will make nations your heritage and the ends of the earth your estate," means anything more than the universal dominion of the historical Davidic king whom the psalm celebrates. And yet, many interpreters speak of this psalm as "messianic," especially Christian scholars who write about "royal messianism" generically in the Old Testament,[43] or specifically in the Psalter.[44] It is better, however, to hold with H. Gressmann, S. E. Gillingham, and others that Psalm 2 is not "messianic" in any sense,[45] because there is no evidence that the religious literal sense of Psalm 2 was ever considered as such in pre-Christian Judaism, and something more than mere assertion is needed to show that the words "This day I have begotten you" mean more than adoptive sonship or imply the divine filiation of a coming Messiah.[46]

43. E.g., E. W. Hengstenberg, *Christology of the Old Testament and a Commentary on the Messianic Predictions* (Grand Rapids: Kregel, 1970) 42-50; J. de Fraine, *L'Aspect religieux de la royauté israélite: L'institution monarchique dans l'Ancien Testament et dans les textes mésopotamiens.* AnBib 3 (Rome: Biblical Institute, 1954) 274-76 ("directement messianique"); H. Gross, *Weltherrschaft als religiöse Idee im Alten Testament.* BBB 6 (Bonn: Hanstein, 1953) 89-90 (". . . dem messianischen König der Zukunft, der Endzeit, der mehr ist als nur Adoptivsohn Gottes"); J. L. McKenzie, "Royal Messianism," *CBQ* 19 (1957) 25-52, esp. 32-33 (Psalm 2 is "better understood as not directly messianic, except in the sense that the king has become a messianic figure, himself the living pledge of the hope of the eternal dynasty of David" [33]); W. C. Kaiser, Jr., *The Messiah in the Old Testament.* Studies in Old Testament Biblical Theology (Grand Rapids: Zondervan, 1995) 90; M. García Cordero, "El mesianismo en los salmos," *Ciencia Tomista* 127 (2000) 5-58.

44. See G. Dahl, "The Messianic Expectation in the Psalter," *JBL* 57 (1938) 1-12; he complains against a "purely secular interpretation" of "many Psalms, especially the so-called Royal Psalms" (p. 2), but such an interpretation is not secular. It is rather the religious, literal meaning of the psalms that is at stake, and that is what the so-called messianic interpretation of them violates. See also A. Miller, "Gibt es direkt messianische Psalmen?" in *Miscellanea Biblica B. Ubach,* ed. R. M. Díaz (Montserrat: Abadia de Montserrat, 1953) 201-9 (yes [205]); A. Robert, "Considérations sur le messianisme du Ps. II," *RSR* 39 (1951) 88-98, esp. 95-96 ("un messianisme direct").

45. See Gressmann, *Der Messias,* 13-14 ("In reality, nothing refers to an endtime Messiah. What the poet describes is not the future, but the present"). Gillingham ("The Messiah in the Psalms," 213) finds fault with the "eisegetical concerns" of those who so read it. Cf. A. A. Anderson, *The Book of Psalms.* NCBC (Grand Rapids: Wm. B. Eerdmans, 1981) 1:66-68.

46. Note the comment of two Jewish interpreters of Ps 2:2: "*His anointed* may refer to the king. The same term 'mashiaḥ' is used in postbiblical literature (but never in the Bible)

(16) Ps 18:50-51(Eng. 49-50) (another preexilic composition) has the same thanksgiving as that in 2 Sam 22:51 and has been treated above (see §7).

(17) Psalm 20 seems to be a late preexilic liturgical composition, written as a petition to accompany an offering being made in the Temple before a king sets out for war; it expresses hope for his victory (as Samuel did in 1 Sam 7:9; cf. 13:9-12; 30:8). The psalmist sings, "Now I know that the LORD gives victory to his Anointed One; He will answer him from His holy heaven, with mighty saving deeds of His right hand" (20:7). The unnamed reigning king is called the LORD's Anointed, i.e., enthroned by the LORD, as in Ps 2:2, but מָשִׁיחַ is not meant in a "messianic" sense. The meaning of the verb may be future, but that is part of a prayer being uttered for a king about to enter into battle, and help from the LORD is scarcely being sought for a remote figure awaited in the end time, even though the wording of the answer may be open to a more remote effect. What one detects here is what Mowinckel calls "the future hope," i.e., that the ideal of kingship in ancient Israel was never fully realized and consequently "had a certain relation to the future."[47] That relation, however, is vague and cannot yet be said to be a "messianic" hope, because the psalm is expressing the might of the divine presence over military force and stressing that the king should not put any confidence in his own prowess, because יְשׁוּעָה, "victory," comes only from the LORD.[48]

(18) Psalm 89, in the final form of the MT, is often considered to be an exilic or postexilic royal psalm, but it actually is a mixed composition, which, some would say, should rather "be dated in the time of the kings."[49] It opens with a hymn of praise addressed to God (vv. 2-19[Eng. 1-18]) and continues as a royal hymn with an oracle of God about stipulations of the

---

to refer to the ideal future Davidic king, and is the origin of the term 'Messiah'"; A. Berlin and M. Z. Brettler, "Psalms," in *The Jewish Study Bible*, ed. Berlin and Brettler (Oxford: Oxford University Press, 2004) 1285. Cf. H.-J. Kraus, *Psalms 1–59* (Minneapolis: Augsburg, 1988) 134.

47. *He That Cometh*, 96. To this topic Mowinckel devotes two whole chapters, pp. 96-154, in which he sets out the conditions under which that future help is spelled out.

48. See further Kraus, *Psalms 1–59*, 282; Gillingham, "The Messiah in the Psalms," 214.

49. H.-J. Kraus, *Psalms 60–150* (Minneapolis: Augsburg, 1989) 203. The mixed character of Psalm 89 may be due to different stages of composition; see E. Lipiński, *Le Poème royal du Psaume LXXXIX, 1-5, 20-38*. CahRB 6 (Paris: Gabalda, 1967); also J. T. Milik, "Fragment d'une source du Psautier (4Q Ps 89) et fragments des Jubilés, du Document de Damas, d'un phylactère dans la grotte 4 de Qumran," *RB* 73 (1966) 94-106 (+ pl. I-III), esp. 95-104; E. Ulrich et al., "98g. 4Qps^x," in *Qumran Cave 4: XI, Psalms to Chronicles*. DJD 16 (Oxford: Clarendon, 2000) 163-67.

covenant established by Him with the Davidic dynasty (vv. 20-38[19-37]). Especially important is v. 37(36): "his offspring shall endure forever, and this throne as long as the sun before me" (again an expression of "the future hope"). The psalm ends, however, with a lament of the community over the decline of the Davidic dynasty since an enemy has prevailed, the throne has fallen, and the covenant has been renounced by God (vv. 39-52[38-51]).[50]

Verses 39-40(38-39) begin the lament, "But You, You have cast off and rejected and burned with wrath against Your Anointed One. You have renounced the covenant with Your servant. . . ." The lament concludes with words of the king speaking and calling himself מְשִׁיחֶךָ, "Recall, O LORD, the mockery of Your servant, my bearing in my bosom the insults of nations, with which Your enemies mock, O LORD, with which they mock the footsteps of Your Anointed One" (vv. 51-52[50-51]). Implied, but not mentioned, are the destruction of Jerusalem and the deportation of many of the people of Judah.

Here the communal lament of Israel utters its incomprehension about the defeat of its Davidic king in battle and the victory of its enemies: "Where is Your loving kindness of old, O LORD, which You swore to David in Your faithfulness?" (89:50[49], an allusion to the Oracle of Nathan, 2 Sam 7:11bc).[51] The phrases "Your servant" and "Your Anointed One" refer in the past tense to some historical king of Israel (the death of Josiah?, the exile of Jehoiachin?, or the capture of Zedekiah?) and mourn the demise of the Davidic monarchy. There is not a hint, however, of a "Messiah," even in vv. 21-24(20-23), which tell in the past tense of God's anointing David, His servant; and this has to be acknowledged despite what has been called "the idealization of David in Psalm 89."[52] The one of whom מָשִׁיחַ is predicated is an unnamed anointed figure in the lineage stemming from David.[53]

(19) In the preexilic royal Psalm 132, the psalmist, echoing the chorus

---

50. See further N. M. Sarna, "Psalm 89: A Study in Inner Biblical Exegesis," in *Biblical and Other Studies* (ed. A. Altmann; Cambridge, MA: Harvard University Press, 1963) 29-46; R. J. Clifford, "Psalm 89: A Lament over the Davidic Ruler's Continued Failure," *HTR* 73 (1980) 35-47.

51. For the debate about whether Psalm 89 alludes to 2 Samuel 7, see Sarna, "Psalm 89," 36-45; K. M. Heim, "The (God-)Forsaken King of Psalm 89: A Historical and Intertextual Enquiry," in J. Day, *King and Messiah in Israel*, 296-322, esp. 299-303.

52. Heim, "The (God-)Forsaken King," 314-15; he also discusses the use of Psalm 89 in the book of Revelation (316-21).

53. See Gillingham, "The Messiah in the Psalms," 216.

of priests and people who accompany the ark of the covenant to its resting place in Zion (cf. 2 Sam 7:1-2), as a sanctuary is founded for it, sings accordingly, "For the sake of David your servant, reject not the plea of your Anointed One" (132:10), i.e., of the king, the descendant of David, who is a contemporary of the psalmist praying for him. The psalmist recasts as a divine "oath" the Oracle of Nathan (2 Sam 7:12-13), thus insuring the continuation of the Davidic dynasty and putting on God's lips the words, "There will I make a horn sprout for David.[54] I have set up a lamp for my Anointed One" (132:17). The psalmist thus recalls the past divine promise concerning Jerusalem and David's dynasty that is ruling there (cf. 2 Sam 21:17). The two verses (10, 17) refer to a king, called מָשִׁיחַ, a "horn" that has sprouted from David's line, and a "lamp" (cf. 2 Sam 21:17). He reigns in Zion (Jerusalem), the place which God chose for his dwelling among the children of Israel.[55] In 2 Chr 6:41-42, the words of Ps 132:8-10 are quoted and used of Solomon (cf. §9 above).

These, then, are the royal psalms in which מָשִׁיחַ occurs. Concerning them in general Mowinckel has rightly noted:

> they are in fact not prophecies but prayers, issuing from a real, contemporary situation, that of the poet or the worshipper himself; and they express what he then felt, and thought, and said. The fact that the worshipper is in many instances a historical king of Israel does not alter the fundamental fact that the psalms are not prophecies but prayers with contemporary reference.[56]

What Mowinckel has said is echoed by other writers too.[57]

The term מָשִׁיחַ is found also in the following three psalms, which are not usually considered to be royal, but are of different sorts.

(20) Psalm 28, a "psalm of David," is regarded mainly as one of individual lament, in which a bit of thanksgiving has also been mixed; it may date from preexilic times, but is hardly from the time of David. The psalm-

---

54. The MT says, *šām 'aṣmîăḥ qeren lĕdāwīd,* which symbolically promises a kingly succession to David.

55. See Mowinckel, *He That Cometh,* 98-99, 117; Gillingham, "The Messiah in the Psalms," 216-17.

56. Mowinckel, *He That Cometh,* 12.

57. E.g., Gillingham, "The Messiah in the Psalms," 220; Becker, *Messianic Expectation in the Old Testament,* 38.

ist prays in the Temple for deliverance from personal enemies who torment him and pleads that Yahweh will punish those who are truly wicked and do not recognize His rule on earth. As his prayer is heard, he gives thanks (vv. 6-7), and then adds: "The LORD is the strength of His people; He is the saving stronghold of His Anointed" (28:8).[58] Because the psalm is ascribed to David, the term "His Anointed" (מְשִׁיחוֹ) might refer to him; but that is far from certain, for it could refer either to an unnamed king on his throne or even to God's people, as the poetic parallelism itself suggests. Mowinckel maintains that the last-named interpretation is "based on erroneous exegesis,"[59] but compare Hab 3:13, where the same parallelism is found. In any case, there is no hint here of any "messianic" connotation of the term.[60]

(21) Psalm 84 is generally understood as a hymn of praise, the song of pilgrims making their way to the Jerusalem Temple on some feast day. It expresses the pilgrims' longing, as they stand at the Temple gates, to enter the courts of the LORD (vv. 3-5[Eng. 2-4]); then it invokes blessings on those who serve there (vv. 6-9[5-8]), utters a prayer for the king (vv. 9-10[8-9]), and repeats the longing to dwell there (vv. 11-13[10-12]). The prayer for the king runs as follows: "O LORD, God of hosts, listen to my prayer; give ear, O God of Jacob! Look, O God, upon our shield,[61] and gaze upon the face of Your Anointed One" (84:9-10[8-9]). Here מְשִׁיחֶךָ stands in poetic parallelism to "our shield," i.e., the reigning king, who affords protection for the pilgrims. This may refer to David, but more probably to one of his descendants in preexilic times. In any case, it lacks all "messianic" connotation, *pace* D. M. Williams.[62]

---

58. The Hebrew text is problematic: יהוה עֹז־לָמוֹ וּמָעוֹז יְשׁוּעוֹת מְשִׁיחוֹ הוּא, lit., "Yahweh (is) strength for them, and He (is) the stronghold of victories of His Anointed." Some Hebrew mss, however, read לְעַמּוֹ, "for His people," instead of לָמוֹ, "for them," and they are supported by the LXX (τοῦ λαοῦ αὐτοῦ) and the Syriac.

59. *He That Cometh*, 7.

60. See Kraus, *Psalms 1–59*, 342; Maillot-Lelièvre, *Les Psaumes*, 1:178; Anderson, *The Book of Psalms*, 1:232; Gillingham, "The Messiah in the Psalms," 220.

61. See Ps 89:19(Eng. 18), where the king again is called "our shield"; cf. Ps 47:10(9). This meaning of *māgēn* is disputed. Some would rather translate it "benefactor, suzerain" (M. Dahood, *Bib* 47 [1966] 414); others, "donor" (M. O'Connor, "Yahweh the Donor," *AuOr* 8 [1988] 46-70; D. N. Freedman and O'Connor, "māgēn," *TDOT* 8 [1997] 86). Note that God Himself is called *šemeš ûmāgēn*, "sun and shield," in Ps 84:12(11).

62. D. M. Williams, *Psalms 73–150*. Communicator's Commentary 14 (Dallas: Word, 1989) 112: "Prayer for the (Messianic) King." See rather Kraus, *Psalms 60–150*, 169: "the reigning king"; similarly, Gillingham, "The Messiah in the Psalms," 220.

(22) Psalm 105:15 is of postexilic origin and has been treated in §14 above.

The attempt to interpret these psalms anachronistically in a "messianic" sense is misguided. As we shall see, some of these passages will be given an allegorical or typological understanding either in later Judaism or in Christianity, but that is a later development in the history of their interpretation. The same has to be said about the "canonical" sense of such passages, i.e., the sense that such psalms take on when considered as part of the Christian Bible. That sense will be discussed in due course, but for the moment the discussion is limited to the original literal and religious sense of these Old Testament passages, where a "messianic" meaning is still out of place.

Two further Old Testament verses use מָשִׁיחַ, Dan 9:25-26, but before we discuss its use in this late writing, a number of other Old Testament passages often regarded as "messianic prophecies" have to be treated, which will be done in the next chapter.

CHAPTER 3

Other Old Testament Passages
Often Regarded as the Background
of the Term "Messiah"

The previous chapter treated the Old Testament passages that use משׁיח in various forms. In all of them it must be translated "Anointed One," and not "Messiah," because they all refer to historical figures in the period of the monarchy of Israel or later and denote God's anointed agents who served His people. In a few instances we noted how reference was made to an unnamed descendant of David on his throne and even to a divine promise to make a horn sprout for David (Ps 132:17), without any indication that that king was to be a Messiah in the sense of an awaited future anointed agent of God.

Now we turn to other Old Testament passages, which have often been said to be part of its "messianic" hope or have been called "messianic prophecies." They are of two kinds and have to be discussed separately: (a) those that have nothing to do with "Messiah" in the strict sense and refer to the premonarchic period of Israel; and (b) those that reveal a development in the understanding of the continuation of the Davidic dynasty, or "the future hope," as Mowinckel has called it. Passages of the latter kind form a transition from the texts discussed in chapter 2 to the use of משׁיח in Dan 9:25-26 and to the historic emergence of a Messiah in Jewish belief. In this chapter the passages of the first type (a) will be discussed.

Among the texts that Mowinckel lists as having "nothing to do with the subject of this book" are Gen 3:15; 49:10; Num 24:17, and a number of royal psalms.[1] The first three of these passages mentioned and some others call for particular comment.

---

1. *He That Cometh,* 11-15. Some of the royal psalms that he mentions (Psalms 2, 18, 20, 89, 132) have been treated in chapter 2, and the rest will be taken up in chapter 4.

Other OT Passages Regarded as the Background of the Term "Messiah"

(1) In Genesis 3 one finds an etiological story of the beginning of evil and sin in human life. After the Yahwist account of the creation of Adam and Eve, that chapter continues with the narrative of the seduction of them by the serpent and of their consequent loss of intimacy and friendship with God. In vv. 14-15, the LORD God reacts and levels a curse against the serpent that seduced Eve. Among other things, He says to the serpent:

> Because you have done this, more cursed are you than all cattle and all wild animals; on your belly shall you crawl, and dirt shall you eat all the days of your life. I will put enmity between you and the woman, and between your offspring and hers; it shall trample your head, and you shall snap at its heel.[2]

The "it" is expressed in Hebrew by the masculine pronoun הוא (*hû'*), which refers to the masculine collective noun זרע (*zeraʿ*, "seed, offspring").[3] The pronoun should not be rendered "he," because that immediately specifies an individual male, whereas the Hebrew speaks of a collectivity, "your seed, your offspring." In cursing the serpent,[4] God speaks clearly of the struggle that will ensue between human beings, born of the woman, and the slithering, often poisonous, member of the animal world, whenever they meet. As in a number of other incidents in the book of Genesis, the episode symbolically recounts the *beginning* of evil and sin among humans in their hostile encounter with the serpent that symbolizes the evil that confronts them.[5] Being an etiology, the account has a signifi-

---

2. Lit., "it shall trample you as to the head, and you shall snap at it as to the heel." The meaning of the verb שׁוף has been debated for a long time, but the meaning "bruise, crush, trample" is often used today. Part of the problem is whether there are one or two verbal roots involved. *HALOT* (1446) treats all the forms as of one verb שׁוף, whereas KBL (956) distinguishes two such verbs, one meaning "trample" and the other "snap at." See further C. Westermann, *Genesis 1-11.* BKAT 1/1 (Neukirchen-Vluyn: Neukirchener, 1974) 353-56; Eng. trans. *Genesis 1–11* (Minneapolis: Augsburg, 1984) 258-61. V. P. Hamilton (*The Book of Genesis: Chapters 1-17.* NICOT [Grand Rapids: Wm. B. Eerdmans, 1990] 198) would render the two verbs alike: "He shall lie in wait for your head" and "you shall lie in wait for his heel."

3. "Seed" is often used as "offspring" in a collective sense: e.g., Gen 9:9; 12:7; 13:16; 15:5, 13, 18; 2 Sam 7:12.

4. The curse is similar to the prohibition of Lev 11:41, "Every creeping thing that creeps upon the earth is an abomination and shall not be eaten."

5. See G. von Rad, *Genesis.* OTL (Philadelphia: Westminster, 1972) 92-93; J. Chaine, *Le livre de la Genèse.* LD 3 (Paris: Editions du Cerf, 1951) 50-51; E. A. Speiser, *Genesis.* AB 1 (Garden City: Doubleday, 1964) 24 (". . . 'seed,' used normally in the collective sense of

cance that transcends the immediate *dramatis personae* and is telling human beings that evil and sin entered their lives apart from God who created them. Evil did not come from Him, but from them who allowed themselves to be seduced by a creature. (That is the simple meaning of this verse in Genesis, even apart from a later Christian identification of the serpent of Genesis 3 with "the ancient serpent, who is called the Devil and Satan" [Rev 12:9], who shall be defeated by Michael in the end time. In that sense, this verse of Genesis 3 *will become* the *Protevangelium,* as Christians have read it for centuries, but it was not such in pre-Christian times.)

Although the curse is formulated for the future, it contains no hint of a coming human victory.[6] Not even the contrast of "head" and "heel" necessarily connotes victory, because they are merely the two anatomical parts of a human being and a serpent that would be involved in such an encounter.[7] "The poisonous serpent strikes at man's foot whenever he is unfortunate enough to come too near to it; and always and everywhere man tries to crush the serpent's head when he has the chance."[8] There is rather only a promise of everlasting hostility between humanity, as the offspring of the woman, and the evil (serpent), as it lies ever in wait for human beings.

Moreover, this verse does not mention מָשִׁיחַ, or even have a hidden reference to a coming Messiah, despite the later interpretations often given to it in both the Jewish and Christian tradition.[9] J. Becker

---

progeny. The passage does not justify eschatological connotations. As Dr. [S. R. Driver] put it, 'We must not read into the words more than they contain'").

6. This point must be stressed, because the verse has often been interpreted as predicting victory. E.g., F. Delitzsch, *Messianic Prophecies in Historical Succession* (New York: Scribner's, 1891) 35 ("in the midst of the curse on the tempter the hope of a victory in the contest with the power of evil rises upon mankind"); Cf. E. Lipiński, "Études sur des textes 'messianiques' de l'Ancien Testament," *Sem* 20 (1970) 41-57, esp. 45; C. Hauret, *Beginnings: Genesis and Modern Science* (Dubuque: Priory, 1964) 155.

7. *Pace* J. Haspecker and N. Lohfink, "Gn 3,15: 'weil du ihm nach der Ferse schnappst,'" *Scholastik* 36 (1961) 357-72, esp. 370-72. Cf. Lipiński, *Sem* 20 (1970) 46-47, where he criticizes the interpretation of Haspecker and Lohfink, but also rightly counters the eschatological and messianic nuances read into Gen 3:15. See also H. Gunkel, *Genesis* (Macon: Mercer University Press, 1997) 20: "Nothing is said of an end to the struggle, of a victory." Cf. D. Castelli, *Il Messia secondo gli Ebrei* (Florence: Le Monnier, 1874) 34-36.

8. S. Mowinckel, *He That Cometh,* 11.

9. Such Jewish interpretation begins in the LXX, and it will be discussed in due course. Such a Christian interpretation can be found, e.g., in B. Rigaux, "La femme et son lignage dans Genèse III, 14-15," *RB* 61 (1954) 321-48, esp. 337, 343; D. I. Block, "My Servant David: Ancient Israel's Vision of the Messiah," in *Israel's Messiah in the Bible and the Dead Sea*

rightly notes that "a preexilic messianic movement is an untenable hypothesis."[10]

(2) The ancient poem of Genesis 49 depicts the dying patriarch Jacob blessing his sons, and in v. 10 he says about Judah among other things, "The scepter shall not depart from Judah, nor the mace from between his feet, until tribute comes to him, and his is the obedience of peoples." The blessing is meant to emphasize the ascendancy of the tribe of Judah among the twelve tribes. The meaning of the last half of the verse, however, is problematic: עד כי יבא שילה ולו יקהת עמים, lit., "until there comes *šîlōh*, and to him/it (is) the obedience of peoples." The problem is the meaning of שִׁילֹה, which has been explained in various ways: (a) as a personal name, "until Shiloh comes" (otherwise not identified[11]). (b) as a place name, "until he comes to Shiloh," presumably the city in Ephraim, north of Bethel, where the ark of the covenant rested from the time of Joshua to the days of Samuel; then ולו would mean "and to it" (but that city's name is usually spelled שילו, שלו, or שלה[12]). (c) as an alleged Akkadian loanword, *šīlu*, often said to mean "ruler, prince" (but it has been shown to be a fiction of lexicographers[13]). (d) as a way of writing *šellōh*, "(until he comes) to whom it [the scepter or mace] belongs," as the RSV and NIV render the clause, following the ancient Syriac version *(man dĕdîlēh hî);* "he comes" is then often taken in a "messianic" sense, meaning that, after Judah's reign has lasted an indefinite time, it will be followed by a Messiah, whom "peoples" will obey (but that syntax is impossible, because *šellōh* would have to be followed by *hû'* in that case[14]). (e) as two words, *šay lōh*, "tribute to him" (the ה is taken as the older spelling of the 3rd person sing. masc. pronominal suffix). This interpreta-

Scrolls, ed. R. S. Hess and M. D. Carroll R (Grand Rapids: Baker, 2003) 17-56, esp. 22 ("Explicit references to the messiah in the Pentateuch"), 37, 56 ("Gen. 3:15 . . . 49:10"); E. W. Hengstenberg, *Christology of the Old Testament and a Commentary on the Messianic Predictions* (Grand Rapids: Kregel, 1970) 13-24.

10. Joachim Becker, *Messianic Expectation in the Old Testament* (Philadelphia: Fortress, 1980) 35.

11. In later Jewish tradition it will be identified as a name of the Messiah (e.g., in *b. Sanh.* 98b).

12. In some MSS of Ps 78:60, however, the city's name is spelled שילה.

13. This meaning was adopted by Mowinckel, *He That Cometh,* 13 n. 2.

14. For the difficulties attending meanings (b), (c), (d), see W. L. Moran, "Gen 49, 10 and Its Use in Ez 21, 32," *Bib* 39 (1958) 405-25. He supports the meaning (e) and explains its use in Ezek 21:32(Eng. 27).

tion is often preferred today and can be found in the NJV: "so that tribute shall come to him" (i.e., to Judah); NAB: "while tribute is brought to him"; NRSV: "until tribute comes to him."[15] Jacob's blessing thus enhances Judah's dominion and undoubtedly hints at the supremacy that that tribe will assume in the time of David, whose dynasty would rule for centuries in Jerusalem and who would receive the homage and tribute of surrounding peoples, before it meets its demise in Zedekiah in the early sixth century.[16] In time this problematic verse was to be given a messianic interpretation in the Jewish tradition.[17] In the preexilic period, however, it was not a "messianic prophecy," and it does not even hint at such a notion, despite modern anachronistic attempts to read such an idea into the text.[18] "In a poem that is manifestly pre-Davidic on every apparent count, one does not strain for veiled references to David,"[19] and *a fortiori* to a "Messiah."

(3) Num 24:17, which is a verse in the fourth oracle of Balaam, son of Beor (24:15-19), who was summoned by Balak, king of Moab, to curse the oncoming Israelites and give advantage to the Moabites: Balaam utters instead a blessing on Israel. In this verse, which appears today in a text from the Yahwistic source, but may be a later addition to it,[20] the seer says, "I see him, though not now; I behold him, though not close at hand: a star shall stride forth from Jacob, and a scepter[21] shall arise from Israel; it shall smite

---

15. See Isa 18:7; Ps 68:30(Eng. 29); 76:12(11) for other instances of *šay* in this sense. For different and more problematic interpretations of שׁילה, see B. Margulis, "Gen. XLIX 10 / Deut. XXXIII 2-3: A New Look at Old Problems," *VT* 19 (1969) 202-10; L. Sabottka, "Noch Einmal Gen 49, 10," *Bib* 51 (1970) 225-29 (understanding עד, "throne," as in Ugaritic).

16. Note the reverse interpretation given to Gen 49:10 in Ezek 21:32(Eng. 27), where the prophet alludes to the Genesis verse and shows how its meaning is turned upside down in King Zedekiah (see Moran, *Bib* 39 [1958] 416-25).

17. See the Qumran interpretation and that in rabbinical literature below, pp. 95-96, 154-55.

18. E.g., W. Brueggemann, *Genesis*. Interpretation (Atlanta: John Knox, 1982) 366: "hints at Messianic dimensions"; Chaine, *Le livre de la Genèse*, 435.

19. Speiser, *Genesis*, 366.

20. See J. A. Hackett, "Balaam," *ABD*, 1:569-72; L. Schmidt, "Die alttestamentliche Bileamüberlieferung," *BZ* 23 (1979) 234-61.

21. The Hebrew word is שׁבט, *šebeṭ*, which is understood to mean "comet" by some interpreters (e.g., B. Gemser, "Der Stern aus Jakob (Num 24,17)," *ZAW* 43 [1925] 301-2; Mowinckel, *He That Cometh*, 12, 102). That meaning would suit the context better, being parallel to "star" in the first clause.

the brows of Moab and the skulls of all the sons of Sheth."[22] Sheth is probably the Hebrew form of an ancient name for Moab, viz. *Šütu.*[23] In any case, the Aramean seer's vision refers to a coming victory of Israel over Moab (and Edom),[24] such as was to be achieved under David (2 Sam 8:2, 13-14). The oracle makes known the future blessings and good fortune coming to Israel, possibly in the person of David, the king who comes forth from Jacob.[25]

Despite the future sense of the verbs, there is neither mention nor hint of a Messiah in this text,[26] even though it came to be so read in the later Jewish tradition and in patristic literature among Christians.[27] Along with Gen 49:10, this text is *vaticinium ex eventu,*[28] and the "event" antedates any putative messianic figure by a millennium.

In addition to these three passages mentioned by Mowinckel, the same caveat has to be expressed also about a number of texts which have been included at times by various writers among "messianic prophecies" of the Old Testament. Among such texts in the Pentateuch, where no occurrence of משיח is ever found, one cites at times the following:

22. The last clause (וקרקר כל בני שת) is difficult to interpret, and I have followed the reading קדקד, "skull" (a collective sing.), which suits the poetic parallelism. So it is read in the Samaritan Pentateuch, and it is supported by Jer 48:45. For this passage, see H. Rouillard, *La péricope de Balaam (Nombres 22-24): La prose et les "oracles."* EBib N.S. 4 (Paris: Gabalda, 1985) 489-506 (bibliog.).

23. See *IDB* 4:326. In the later Jewish tradition, the name "Sheth" will be confused with that of "Seth," son of Adam. Cf. J. de Vaulx, *Les Nombres.* SB (Paris: Gabalda, 1972) 290.

24. See W. Gross, *Bileam: Literar- und formkritische Untersuchung der Prosa in Num 22-24.* SANT 38 (Munich: Kösel, 1974).

25. So it is understood by M. Noth (*Numbers.* OTL [Philadelphia: Westminster, 1968] 192-93); Mowinckel, *He That Cometh,* 13; J. Becker, *Messianic Expectation in the Old Testament,* 37.

26. See J. Coppens, "Les oracles de Biléam: Leur origine littéraire et leur portée prophétique," *Mélanges Eugène Tisserant.* Studi e testi 231 (Vatican City: Biblioteca Apostolica Vaticana, 1964), 1:67-80, esp 79. Cf. D. Castelli, *Il Messia secondo gli Ebrei,* 43-44.

27. E.g., H. Gross, "'Ein Zepter wird sich erheben aus Israel' (Num 24,17): Die messianische Hoffnung im Alten Testament," *BK* 17 (1962) 34-37 (this article discusses many alleged messianic texts, but it hardly explains how Num 24:17 or the others can be called "messianic"). So it still is interpreted at times today; e.g., T. R. Ashley, *The Book of Numbers.* NICOT (Grand Rapids: Wm. B. Eerdmans, 1993) 503. Cf. K. J. Cathcart, "Numbers 24:17 in Ancient Translations and Interpretations," in *The Interpretation of the Bible,* ed. J. Krašovec. JSOTSup 289 (Sheffield: Sheffield Academic, 1998) 511-20.

28. So Becker, *Messianic Expectation in the Old Testament,* 37.

(4) Gen 9:25-27: Noah's curse of Canaan and his blessing of Shem and Japheth, which implies the subjugation of Canaan to Israel, and nothing more.

(5) Gen 12:3: the blessing of Abraham and all families of the earth through him, which implies the divinely destined role that Israel was to play among other peoples of the ancient world.

(6) Exod 12:42: the passover as "a night of vigil to be kept for the LORD by all the Israelites throughout their generations."

(7) Deut 18:15-18: God's promise to Moses to raise up a prophet like him from among his brothers who will listen to God's words and transmit them.[29] In the later Jewish tradition, this prophet like Moses will have a role with the Messiah(s) that emerge in due course (especially in the sectarian texts from Qumran), but he is not understood even then as a Messiah, and certainly cannot be so understood in the book of Deuteronomy itself.[30]

What one reads in the foregoing Old Testament texts are diverse forms of the promise that God has made to bless Israel and of ways in which Israel is called to be mindful of His continuous providence for it. It is an unwarranted stretch of interpretation to regard such promises as early instances of "messianic prophecies" or expressions of a "messianic hope." Similarly, other texts, such as Exod 40:9-11 (the anointing of the tabernacle), Num 23:21 (the shout of the king), Deut 25:19 (the blotting out of all remembrance of Amalek), and Deut 30:4 (the gathering in of the dispersed) must also be dismissed, even if some of them have preternatural or mythical traits that transcend the ordinary human condition. Such traits do not make them "messianic."[31]

---

29. See chapter 2, n. 24 on the Samaritans and their expectation. Cf. M. Sabbe, "Het tema van de Messias, profeet zoals Mozes," *Collationes Brugenses* 50 (1954) 148-65; H. M. Teeple, *The Mosaic Eschatological Prophet.* JBL Monograph 10 (Philadelphia: Society of Biblical Literature, 1957).

30. See Block, "My Servant David," 31-32.

31. See further Mowinckel, *He That Cometh,* 14-15.

Old Testament Passages That Reveal a Developing Understanding of the Davidic Dynasty

In chapter 2 we saw that the noun מָשִׁיחַ was used most frequently of historical kings of Israel, especially of Saul, David, and unnamed kings of the dynasty that emerged from the latter. Because the Messiah in the Jewish tradition is intimately related to that dynasty, it is necessary to look at further passages in the Old Testament that tell about the dynasty and its development in the preexilic, exilic, and postexilic periods.[1] This is what Mowinckel has called "a preliminary stage of the true Messianic faith,"[2] even though it is not yet the period in the history of Judaism when "messianism" fully emerges.

(1) Although David's role as king of Israel is mentioned in various passages (e.g., 2 Sam 2:4; 5:3), the most important passage in the Old Testament that tells of the dynasty that comes from him is the Oracle of Nathan in 2 Samuel 7.[3] There one learns that King David, who was dwelling

1. See K. E. Pomykala, *The Davidic Dynasty Tradition in Early Judaism: Its History and Significance for Messianism.* SBLEJIL 7 (Atlanta: Scholars, 1995); E.-J. Waschke, "The Significance of the David Tradition for the Emergence of Messianic Beliefs in the Old Testament," *WW* 23 (2003) 413-20.

See further S. Amsler, *David, roi et messie: La tradition davidique dans l'Ancien Testament.* CahT 49 (Neuchâtel: Editions Delachaux et Niestlé, 1963); J. L. Sicre, *De David al Mesías: Textos básicos de la esperanza mesiánica.* Collección 'El Mundo de la Biblia' (Estella: Editorial Verbo Divino, 1995).

2. *He That Cometh,* 99.

3. It is sometimes thought that ch. 7 is a late insertion into the Early Source that is otherwise being used at this part of 2 Samuel, but see A. Laato, "Second Samuel 7 and Ancient Near Eastern Royal Ideology," *CBQ* 59 (1997) 244-69; also F. M. Cross, *Canaanite Myth*

in a fine house of cedar and wanted to build a house for God's ark, is told by the prophet Nathan that God has taken David from pasturing sheep to be a prince over His people and to make for him a great name. Moreover,

> the LORD declares that He will make a house for you: 'When your days are complete and you lie down with your ancestors, I will raise up your offspring after you, which shall come forth from your loins, and I will establish his kingship forever. He shall build a house for my name, and I will establish the throne of his kingship forever. I will be his father, and he shall be my son. (7:11-14)[4]

This oracle is repeated in the postexilic writing, 1 Chr 17:10b-14, in a slightly embellished form, in which God explains the "offspring" as "one of your own sons," and assures David that He shall not take away from him His "steadfast love" (חסדי).

The term "house" in this passage is important because of the play on its various meanings. The "house" of cedar in which David is dwelling is his palace, and he wants to build for the LORD and His ark a similar "house," i.e., a temple; but the LORD says that He will build instead for him a "house," i.e., a dynasty that will endure in Israel.[5] To this dynastic house several royal psalms refer, where an heir of David is called משיחך, "your Anointed One" (89:39, 52[Eng. 38, 51]; 132:10), as discussed in chapter 2 above. This passage is seen, then, "as the Magna Charta of the Davidic

---

and Hebrew Epic: Essays in the History of the Religion of Israel (Cambridge, MA: Harvard University Press, 1973) 241-64. Cf. M. Avioz, "Nathan's Prophecy in II Sam 7 and in I Chr 17: Text, Context, and Meaning," ZAW 116 (2004) 542-54.

4. See L. Rost, Die Überlieferung von der Thronnachfolge Davids. BWANT 3/6 (Stuttgart: Kohlhammer, 1926); Eng. trans. The Succession to the Throne of David (Sheffield: Almond, 1982); M. Noth, "David und Israel in 2. Samuel 7," in Mélanges bibliques rédigés en l'honneur de André Robert. TICP 4 (Paris: Bloud & Gay, 1957) 122-30; J. Becker, Messianic Expectation in the Old Testament (Philadelphia: Fortress, 1980) 25-31.

5. Cf. also the related "law of the king" in Deut 17:14-20, esp. v. 15, "You shall indeed set over you as king him whom the LORD your God chooses," even though it does not mention David and his royal line. For the relation of this text and the Oracle of Nathan to Deuteronomistic History, see J. G. McConville, "King and Messiah in Deuteronomy and the Deuteronomistic History," in King and Messiah in Israel and the Ancient Near East, ed. J. Day. JSOTSup 270 (Sheffield: Sheffield Academic, 1998) 271-95, but note how unclear are what he calls "the parameters of a messianic theology" (293); they are nonexistent in the book of Deuteronomy itself.

monarchy, fixed and effectual since the days of David, impressively documenting its monopoly on legitimacy."[6]

That dynasty continued, even after Solomon succeeded David and built the Temple in Jerusalem, with Rehoboam as king of Judah (922-915 B.C.), and after the revolt when Jeroboam became king of Israel (922-901 B.C.). The dynasty continued to thrive in Judah (see 1 Chr 3:1, 5, 10-16) through the kings Abijah, Asa, Jehoshaphat, Jehoram (Joram), Ahaziah, Jehoash (Joash), Amaziah, Uzziah (Azariah), Jotham, Ahaz (Jehoahaz I), Hezekiah, Manasseh, Amon, Josiah, Jehoahaz II (Shallum), Jehoiakim (Eliakim), Jehoiachin (Jeconiah), and Zedekiah (Mattaniah [597-587 B.C.]), until the time of the Babylonian Captivity, when the monarchy came to an end. Of these kings after David, only Solomon and Zedekiah specifically bear the title מָשִׁיחַ in Old Testament passages (2 Chr 6:42; Lam 4:20), although they all were anointed presumably at their accession to the throne. Some of them were among the unnamed kings who are given the title (as in 1 Sam 2:35; Ps 18:51[Eng. 50]), and Josiah was meant undoubtedly in some of the references to unnamed kings.[7] After the Captivity, the restored dynasty is continued in Shealtiel and Zerubbabel (1 Chr 3:17, 19). (See also Matt 1:12-13, which continues in vv. 13-16 with further names: Abiud, Eliakim, Azor, Zadok, Achim, Eliud, Eleazar, Mattan, Jacob, Joseph, which are unknown in the Old Testament and differ from those given in Luke 3:23-27;[8] and some of them may not even be regal names.)

Passages in some of the preexilic prophetic writings refer to the continuous endurance of this Davidic dynasty.

(2) In the eighth century B.C., the prophet Isaiah was sent to King Ahaz of Judah to reassure him about the continuation of the Davidic monarchy. Three passages in particular tell about it (7:1-9; 8:23–9:6; 11:1-10), and H. G. M. Williamson rightly has stressed not only their interrelationship, but also their relation to the context in the first part of Isaiah.[9] In the first of these passages, the Davidic monarchy is threatened by

---

6. Becker, *Messianic Expectation in the Old Testament,* 25.

7. See A. Laato, *Josiah and David Redivivus: The Historical Josiah and the Messianic Expectations of Exilic and Postexilic Times.* ConBOT 33 (Stockholm: Almqvist & Wiksell, 1992).

8. See J. A. Fitzmyer, *The Gospel According to Luke I–IX.* AB 28 (Garden City: Doubleday, 1981) 492-94.

9. H. G. M. Williamson, "The Messianic Texts in Isaiah 1–39," in Day, *King and Messiah in Israel and the Ancient Near East,* 238-70, esp. 241-44.

attack from Rezin of Damascus and Pekah of Israel (Isa 7:1-9; the details are described in 2 Kgs 16:1-20). They had conspired against Ahaz to set up in his stead an Aramean usurper, the son of Tabeel, but God reassures Ahaz, "It shall not come to pass" (v. 7). Then through Isaiah God offers Ahaz and the house of David a further sign: "Therefore the LORD himself will give you (plural) a sign. Look! The young woman is with child and bearing a son. She shall name him Immanuel" (7:14).[10] Here the emphasis falls not on the woman (despite the definite article) but on the birth and naming of a child ("God with us").[11] He will grow up, but before he can distinguish right from wrong, God will see to the desolation of the lands that threaten Ahaz. Thus the sign is to make Ahaz trust in God. The name given to the child emphasizes the way God is providing for the continuation of the Davidic dynasty in these trying circumstances.[12] Whether the child is to become a leader of God's people in such historical circumstances is of less concern, but in any case there is not a hint of a future "Messiah" in this passage, for the child to be born is to be no more than a successor of King Ahaz. The greatest objection to the messianic interpretation of this passage is this: "How can Emmanuel, the Messianic child of the distant and impenetrable future, be a true sign for the eighth century king, Ahaz?"[13]

(3) In the second passage, when the Assyrian king Tiglath-pileser III in 733 B.C. invaded Zebulun and Naphtali, provinces of the Northern Kingdom (Israel), and deported its inhabitants to exile in Assyria (2 Kgs 15:29), words of Isaiah promised that God would restore that land's former glory (Isa 8:23–9:6[Eng. 9:1-7]): "the people who walked in darkness have seen a great light . . . and the rod of its oppressor has (been) broken." God's activity in their deliverance is the main reason for the rejoicing of the people

10. See A. Laato, *Who Is Immanuel? The Rise and the Foundering of Isaiah's Messianic Expectations* (Åbo: Åbo Akademis, 1988); M. R. Adamthwaite, "Isaiah 7:16: Key to the Immanuel Prophecy," *RTR* 59 (2000) 65-83.

11. *Pace* S. Mowinckel, העלמה does not refer to "a supernatural woman," allegedly known from "a well-known popular belief," which he does not identify further; *He That Cometh*, 113.

12. The verse is "usually not considered messianic" (Becker, *Messianic Expectation in the Old Testament*, 37; similarly Mowinckel, *He That Cometh*, 17, 111-19. For a different interpretation of Isa 7:1-17, which stresses more the discontinuity and with "somewhat more of a 'messianic' flavour," see Williamson, "The Messianic Texts in Isaiah 1–39," 244-54.

13. F. L. Moriarty, "The Emmanuel Prophecies," *CBQ* 19 (1957) 226-33, esp. 232.

(vv. 2-4[3-5]), but their joy is further created by the birth of a king, who is to rule this people as God's agent and deliver them from oppression:

> For a child has been born to us, a son has been given to us; upon his shoulder dominion has settled; one has named him Wonderful Counselor, Warrior God, Everlasting Father, Prince of Peace. Of the vastness of (his) dominion and of peace there shall be no end, upon David's throne and over his kingdom, to establish it and to sustain it in justice and righteousness from now and for ever. The zeal of the LORD of hosts shall do this. (9:5-6[6-7])

The stress in these verses is still on the activity of God, who through the royal figure that has been born will bring about the kind of human society that the prophet Isaiah has always been advocating, one marked by "justice and righteousness" (9:6[7]); this pair of qualities is often met in his words (e.g., 1:21, 27; 5:7, 16; 28:17; 32:1, 16; 33:5). Even though the passage began with a reference to the Northern Kingdom, it ends with a clear reference to the Davidic dynasty (and with vocabulary echoing the Oracle of Nathan: throne, kingdom, establish, forever [2 Sam 7:11-14]). "It is the birth of a prince in Jerusalem which has occasioned this promise."[14] The four titles that are given to the child are to be understood as symbolic throne-names, rhetorically summing up the names that he will win for himself in the people's estimation, when he sits upon the throne.[15] Attempts have been made at times to interpret them as names of God, describing what God will be for the child: "One who plans a wonder is the warrior God; the father for ever is a commander who brings peace."[16] In any case, "the predominant thought of the passage neither demands, nor is even particularly suitable to, a postexilic date."[17] Hopes vested in the early Hezekiah or in the early Josiah would exemplify the saying, and a case has been made for both of

---

14. Mowinckel, *He That Cometh,* 109. "But *who* the child should be, was still hidden from him [i.e., the prophet]" (p. 110).

15. For an explanation of the names, see Mowinckel, *He That Cometh,* 105.

16. J. Goldingay, "The Compound Name in Isaiah 9:5(6)," *CBQ* 61 (1999) 239-44. Cf. J. J. M. Roberts, "Whose Child Is This? Reflections on the Speaking Voice in Isaiah 9:5," *HTR* 90 (1997) 115-29; H. Wildberger, "Die Thronnamen des Messias, Jes. 9,5b," *TZ* 16 (1960) 314-32; E. Lipiński, "Études sur des textes 'messianiques' de l'Ancien Testament," *Sem* 20 (1970) 41-57, esp. 50-53.

17. See Williamson, "The Messianic Texts in Isaiah 1-39," 257; cf. Becker, *Messianic Expectations in the Old Testament,* 44-45.

them in recent major studies.[18] Others would maintain that it merely refers to an ideal future king, without calling him a "Messiah."[19] Yet many read that meaning into this (and the next) Isaian passage![20]

(4) Again, in the third passage, a similar promise about the continuation of the Davidic dynasty is made in Isa 11:1-10, where a future heir of the throne is described and his reign is said to be accompanied by righteousness, equity, and fidelity. The promise follows upon 10:33-34, where God is depicted as a forester who lops off the boughs of trees and cuts down the thickets that symbolize Assyria, the invader coming from the north. Verses 1-3a of ch. 11 begin with a conjunction *(wĕ-),* which connects them to the end of ch. 10.[21] They run as follows:

> But a shoot shall come forth from the stump of Jesse, and a sprout shall bloom from his roots. The spirit of the LORD shall alight upon him, a spirit of wisdom and understanding, a spirit of counsel and might, a spirit of knowledge and fear of the LORD. And his delight shall be in the fear of the LORD.

Verses 3b-9 then give an idyllic description of the reign of this Davidic descendant, and v. 10 concludes it, "On that day the root of Jesse shall stand as a signal for nations: Gentiles shall seek him out, for his dwelling shall be glorious." Jesse, the Bethlehemite, the father of David (1 Sam 16:11-13), is said here to be the "stump" and "root" from which the dynastic line of David is derived. The "spirit of the LORD," which is said to alight upon the "shoot" (חטר, *ḥōṭer*) and the "sprout" (נצר, *nēṣer*), is like the spirit transferred from Moses to the seventy elders in Num 11:25-26 or like that of Elijah given to Elisha in 2 Kgs 2:15. Hence it denotes the succession of David's heir to the throne and God's blessing of him.[22] The king is thus described as God's agent in administering justice, as was the child in Isaiah 9. It is,

---

18. Williamson, "The Messianic Texts in Isaiah 1–39," 257.

19. Mowinckel, *He That Cometh,* 17.

20. See J. Coppens, "Le roi idéal d'Is. ix, 5-6 et xi, 1-5 est-il une figure messianique?" *À la rencontre de Dieu: Mémorial Albert Gelin.* Bibliothèque de la Faculté Catholique de Théologie de Lyon 8 (Le Puy: Xavier Mappus, 1961) 85-108.

21. As Williamson rightly stresses; "The Messianic Texts in Isaiah 1–39," 260-64.

22. See Williamson, "The Messianic Texts in Isaiah 1–39," 258-59. Cf. M. A. Sweeney, "Jesse's New Shoot in Isaiah 11: A Josianic Reading of the Prophet Isaiah," in *A Gift of God in Due Season: Essays on Scripture and Community in Honor of James A. Sanders,* ed. R. D. Weis and D. M. Carr. JSOTSup 225 (Sheffield: Sheffield Academic, 1996) 103-18.

however, a matter of debate among interpreters whether "the stump of Jesse" implies that the Davidic monarchy has come to an end (e.g., in King Zedekiah) or not. If it does imply that, the "shoot" and the "sprout" would then mean the continuation of the dynasty after the Babylonian Captivity, in some sense, but without immediately implying a "messianic" ruler.[23]

(5) There are a few other passages in Isaiah that are at times considered to be like the three main ones discussed so far, e.g., 2:2-4; 4:2; 16:1-5 (especially vv. 4-5); 32:1-5. They are only minimally the same and need no further discussion, since none of them has a "messianic" connotation, even remotely.[24]

One passage may call for some discussion, however, Isa 51:5, which is now read in the Qumran Isaiah Scroll A (1QIsa[a] 42:19) with 3rd person sing. suffixes instead of 1st person sing. suffixes of the MT (referring to God): "His arm shall govern peoples; coastlands shall wait for him; for his arm they shall hope."[25] M. Hengel is undoubtedly right in interpreting the 3rd person suffixes as referring to the Servant mentioned in Isa 50:10, but by no means right in saying that it is "probably to be interpreted messianically."[26] After all, there is only one person who bears the title מָשִׁיחַ (māšîaḥ) in the writings of this prophet, and that is the Persian King Cyrus (45:1), as we have seen. So it is sheer eisegesis to introduce a "messianic" nuance here.[27] This leads us to the major exegetical problem of Deutero-Isaiah.

(6) Many interpreters give a "messianic" interpretation to the Ser-

---

23. Mowinckel, *He That Cometh*, 17; Becker, *Messianic Expectation in the Old Testament*, 37.

24. As Williamson rightly notes ("The Messianic Texts in Isaiah 1–39," 269-70). See, however, E. Barthold, "Der Messias im Buche Isaias," *TGl* 38 (1948) 228-43; A. Feuillet, "Le messianisme du Livre d'Isaïe: Ses rapports avec l'histoire et les traditions d'Israël," *RSR* 36 (1949) 182-228; H. Junker, "Ursprung und Grundzüge des Messiasbildes bei Isajas," *Volume du congrès, Strasbourg 1956*, ed. P. A. H. De Boer. VTSup 4 (Leiden: Brill, 1957) 181-96.

25. See D. W. Parry and E. Qimron, *The Great Isaiah Scroll (1QIs[a]): A New Edition.* STDJ 32 (Leiden: Brill, 1999) 84-85. The shift of the suffix from ו *(waw)*, "his," to י *(yodh)*, "my," is caused often by the careless writing of a copyist.

26. M. Hengel, "The Effective History of Isaiah 53 in the Pre-Christian Period," in *The Suffering Servant: Isaiah 53 in Jewish and Christian Sources*, ed. B. Janowski and P. Stuhlmacher (Grand Rapids: Wm. B. Eerdmans, 2004) 103.

27. Williamson, however, tries to play down the significance of the solitary use of מְשִׁיח for Cyrus in Deutero-Isaiah ("The Messianic Texts in Isaiah 1–39," 239), whereas the fact remains that there is no use of that word, either as an adjective or a title, in Isaiah 1–39, or elsewhere in Deutero-Isaiah, which reveals that it is a deliberate omission, when it could have been employed so easily.

vant Songs of Isaiah, especially to the Fourth Servant Song (Isa 52:13–53:12).[28] That mode of interpretation, however, is tendentious and problematic, because, to begin with, מָשִׁיחַ is not found in any of the Servant Songs; nor is the verb מָשַׁח used in any of them.[29]

Moreover, it does not suffice to show that עַבְדִּי (ʿabdî, "my servant") predicated of someone makes him a "Messiah," pace J. Jeremias.[30] In reality, that mode of interpretation is a refusal to let an important passage in the prophecy of Deutero-Isaiah speak for itself.[31]

28. I am prescinding from discussion of the first three Servant Songs. See, e.g., M. Black, "Servant of the Lord and Son of Man," *SJT* 6 (1953) 1-11; J. Cunningham, "The Suffering Servant," *JRR* 8/1 (1998) 14-28; I. Engnell, "The ʿEbed Yahweh Songs and the Suffering Messiah in 'Deutero-Isaiah,'" *BJRL* 31 (1948) 54-93; P. Stuhlmacher, "Der messianische Gottesknecht," *JBT* 8 (1993) 131-54; Feuillet, *RSR* 36 (1949) 182-228.

29. In 1QIsaᵃ 44.2 (= MT 52:14), however, משחתי is read (see Parry and Qimron, *The Great Isaiah Scroll*, 88-89). Although it looks like the 1st sing. perf. qal of משח, "I have anointed," the form is anomalous in this context.

In the MT, a description is being given of the suffering Servant, which reads כֵּן־מִשְׁחַת מֵאִישׁ מַרְאֵהוּ, "his appearance was so marred beyond human resemblance" *(RSV)*, or lit., "was a disfigurement beyond a human being." This grammatically anomalous Hebrew phrase has a noun in the construct state followed by a prepositional phrase; the form מִשְׁחַת is a *hapax legomenon* and normally understood as a *miqtal* derivative of the root שׁחת, "mar, mutilate." The form מִשְׁחַתִּי in 1QIsaᵃ 44:2 replaces that form, but no English version of the Bible has preferred it to the reading of the MT. Even *The Dead Sea Scrolls Bible* (ed. M. Abegg, Jr., P. Flint. and E. Ulrich [San Francisco: HarperSanFrancisco, 1999]) translates the words, "so was *he marred* in his appearance, more than any human" (p. 359). Hengel, however, has used the Qumran reading, translating it: "so have I anointed his appearance beyond that of any (other) man. . . ." ("The Effective History of Isaiah 53 in the Pre-Christian Period," 104). Hengel comments: "The Servant's unique exaltation and his anointing by God correspond to one another." Nevertheless, it is far from clear. What would an anointing "beyond that of any (other) man" be? And what would the "anointing" of someone's "appearance" mean?

30. Jeremias maintains, "Already in the OT the Messiah is 5 times called 'my servant': Ez. 34:23 f.; 37:24 f. (in all 4 verses עַבְדִּי דָוִד); Zech. 3:8 (עַבְדִּי צֶמַח)" ("παῖς θεοῦ," *TDNT*, 5:681). Later in the same paragraph, Jeremias explains that later (in rabbinic Jewish literature) "the description of the Messiah as God's servant occurs only in the form 'my servant' and only on the lips of God." This usage "persisted . . . only in quotations from Scripture" and "was never at any time a true title of the Messiah in Judaism" (p. 682). Jeremias should have said that it was never a title of the Messiah even in Scripture, because in none of the passages that he has cited (given above) does one find מָשִׁיחַ, and it is simply eisegetical to speak of "Messiah" there. The meaning of such passages will be discussed below, when we come to Old Testament texts that mention a coming or future "David."

31. See P. D. Hanson, "The World of the Servant of the Lord in Isaiah 40–55," in *Jesus*

The passage is important because the Fourth Servant Song depicts God uttering the opening lines (52:13-15) in a lament about the suffering of His "Servant," who, though he grew up like a sapling, now has no stately bearing and is spurned and shunned by all, "a man of suffering, acquainted with infirmity" (53:3). But it was "our infirmities" that he bore, "our offenses" for which he was pierced, and "our sins" that crushed him. "The LORD laid upon him the iniquity of us all" (53:6), "though he had done no wrong, and there was no deceit in his mouth" (53:9cd). The Servant is thus presented as a stand-in, a model of vicarious suffering for others, but the LORD also tells of the reward that His Servant will receive, to the amazement of many peoples (52:15):

> And he made[32] his grave among the wicked and with the rich in his death, though he had done no wrong, and there was no deceit in his mouth. But the LORD was pleased to crush him with infirmity,[33] that if he made himself an offering for sin, he might see offspring and prolong his days, and that the will of the LORD might be implemented through him. Out of his anguish he shall see light[34] and find satisfaction. In his knowledge, my servant,[35] the righteous one, shall make many righteous, and he shall bear their iniquities. Therefore I will allot him a portion with the many, and he shall acquire the multitude as his spoil, seeing that he surrendered himself to death and was numbered with transgressors. Yet he bore the sins of many and made intercession for their transgressions.[36] (Isa 53:9-12)

So ends the Fourth Servant Song about the suffering and triumphant עבד יהוה (‘ebed Yahwēh), which teaches how a faithful and righteous Servant

---

and the Suffering Servant: Isaiah 53 and Christian Origins, ed. W. H. Bellinger, Jr., and W. R. Farmer (Harrisburg: Trinity Press International, 1998) 9-22; R. E. Clements, "Isaiah 53 and the Restoration of Israel," in Bellinger and Farmer, 39-54; O. H. Steck, "Aspekte des Gottesknechts in Jes 52,13-53,12," ZAW 97 (1985) 36-58.

32. The MT and 4QIsa[d] read the sing. ויתן (wayyittēn), but 1QIsa[a] has the plur. ויתנו (wayyittĕnû), "and they made."

33. The MT and 4QIsa[d] read החלי, but 1QIsa[a] reads ויחללהו, "and he made him suffer."

34. Reading אור with 1QIsa[a,b], 4QIsa[d], and the LXX (φῶς).

35. The MT and 4QIsa[d] read עבדי, "my servant," but 1QIsa[a] has עבדו, "His servant."

36. The MT reads לפשעים (lappōšĕ‘îm), "for transgressors," but 1QIsa[a,b] and 4QIsa[d] read לפשעיהמה (lĕpiš‘êhemmāh), "for their transgressions."

can suffer and offer his suffering in expiation of the wrongs of other human beings.[37] As Mowinckel remarks, "what is here described is an act of free grace on God's part. It is His plan that is realized; and it is for this that He has created and equipped the Servant. In order to make this thought clear, the poet naturally uses metaphors from current contemporary ideas about atonement and the forgiveness of sins, i.e., sacrificial language."[38]

The major problem is to explain whom the Servant represents: the people of Israel as a whole? or an individual like the prophet himself? or both an individual and Israel?[39] It seems preferable to understand the "Servant" as an individual, e.g., a future prophet, even if the description of him in the Fourth Song goes "beyond the usual picture of the Old Testament prophet."[40] (How he will be interpreted in later Judaism and Christianity is another matter, which will be discussed in due course.) In any case, the important teaching in the Fourth Servant Song is that "God provides the very sin-offering by which Israel can be healed, cleansed, and forgiven."[41]

As the Fourth Song stands in its present Deutero-Isaian context, however, "there is no room for an expected Messiah as the ruler of the age of salvation."[42] In fact, the passage does not envisage the Servant even as a royal figure, or as a scion of David, or associate with him any political role.[43]

If the reader wonders, then, why the Fourth Servant Song has been introduced into this discussion at this point, it is simply to stress once again that there is no passage in the book of Isaiah that mentions a "Mes-

37. See further B. Janowski, "He Bore Our Sins: Isaiah 53 and the Drama of Taking Another's Place," in Janowski and P. Stuhlmacher, *The Suffering Servant*, 48-74.

38. *He That Cometh*, 210.

39. For a survey of the interpretations across the centuries, see C. R. North, *The Suffering Servant in Deutero-Isaiah*, 2nd ed. (London: Oxford University Press, 1956) 6-116. Cf. Mowinckel, *He That Cometh*, 213-25.

40. Mowinckel, *He That Cometh*, 230.

41. Clements, "Isaiah 53 and the Restoration of Israel," 54.

42. H.-J. Hermisson, "The Fourth Servant Song in the Context of Second Isaiah," in *The Suffering Servant: Isaiah 53 in Jewish and Christian Sources*, ed. B. Janowski and P. Stuhlmacher (Grand Rapids: Wm. B. Eerdmans, 2004) 16-47, esp. 45.

43. Mowinckel sees the difference between the Servant and the Messiah thus: "In the Old Testament period, no one expected the Messiah to be instrumental in establishing the kingdom of God. What the Messiah cannot do, the Servant of the Lord will do. Therefore the thought of the Servant is in itself compatible with the idea of a future king as the supreme figure in the restored kingdom. The poet-prophet would hardly think of the two conceptions as overlapping. Probably he never consciously thought of the relationship between them"; *He That Cometh*, 256.

siah" in the narrow sense, and all attempts to speak of Isaiah's "messianic prophecies" are still-born. Even though passages dealing with a Davidic heir and the suffering Servant of Isaiah 53 share at times an eschatological reference in ushering in the age when God's will shall prevail in Israel, they are discrete in their modes of doing so. The same has to be said also about the predicates attributed to the two figures, which may be drawn from a common stock, for משיח יהוה, "the LORD's Anointed," is different from עבד יהוה, "Servant of the LORD."[44]

Certain psalms mention or allude to the continuation of the Davidic dynasty, especially the six royal psalms that lack the term משיח but pray for the king or some aspects of his role, and thus they reveal how the enduring dynasty has been developing, e.g., Psalms 21, 45, 72, 101, 110, and 144:1-11. Three of them celebrate the enthronement of a Davidic king.

(7) "Endow, O God, the king with your justice and the king's son with your righteousness, that he may govern your people with righteousness, and your afflicted ones with justice" (72:1-2). So begins the psalm composed for the enthronement of a Davidic king, which then goes on to extol the qualities of the equitable rule of the kingly figure (vv. 3-4): his long, renowned reign (vv. 5-7), the extent of his dominion and his relations with foreign nations (vv. 8-11), his defense of the poor and afflicted among his people (vv. 12-14). It ends with prayers for the abundant prosperity of his kingdom (vv. 15-17). The psalm, then, is an intercession for a preexilic reigning king, which contains no divine promise about a coming heir of David. The rhetorical hyperbole (especially of vv. 3, 5-6) makes some commentators hesitate to ascribe all of the description to an earthly king, and so they claim that the psalm is "messianic." The psalm, however, is simply making use of a well-known rhetorical court-style and echoing some of the phraseology of 2 Sam 7:11-16, which makes it more "open" to further interpretation later on in the Jewish tradition.[45] (Verses 18-20 are not really

---

44. See H. H. Rowley, "The Suffering Servant and the Davidic Messiah," *The Servant of the Lord and Other Essays on the Old Testament* (Oxford: Blackwell, 1965) 63-93.

45. E.g., in *Pss. Sol.* 17, as C. C. Broyles has shown; "The Redeeming King: Psalm 72's Contribution to the Messianic Ideal," in *Eschatology, Messianism, and the Dead Sea Scrolls*, ed. C. A. Evans and P. W. Flint. SDSSRL (Grand Rapids: Wm. B. Eerdmans, 1997) 23-40. Cf. R. E. Murphy (*A Study of Psalm 72 (71)*. CUA Studies in Sacred Theology, 2nd ser. 12 [Washington: Catholic University of America Press, 1948]), who interpreted it as messianic. Similarly, E.-J. Waschke, "Die Stellung der Königstexte im Jesajabuch im Vergleich zu den Königspsalmen 2, 72 und 89," *ZAW* 110 (1998) 348-64; E. Zenger, "So betete David für seinen

part of Psalm 72, but form a doxology and a conclusion that mark the end of Book II of the Psalter.)

(8) Psalm 101 is a short utterance of eight verses, pronounced by a Davidic king as he is enthroned or perhaps at a later feast that commemorates his enthronement. It describes the life of integrity that he is expected to lead. The future sense of some verbs does not imply anything "messianic," even if they help to express the Davidic king's continuing loyalty and commitment to rule with justice.[46]

(9) Psalm 110 is another royal psalm for the enthronement of a Davidic king who is to rule in Jerusalem (cf. 2 Chr 9:8 [Yahweh seating Solomon]; 1 Chr 28:5). The court poet recites an oracle addressed to the king, as he is promised victory over his foes:

> 1 An oracle of Yahweh for my lord, 'Sit at my right hand, till I make your enemies a stool for your feet.' 2 The LORD will stretch forth from Zion the scepter of your might: so rule in the midst of your enemies. 3 Your people offer themselves willingly on the day of your power. In majestic holiness, from the womb of the morning, like dew, have I begotten you.[47] 4 Yahweh has sworn and shall not renege, 'You are a priest forever after the manner of Melchizedek.' 5 The LORD is at your right hand; He smote kings on the day of His wrath. (110:1-5)

What is striking in this poorly transmitted royal psalm is not only the cultic language that it employs but also the recognition of the priestly dignity of the new king.[48] He is envisaged to be like the ancient priest-king of Canaanite Jerusalem mentioned in Gen 14:18 (cf. 1QapGen 22:14-17), hence a figure in a special priesthood, different from that of the sons of Aaron.[49] S. E. Gillingham emphasizes the relation of this psalm to Psalm 132 in its connection with Zion or Jerusalem, and "within such a religio-

---

Sohn Salomo und für den König Messias: Überlegungen zur holistischen und kanonischen Lektüre des 72. Psalms," *JBT* 8 (1993) 57-72. But see S. E. Gillingham, "The Messiah in the Psalms," in Day, *King and Messiah in Israel and the Ancient Near East*, 222-23, who rightly interprets the psalm in and for itself.

46. Mowinckel, *He That Cometh*, 91; S. E. Gillingham, "The Messiah in the Psalms," 223.

47. Verse 3 is poorly transmitted not only in the MT, but also in the ancient versions.

48. See Mowinckel, *He That Cometh*, 71-74.

49. For a "messianic" interpretation, see B. C. Davis, "Is Psalm 110 a Messianic Psalm?" *BSac* 157 (2000) 160-73. Cf. Lipiński, *Sem* 20 (1970) 56-57.

political context it could hardly refer to any eschatological ideal in the distant future."[50]

(10) Psalm 21 is also a royal psalm, but it has nothing to do with enthronement. It begins, "O LORD, the king delights in Your might; in Your victory how greatly he exults" (21:2[Eng. 1]). It is an utterance of a court poet who gives thanks to God for his king's victory in battle, ending with "The king trusts in the LORD; through the loving kindness of the Most High he stands unshaken" (v. 8[7]). Afterwards the people of the realm invoke blessings on the king (vv. 9-13[8-12]). This psalm is paired with and similar in structure to Psalm 20, which was composed rather to ask for divine assistance as the "Anointed One" sets out to do battle.[51] The king is an unnamed monarch reigning on David's throne, and there is no hint of him as a "Messiah."[52]

(11) Psalm 45 is yet another royal psalm, but now a nuptial ode composed by a court poet for a royal wedding, as one celebrates the marriage of some Davidic king (Solomon?), apparently to a Phoenician princess (see 45:13[Eng. 12]; the MT has בת צר, "daughter of Tyre"). Verses 3-10(2-9) sing of the royal bridegroom's handsome look, virtue, and military ability; vv. 11-12(10-11) urge the bride to wifely devotion; vv. 13-16(12-15) describe the bridal raiment and procession; and vv. 17-18(16-17) wish the king suitable offspring. The verses often considered important in this psalm are the following:

> Your throne, O God, stands forever and ever; your royal scepter is a scepter of equity. You have loved righteousness and hated wickedness. Therefore God, your God, has anointed you with the oil of gladness above your peers. (45:7-8[6-7])

In v. 7(6), the king seems to be addressed as אלהים (*'ĕlōhîm*, "God"), which makes him superhuman or godlike; that is, again, part of the elevated rhetoric of the court style that one meets at times in the Psalter. In v. 8(7) it is said that God "has anointed" him (אלהיך על־כן משחך אלהים). So it is

---

50. "The Messiah in the Psalms," 222. Although it sounds like a good instance of the sacral kingship of the preexilic period, the psalm probably dates from the postexilic age (see Becker, *Messianic Expectation in the Old Testament,* 43-44). *Pace* D. Kidner (*Psalms 1-72.* TOTC [Leicester: Inter-Varsity, 1973] 391-92), it is far from "an implicit prophecy about a future Messianic King."

51. See p. 21 above.

52. See Gillingham, "The Messiah in the Psalms," 221.

often concluded that vv. 7-8(6-7) are already speaking of the "Messiah."[53] The anointing, however, is spoken of in the past tense and recalls that of someone who has mounted the Davidic throne, for whose marital welfare the psalmist is now praying. It is another instance of sacral kingship of the preexilic period, but the dating of this psalm is debated; even if it comes from the postexilic period, nothing in it bears a remote future reference, not even vv. 17-18(16-17), which speak of the king's sons as "princes throughout the land" and of his inevitable celebrated notoriety: "peoples will praise you for ever and ever."[54]

(12) The last royal psalm to be considered is Ps 144:1-11, which seems to be a lament in which a Davidic king prays for deliverance from enemies, but its classification is disputed, because the psalm ends with a blessing in vv. 12-15. After he (the king?) praises God for victory (vv. 1-2), he meditates on human frailty and pleads for deliverance (vv. 3-8), and then he acknowledges his God-given victory over foreigners (vv. 9-11).[55] It seems to be a royal psalm that again reflects the continued divine blessing of the Davidic dynasty, but there is nothing "messianic" in it. In fact, almost every verse in it looks like a borrowing from other psalms or kindred passages.[56]

These six royal psalms, each in its own way, carry on the idea of the continuation of the Davidic dynasty, because they refer to a contemporary ruler with historical, political roots. There are, however, some other psalms that are neither royal by classification nor contain the title משיח, but have at times been given the designation "messianic," e.g., Psalms 22 and 69,[57] but that is because of the later New Testament use of them, not because of what they say in themselves (both being psalms of individual lament). Those who

---

53. See P. King, *A Study of Psalm 45 (44)* (Rome: Pontificia Universitas Lateranensis, 1959) 73-84, for a survey of the various ways אלהים in v. 7 has been interpreted. Cf. R. Tournay, "Les affinités du Ps. xlv avec le Cantique des Cantiques et leur interprétation messianique," *Congress Volume Bonn 1962.* VTSup 9 (Leiden: Brill, 1963) 168-212; J. Hoftijzer, "Remarks on Psalm 45:7a," *Frank Moore Cross Volume,* ed. B. A. Levine et al. ErIsr 26 (Jerusalem: Israel Exploration Society, 1999) 78*-87*.

54. See Mowinckel, *He That Cometh,* 100; Gillingham, "The Messiah in the Psalms," 217-18.

55. Verses 12-15 of this psalm are a prayer for a year of prosperity. They are usually thought to be a separate composition, which has been attached in some strange way to vv. 1-11.

56. See Gillingham, "The Messiah in the Psalms," 221-22.

57. See *The Catholic Study Bible,* ed. D. Senior (Oxford: Oxford University Press, 1990) 658 ("Psalm 22: Passion and Triumph of the Messiah"), 690 (Psalm 69 is said to be "at least indirectly messianic").

regard some other psalms as prophetic and messianic would include Psalms 9-10, 40, 41, 49, 55, 56, 59, 68, 71, 86, 88, 91, 116, but once again one has to ask whether any of these psalms, when considered in and for themselves, are to be understood as such. Rather, most of them stress the abiding significance of the enthronement and reign of both Yahweh and David or his heirs.[58]

Prior to and during the period of the exile, some of the prophets of Israel stirred up the hope for the eventual restoration of the Davidic dynasty, for the divine promise in the Oracle of Nathan, "I will establish his kingship forever . . . , (and) I will establish the throne of his kingship forever" (2 Sam 7:12-13), had not been forgotten. Especially after 586 B.C., there arose a national hope for the restoration of the Davidic monarchy along with a proper awareness of God's rule. That hope, however, was not yet a hope for a Messiah, and so the two ideas did not immediately emerge.

(13) The earliest such reference is found in the writings of Hosea, who prophesied in the Northern Kingdom of Israel, about the time of the fall of Samaria in 721 B.C. and the subsequent Assyrian deportation of its people under Tiglath-Pileser III. It reads:

> For many days the Israelites will dwell without a king or prince, without sacrifice or pillar, without ephod or teraphim. After that the Israelites will return and seek for the LORD their God and David their king, and they will come in fear to the LORD and His goodness at the end of days. (Hos 3:4-5)

Many commentators believe that the reference to David is a later addition, echoing what is found in prophetic writings related to the Babylonian Captivity, because the missing "king or prince" in Hosea's oracle about the Northern Kingdom and the Assyrian deportation would not have been of Davidic lineage. However, the words of Hosea, as they stand, reflect not only the restoration of the Davidic dynasty but also the reunion of the two kingdoms. In any case, the mention of Israelites seeking for "David their king" is similar to the idea of "a coming David" that emerges in exilic and postexilic writings. However, even a future David is not yet a "Messiah," *pace* E. H. Maly.[59]

---

58. See J. J. M. Roberts, "The Enthronement of Yhwh and David: The Abiding Theological Significance of the Kingship Language of the Psalms," *CBQ* 64 (2002) 675-86; Gillingham, "The Messiah in the Psalms," 224-25.

59. See E. H. Maly, "Messianism in Osee," *CBQ* 19 (1957) 213-25. Compare Mowinckel, *He That Cometh*, 19 (who recognizes that Hosea's words "have been modified in the light of the conditions and needs of later Judaism").

(14) Jeremiah, in writing from Jerusalem to the elders of the exiles, priests, and prophets whom Nebuchadnezzar had carried off to Babylon in 586 B.C., among other things, assures them of God's message: "When seventy years are completed in Babylon, I will visit you, and I will fulfill my promise and bring you back to this place" (Jer 29:10; cf. 25:11). Jeremiah thus seeks to console the exiles of Judah in their travail, during that "time of distress for Jacob":

> On that day it shall come to pass, says the LORD of hosts, that I will break the yoke off their necks and burst their bonds; and strangers shall no more make slaves of them. Instead they shall serve the LORD, their God, and David their king, whom I will raise up for them. (Jer 30:8-9)

With such prophetic utterances, we begin to see an important development in the understanding of the continuation of the Davidic dynasty. Jeremiah now speaks about the coming of a future "David" (ואת דוד מלכם אשר אקים להם, "and [they shall serve] David their king, whom I will raise up for them"). This does not mean that God plans to resuscitate King David of old; it is not a resuscitated David, a reincarnated David, a *David redivivus*.[60] Rather, God will see to the restoration of the Davidic dynasty by raising up an heir of David who will continue his spirit and influence.[61] This notion of "a coming David" corresponds to what Mowinckel has called "the early Jewish future hope."[62] Significantly, however, the coming king is not yet called משיח, but is given the name "David," and so, even with this noteworthy development, "messianism" has not yet emerged in the history of Judaism. This utterance of Jeremiah is not an isolated prophecy, because there are others like it.

(15) In Jer 23:5-6 the prophet similarly proclaims:

> Look! Days are coming, says the LORD, when I will raise up for David a righteous scion, and he shall rule as king and deal wisely, executing justice and righteousness in the land. In his days Judah shall be saved,

---

60. Mowinckel, *He That Cometh,* 163.

61. See P. Beauchamp, "Pourquoi parler de David comme d'un vivant?" *Figures de David à travers la Bible: XVIIᵉ Congrès de l'ACFEB (Lille, 1ᵉʳ-5 septembre 1997),* ed. L. Desrousseaux and J. Vermeylen, LD 177 (Paris: Cerf, 1999) 225-41; Lipiński, *Sem* 20 (1970) 53-55.

62. *He That Cometh,* 125-54.

and Israel shall dwell in security. This is the name by which he shall be called: "The LORD is our righteousness."

An heir of David will appear, to whom the title is given, צמח צדיק (*ṣemaḥ ṣaddîq*, lit., "righteous branch"); he will be raised up "for David," i.e., for the house of David.[63] His throne name will be יהוה צדקנו (*Yahweh ṣidqēnû*, "Yahweh our righteousness").[64] Again, no mention of משיח, for the same reason. The title, "righteous scion" (צמח צדיק, *ṣemaḥ ṣaddîq*), which is given here to the Davidic heir, conceptually resembles that of Isa 11:1, the "shoot" (חטר, *ḥōṭer*) and the "sprout" (נצר, *nēṣer*), but the terms are different. What is said here is further formulated in different ways by the prophet, e.g., in Jer 17:25, where he depicts God promising that, if the Sabbath is kept, there will always be kings and princes on David's throne.[65]

(16) Moreover, Jeremiah is not the only prophet who has this idea of a "future David," yet to be raised up. Ezekiel, who sees the fall of Jerusalem to the Babylonians in the first decade and a half of the sixth century as God's punishment of his generation of Israelites, levels his lengthy and biting criticism against "the shepherds" (i.e., the kings) of Israel. Ezekiel begins by recalling his own call in the "fifth year of the exile of King Jehoiachin" (Ezek 1:2), which clearly sets the stage for his critical remarks. In 34:1-31 he quotes God's words against the wicked shepherds who have mistreated their flocks (vv. 1-10). Then God announces that He shall provide for the people, and part of that providence is formulated as follows:

I will set over them one shepherd to tend them, my servant David; he shall feed them and be their shepherd. I, the LORD, will be their God, and my servant David shall be prince among them. I, the LORD, have spoken. (Ezek 34:23-24)

Here the future David is called עבדי (*'abdî*), "my slave, servant," and נשיא (*nāśî'*), "prince, leader," but not מלך, "king," much less משיח, again be-

63. See J. Dubbink, "Cedars Decay, a Sprout Will Blossom: Jeremiah 23:5-6, Conclusion of the Prophecies on Kingship," *Unless Some One Guide Me . . . : Festschrift for Karel A. Deurloo*, ed. J. W. Dyk et al. ACEBTSup 2 (Maastricht: Shaker, 2001) 157-65.

64. See Jer 33:14-16, where the words of 23:5 are quoted again and commented on. "The Lord is our righteousness" becomes the new name for Jerusalem. In 33:17-26, the words are related further to the covenant. Cf. Zech 3:8-10; 6:12 (quoted below in §18).

65. See also Amos 9:11, where God promises to "raise up the booth of David that has fallen."

cause the time for "messianism" in Judaism has not yet arrived.[66] Ezekiel, however, stresses that under such a "David" the people "shall know that I am the LORD" (7:27).

(17) Later on, the prophet Ezekiel repeats the same message as part of God's instruction to join two sticks that symbolize the joining of the two kingdoms under the coming Davidic rule:

> My servant David shall be king over them; and there shall be one shepherd for all of them. They shall follow my ordinances and be careful to obey my statutes. They shall dwell in the land that I gave to my servant Jacob, in which your fathers dwelt; they and their children and their children's children shall dwell there forever, with David my servant as their prince forever. (37:24-25)

Now the future David is called "king." These passages point significantly to the coming of an individual who will rule as "David" or as "prince/king" over God's people, but in none of them does משיח appear as a title of such a future David, "their prince forever." Yet they express well the "future hopes in royal figures," which is a primary concern of the prophet's theology, as P. M. Joyce has argued.[67] He cites, however, other isolated verses of Ezekiel, namely, 17:22-24 (the allegory of the cedar); 21:32b(Eng. 27b); and 29:21 ("I will make a horn spring up for the house of David," an allusion to Ps 132:17a), and regards them as "potentially messianic references." Yet all these verses express merely the development of the continuing Davidic dynasty, without any remote connection to a "Messiah." Indeed, the last passage mentioned omits v. 17b of Psalm 132 with its mention of משיחי, "my Anointed One," which would have been grist for the mill, if 29:21 were intended in a "messianic" sense. Nor does it help to admit at the end that "the 'messianic' figure is at best on the fringes of what for Ezekiel is the real focus of future expectation, namely the restored sanctuary," as Joyce finally quotes Ezek 37:27.[68] The question is whether "the 'messianic' figure" is there at all.[69]

---

66. For an analysis of the term נשיא in the book of Ezekiel, see P. M. Joyce, "King and Messiah in Ezekiel," in Day, *King and Messiah in Israel and the Ancient Near East*, 323-37, esp. 330-32. Cf. D. I. Block, "My Servant David," 17-56.

67. Joyce, "King and Messiah in Ezekiel," 328-29.

68. Joyce, "King and Messiah in Ezekiel," 337.

69. As M. J. Gruenthaner would have it, "The Messianic Concepts of Ezechiel," *TS* 2 (1941) 1-18. Cf. A. Caquot, "Le messianisme d'Ézéchiel," *Sem* 14 (1964) 5-23.

Finally, when the Persian king Cyrus, who is accorded the title משיח in the historical sense (Isa 45:1), allows the captives to return from exile in Babylon (538 B.C.) in order to rebuild the house of the God of Israel in Jerusalem (Ezra 1:2-4; cf. 6:3-5), the hope for the restoration of the Davidic dynasty is realized. It is continued in Shealtiel and Zerubbabel (1 Chr 3:17, 19), and others whose names are lost. Zerubbabel was the grandson of King Jehoiachin (Jeconiah), who had been deported to Babylon in 597,[70] and his name זרבבל even means "offspring of Babylon" (זרע בבל, *zera' bābel*). Then the Persians appointed him as governor of Judah.

(18) In the clearly postexilic period, the prophet Zechariah alludes to Jer 23:5, as he depicts God saying to Joshua, the newly-clothed High Priest:

> Listen carefully, O Joshua, High Priest, you and your friends who sit with you, for they are men of good omen: Look! I am introducing my servant, the scion. Look at the stone that I have put before Joshua; upon a single stone with seven facets I will engrave its inscription, "Oracle of the LORD of hosts: I will take away the guilt of this land in a single day." "On that day," oracle of the LORD of hosts, "each one of you shall invite his neighbor under his vine and under his fig tree." (Zech 3:8-10)

From Jer 23:5 (and 33:15) one recognizes the "scion" (צמח, *ṣemaḥ*. lit., "branch") as the future David, to whom the title עבדי (*'abdî*, "my servant") is again given, as in Ezek 34:23. For the prophet Zechariah, however, that future David is now present in an heir of the Davidic throne, Zerubbabel, who according to Zech 6:11b is to be crowned.[71] There the MT actually reads ושמת בראש יהושע, "and you will put (it) on the head of Joshua," but commentators generally recognize that the text is quite mixed up and problematic. The *apparatus criticus* in BHS even reads זרבבל בן שאלתיאל, "Zerubbabel son of Shealtiel," instead of "Joshua."[72] Verse 12 continues with

70. Compare Ezra 1:8, 11; 5:14, 16 with 1 Chr 3:18, probably the same son of Jehoiachin (Jeconiah).

71. Cf. Hag 2:23: "On that day, says the Lord of hosts, I will take you, O Zerubbabel my servant, the son of Shealtiel, . . . and make you like a signet ring; for I have chosen you." See R. Mason, "The Messiah in the Postexilic Old Testament Literature," in J. Day, *King and Messiah in Israel,* 338-64, esp. 340-49.

72. There is another problem in the word for "crown," which in v. 11a of the MT is plural (עטרות, *'āṭārôt*). Some commentators think that two crowns are to be made and put on the heads of both Zerubbabel, the king, and Joshua, the High Priest. Normally, however,

הנה־איש צמח שמו ומתחתיו יצמח ובנה את־היכל יהוה, "Here is a man whose name is scion; he will sprout from his place, and he will build the temple of the LORD," i.e., a further reference to Zerubbabel. Then 6:13 announces that "there shall be a priest by his throne," a reference to Joshua. Even with this further development of the continuation of the Davidic dynasty in Zerubbabel as a "future David" and a "scion," who is brought on the scene by God, it is significant that the title משיח does not appear, for it is still too early (520-518 B.C.) for "Messiah" in the narrow sense.

Not only is the Davidic line thus continued, but also the priesthood, because Joshua's "friends," who sit with him, "the men of good omen," are undoubtedly the priests who will serve in the Jerusalem Temple, when it is rebuilt. This restoration is intended by the divine oracle: "I will take away the guilt of this land in a single day." It is further connoted by the following vision of the lampstand and two olive trees in Zech 4:1-14, which ends with the declaration, "These are the two sons of oil (שני בני היצהר, šěnê běnê hay-yiṣhār) who stand by the LORD of the whole earth" (4:14). Even though this phrase implies the anointing of the king and high priest, the declaration of them as "sons of oil" appears again without the title משיח.

Later on in the book of Zechariah, commentators see the influence of the Fourth Servant Song of Isaiah 53 in Zech 12:10-14; 13:7, where a leader in "the family of the house of David" is mourned who is even called "my shepherd," but not Messiah, *pace* Hengel.[73] The reason why that title does not appear in these passages of Zechariah is that "messianism" has not yet appeared on the scene in the history of Judaism.[74]

---

the crown is the kingly prerogative. Whatever the real solution to 6:11 is, the "scion" of Zech 3:8 must refer to the crowned Davidic king because of its allusion to Jer 23:5. See Becker, *Messianic Expectation in the Old Testament,* 64-67.

73. Hengel, "The Effective History of Isaiah 53," 85. Note how Hengel speaks at first of "the violent death of a (messianic?) leader" and then states that Rudolph sees "correctly" a reference "to the Messiah in the shepherd chapter of Zechariah 11:4-17." Yet all the references to "shepherds" in Zechariah 9–11 are to unnamed leaders of the Hellenistic era who rule over the house of David. Then Hengel says, "Admittedly, a 'messianic' interpretation of Zechariah 12:10 first appears again in earliest Christianity and then with the Messiah ben Joseph in Judaism" (p. 89). If Hengel had left out the adverb "again," his statement would be correct. Cf. J. Kremer, *Die Hirtenallegorie im Buche Zacharias auf ihre Messianität hin untersucht: Zugleich ein Beitrag zur Geschichte der Exegese.* ATA 11/2 (Münster/W.: Aschendorff, 1930).

74. See Mowinckel, *He That Cometh,* 119-22, and esp. 122-24. But Mason thinks in Zech 9:9-10 and 12:7–13:1 "the 'messianic' silence is broken" ("The Messiah in the Postexilic Literature of Israel," 351). Yet that is hardly the case, because, although Jerusalem's king may

(19) Likewise from the postexilic period comes a passage in the prophecy of Micah, who is otherwise an eighth-century figure. At least Mic 4:1–5:14(Eng. 15) is frequently so regarded, chiefly because of the reference to exile in "Babylon" in 4:10. The crucial verse for discussion here, however, is 5:1(2), which reads:

> But you, Bethlehem-Ephrathah, too small to be among the clans of Judah, from you shall come forth for Me one who is to be ruler in Israel, whose origin is from of old, from ancient times.

For Bethlehem-Ephrathah, see Gen 35:19; Ruth 4:11 (the site of Rachel's grave). The new "ruler in Israel" will not be born in Jerusalem, but in the tiny insignificant town and clan of Bethlehem-Ephrathah, which is remembered as that from which David came (see 1 Sam 16:18-19). The contrast is between the lowly Bethlehem and the noted Zion. The "Me" refers to the Lord, who utters these words and who thus ratifies the rule of the new Davidic heir. His origin is from "ancient times," because he will be descended from David, who reigned roughly from 1000 to 962 B.C. The future ruler remains unnamed; he is not called "Messiah," and there is no indication that the prophet's words are to be so interpreted. He is merely a Davidic heir to the throne in some coming period. The hope of a restored Davidic dynasty with the associated priesthood is not yet the hope of a Messiah. J. Becker rightly insists:

> What must be objected to is the almost universal equation of restorative monarchism with messianism. There is no evidence for true messianism until the second century B.C. What we are dealing with in the interim is the restoration of preexilic institutions, as a glance at priesthood and prophecy will show.[75]

(20) Lastly, another postexilic prophet, Malachi, brings his oracle to an end with a promise:

> Look! I am sending to you Elijah the prophet before the great and terrible day of the LORD comes; he will turn the hearts of fathers to their children and the hearts of children to their fathers, lest I come and strike the land with doom. (Mal 3:23-24[Eng. 4:5-6])

---

come to it "triumphant and victorious, humble and riding on an ass," the passages do not even consider him to be an anointed agent.

75. *Messianic Expectation in the Old Testament,* 50; cf. also 87-92.

Because Elijah had been carried up "into heaven by a whirlwind" (2 Kgs 2:11) and had not been said to have died, there grew up in postexilic Judaism the belief that he would return, and to that return the end of Malachi's oracle refers. This passage, which is often regarded as a late addition to the original prophetic writing,[76] identifies Elijah as the messenger of Mal 3:1 who is to come "before the great and terrible day of the LORD." Moreover, in his praise of famous men of old (Sir 44:1–50:24), Sirach has a lengthy encomium on Elijah (48:1-11), which slightly reformulates the words of Malachi: "You were taken aloft by a whirlwind of fire, in a chariot with horses of fire; you who were destined to come, it is written, at an appointed time, to put an end to wrath before the day of the LORD, to turn the heart of a father to a son, and to restore the tribes of Jacob" (48:9-10). In time, this belief in the return of Elijah was said to make him a precursor of the Messiah, because the coming of the Messiah depends on whether Israel repents and reforms; so Elijah was thought to come first to bring about that repentance and reformation. Yet neither the oracle of Malachi nor the form of it in Sirach speaks of that role of precursor,[77] for he is expected to return "before the great and terrible day of the LORD" (Mal 3:23[4:5]), which is rather to be understood as the יום יהוה, *yôm Yahweh* or the day of vindication, of earlier prophets (e.g., Amos 5:18-20; 8:9-14; Isa 13:6, 9; Jer 46:10).

Nor is this belief that about which the disciples ask Jesus, "Why do the scribes say that Elijah must come first?" (Mark 9:11; Matt 17:10), when that passage is correctly understood in the Gospels.[78] In the context of the

---

76. See B. V. Malchow, "The Messenger of the Covenant in Mal 3:1," *JBL* 103 (1984) 252-55.

77. Mowinckel errs when he says that Sir 48:10 speaks of Elijah as "the forerunner of the Messiah" (*He That Cometh,* 299). Similarly J. D. Martin, "Ben Sira's Hymn to the Fathers: A Messianic Perspective," *Crises and Perspectives.* OtSt 24 (Leiden: Brill, 1986) 107-23.

78. M. M. Faierstein ("Why Do the Scribes Say That Elijah Must Come First?" *JBL* 100 [1981] 75-86) has shown how many interpreters — what he calls "the consensus of NT scholarship" (e.g., J. Jeremias, G. F. Moore, J. Klausner, S. Mowinckel, L. Ginzberg) — have interpreted that passage in the Gospels as meaning that Elijah is the forerunner of the Messiah. Faierstein insists that such an interpretation is based on "an underlying *a priori* assumption," with hardly any evidence. D. C. Allison. Jr. ("'Elijah Must Come First,'" *JBL* 103 [1984] 256-58) has tried to counteract Faierstein's interpretation and tip the scales in favor of the traditional interpretation; but unsuccessfully (see J. A. Fitzmyer, "More about Elijah Coming First," *JBL* 104 [1985] 295-96). Cf. M. Öhler, "The Expectation of Elijah and the Presence of the Kingdom of God," *JBL* 118 (1999) 461-76, esp. 463-64.

disciples' question, "first" means *before* "the rising from the dead" (Mark 9:10) or *before* "the Son of Man rises from the dead" (9:9).[79] In time, that relation of the return of Elijah to the resurrection of the dead will appear in the postbiblical Jewish tradition (in *m. Soṭah* 9:15).

Finally, there are other postexilic passages that sometimes have been regarded as "messianic," namely, Hag 2:23; Zech 9:9-10; Isa 55:3-5; and various passages in Qoheleth, Chronicles, and Sirach,[80] but the use of that adjective to describe them leaves much to be desired.

Many of the passages that have been discussed above appear in the list of what Mowinckel has called "the Authentic Messianic Prophecies,"[81] which he says all "date from the time after the fall of the monarchy and the destruction of the Israelite states,"[82] except Isaiah 7 and 9:1, which are preexilic. But then he has to qualify the initial statement, because "they are not Messianic in the strict sense." Mowinckel should have been saying that the passages discussed in this chapter are concerned with "actual historical kingship," whether preexilic, exilic, or postexilic. Some of them may indeed present a picture of "the ideal king" on David's throne, but that is not yet a picture of "the Messiah." When the Messiah does appear, however, he will indeed be *"the future, eschatological realization of the ideal of kingship."*[83]

---

79. See further G. Molin, "Elijahu der Prophet und sein Weiterleben in den Hoffnungen des Judentums und der Christenheit," *Judaica* 8 (1951) 65-94.

80. See Mason, "The Messiah in the Postexilic Old Testament Literature," 340-42, 349-51; R. T. Siebeneck, "The Messianism of Aggeus and Proto-Zacharias," *CBQ* 19 (1957) 312-28; A. Bentzen, "Quelques remarques sur le mouvement messianique parmi les juifs aux environs de l'an 520 avant Jésus-Christ," *RHPR* 10 (1930) 493-503; A. Caquot, "Ben Sira et le messianisme," *Sem* 16 (1966) 43-68; "Peut-on parler de messianisme dans l'oeuvre du Chroniste?" *RTP* 16 (1966) 110-20; N. Perrin, "Messianism in the Narrative Frame of Ecclesiastes?" *RB* 108 (2001) 37-60.

81. *He That Cometh*, 15: "the actual Messianic prophecies in the prophetic books."

82. *He That Cometh*, 20.

83. *He That Cometh*, 156 (his emphasis).

CHAPTER 5

The Role of Daniel 9:25-26
in the Emergence of Messianism

The two preceding chapters have discussed various Old Testament passages that describe the Davidic dynasty and the way the continuation of it developed from preexilic to postexilic times in the history of Judaism. Part of the development in the postexilic period can be traced in the oldest Greek translation of the Old Testament, the Septuagint (LXX), and part of it can also be traced in the last book of the Hebrew Scriptures, the book of Daniel, which was finally redacted ca. 165 B.C., about the time when Antiochus IV Epiphanes was trying to hellenize Judah and was desecrating the Temple of Jerusalem. What little is known about the LXX's history places the beginning of the translation in Alexandria in the mid-third century B.C., probably during the reign of Ptolemy II Philadelphus (285-247 B.C.).[1] Since that translation was to be made of "the books of the Law of the Jews," meaning a Greek version of the Pentateuch, it tells us little about the time when the rest of the Hebrew Scriptures was translated. Consequently, the decision to treat the book of Daniel before the evidence of de-

---

1. See the so-called Letter of Aristeas, *To Philocrates* §30-40 (M. Hadas, *Aristeas to Philocrates (Letter of Aristeas)* [New York: Harper, 1951] 111-17). Since this letter was written toward the end of the second century B.C. and is recognized today as an apologetic romance that contains a number of factual errors, its historical value is questioned; yet many scholars tend to follow its dating of the LXX to the time of Ptolemy II Philadelphus (at least in a general sense). Cf. J. W. Wevers, "Septuagint," *IDB*, 4:273-78; D. W. Gooding, "Aristeas and Septuagint Origins: A Review of Recent Studies," *VT* 13 (1963) 357-79; repr. in *Studies in the Septuagint: Origins, Recensions and Interpretations: Selected Essays, with a Prolegomenon*, ed. S. Jellicoe (New York: Ktav, 1974) 158-80.

velopment of traditions about the Davidic dynasty in the LXX is merely one of convenience. The reader will realize that some of the development attested in that ancient Greek version may well antedate what emerges from the book of Daniel, even if one is not sure of its date.

What one finds in this period is not merely aspirations for the restoration of the Davidic dynasty in early postexilic times, but a new development born of anti-Hasmonean tendencies. This is the period in the history of Judaism when belief in the coming David develops into that of a national Messiah, whom God will raise up as a descendant of David, an earthly scion, a future eschatological realization of the ideal of kingship. Such a messianic belief takes shape in the book of Daniel, even though some commentators are reluctant to admit that there is any evidence of it there.[2]

Three passages in the book of Daniel have to be discussed: the Vision of Divine Judgment (7:9-14); the Prophecy of the Seventy Weeks of Years (9:24-27); and the Final Consummation (12:1-3).

(1) In the Aramaic account of ch. 7, the seer has an apocalyptic vision of four beasts (winged lion, bear, leopard, and one unidentified) that rise from the sea. The vision tells of their fate, which symbolizes the passing of four kingdoms (Babylon, Media, Persia, and Greece) that will make way for the coming kingdom of God. In part of the vision, the seer beholds the convening of the heavenly court of judgment, where judgment is to be made on those kingdoms:

> As I gazed, thrones were set up, and an Ancient of Days took his seat. His robe was white as snow, and the hair of his head pure as wool. His throne was flames of fire; its wheels, flashing fire. A stream of fire surged and flowed out before him. Thousands upon thousands were serving him, and myriads upon myriads stood before him. The court was in session, and books were opened. Then, because of the sound of arrogant words that the horn was uttering, I continued to gaze and watched until the beast was slain and its body thrown into burning fire. As for the other beasts, their dominion was taken away, but an extension in life was granted them for a time and a season. During the visions of the night I gazed, and lo, with the clouds of heaven came one

2. See A. Caquot ("Ben Sira et le messianisme," *Sem* 16 [1966] 43-68), who writes, "Un écrit comme le livre de *Daniel* révèle une ferveur eschatologique qui ne fait pas de place à un messie" (43). Similarly, J. Coppens, *Le Fils d'homme vétéro- et intertestamentaire.* BETL 61 (Louvain: Peeters, 1983) 115: "un messianisme sans Messie."

like a son of man. When he reached the Ancient of Days and was presented before him, he was given dominion, glory, and kingship so that all peoples, nations, and tongues might serve him. His dominion is an everlasting dominion, which shall not pass away, and his kingship shall not be destroyed. (7:9-14)

In this vision, God is depicted as the Ancient of Days (see Ps 90:2), who, surrounded by His court (see 1 Kgs 22:19), sits in judgment over the four kingdoms, and the record books about them are consulted. The "horn," its "arrogant words," and the beast that is "slain" represent the persecuting Antiochus IV Epiphanes, one of the Seleucid "Successors" of Alexander the Great (i.e., the kingdom of the Greeks; see 2 Macc 5:15-17). The other beasts represent the Babylonians, Medes, and Persians, who are enemies to be defeated. As such, they are represented by beasts, but the victor is depicted as "one like a son of man," who receives "dominion, glory, and kingship," but the victory itself is ascribed to the Most High.

The identity of "one like a son of man," however, has long been a *crux interpretum*.[3] Four interpretations have been used: (1) *A human individual:* It is so understood by Jewish commentators (*1 Enoch, 4 Ezra*),[4] who sometimes identified him with the Messiah, and also by early Christian writers who used it of Jesus Christ (e.g., Mark 13:26; 14:62). Interpreting the figure as messianic was common among patristic writers and persisted even into the twentieth century. (2) *A collectivity:* Frequently it has been understood according to the description given to the seer by a heavenly courtier in 7:18, 22, 27, "the holy ones of the Most High," i.e., the triumphant righteous people of Israel, destined to become the kingdom of God. This was a rare Christian interpretation first attested in the writings of the fourth-century Ephrem Syrus, which was used subsequently by medieval Jewish interpreters (e.g., Ibn Ezra) and became very common in the nineteenth and early twentieth centuries.[5] (3) *Messiah as Head of the Holy Ones of the Most High:* Or as representing the collectivity. This representative-corporate view was proposed by a good number of interpreters in the twentieth century (e.g., A. Bentzen, L. Denefeld, M.-J. Lagrange, P. Volz). (4) *A heavenly or angelic figure:* It means either an unnamed angel, or Michael, "the great prince,

---

3. See J. J. Collins, *Daniel.* Herm (Minneapolis: Fortress, 1993) 304-10.

4. See pp. 86, 136 below.

5. See, e.g., A. A. Di Lella, "The One in Human Likeness and the Holy Ones of the Most High in Daniel 7," *CBQ* 39 (1977) 1-19.

guardian of Your people" (Dan 12:1), or Gabriel, the "one seen in a vision" (Dan 9:21); and then "the holy ones of the Most High" are understood as the angelic host (cf. the angels of the Qumran War Scroll [1QM]). This interpretation, which builds on many biblical passages where angels are represented by or as human beings (Gen 16:7, 13; 18:2; Josh 5:13; Tob 5:4-5), has become widely used since the discovery of Qumran literature and the light it has shone on Palestinian Jewish angelology. Whereas some commentators have counseled against the fourth interpretation,[6] it has much to be said for it. Collins maintains that "Michael, the prince of Israel, is the more appropriate recipient of the kingdom."[7]

In any case, although the "one like a son of man" is an important figure in this Danielic passage and will become even more important in the "Son of Man" tradition in the New Testament,[8] there is no evidence in the book of Daniel itself for a messianic interpretation of the term, despite the way it will be interpreted in later Jewish literature.[9]

> The background of this scene is to be sought, therefore, not in the later apocalyptic ideas of the coming of the Messiah from heaven, but in the ideas associated in Israelite belief with the reigning king. He was thought of as a mediator, embodying the true welfare and destiny of the People of God and representing God's Rule on earth.[10]

Attempts, however, continue to be made to identify "one like a son of man" here in Daniel 7 with a messianic figure.[11]

6. "No attempt should be made to see in the 'one like unto a son of man' a figure *descending* from heaven. He came not from God but to him"; E. W. Heaton, *The Book of Daniel.* TBC (London: SCM, 1956) 183 (his emphasis).

7. *Daniel,* 310; see also his dissertation, *The Apocalyptic Vision of the Book of Daniel.* HSM 16 (Missoula: Scholars, 1977) 141-47.

8. See J. A. Fitzmyer, "The New Testament Title 'Son of Man' Philologically Considered," *WA,* 143-60; *SBNT,* 143-60; Coppens, *Le Fils d'homme vétéro- et intertestamentaire,* 100-12; J.-C. Loba Mkole, "Une synthèse d'opinions philologiques sur le Fils de l'homme," *JNSL* 22 (1996) 107-23.

9. See J. Klausner, *The Messianic Idea in Israel* (New York: Macmillan, 1955; London: Allen and Unwin, 1956) 230: "in a comparatively short time after the composition of the Book of Daniel it was thought among the Jews that this 'son of man' was the Messiah." Klausner means that it was so interpreted in the Parables of *1 Enoch* 37–71 and in the "hints" of Jesus in the Gospels.

10. Heaton, *The Book of Daniel,* 183.

11. R. D. Rowe, "Is Daniel's 'Son of Man' Messianic?" in *Christ the Lord: Studies in*

(2) Far more important is the Prophecy of the Seventy Weeks of Years in Dan 9:24-27. This passage alludes to a prophetic pronouncement of Jeremiah, as Dan 9:2 makes clear: "In the first year of his reign [i.e., of Darius, called the Mede], I, Daniel, perceived in the books the number of years, of which God spoke to Jeremiah the prophet, which must be completed before the desolation of Jerusalem, namely, seventy years." The prophet Jeremiah recorded God's judgment about all the people of Judah and Jerusalem:

> This entire land shall become a ruin and a waste, and these nations will be enslaved to the king of Babylon for seventy years. Then after seventy years are completed, I will punish the king of Babylon and that nation, the land of the Chaldeans, because of its iniquity, making it an everlasting waste, oracle of the LORD. (Jer 25:11-12)[12]

And again:

> Thus says the LORD, After seventy years have been completed for Babylon, I will visit you and fulfill for you my promise to bring you back to this place. (Jer 29:10)

What the prophet Jeremiah recorded about the desolation and restoration after "seventy years" of Babylonian Captivity for the people of Judah and Jerusalem is interpreted by the angel Gabriel for Daniel as "seventy weeks of years":

> 24 Seventy weeks of years are decreed for your people and for your holy city, to bring an end to transgression, to stop sin, to expiate iniq-

---

Christology Presented to Donald Guthrie, ed. H. H. Rowdon (Downers Grove: InterVarsity, 1982) 71-96. For a survey of interpretations of "son of man" as a messianic title, see W. Horbury, "The Messianic Associations of 'The Son of Man,'" JTS 36 (1985) 34-55 (he claims that "the messianic interpretation of Dan. vii" gave "'the son of man' a messianic association at the beginning of the Christian era" [36], but he never answers the question whether "son of man" in Daniel 7 itself connoted "Messiah," which is the real problem, because by the beginning of the Christian era, the term was clearly given to one called "Messiah," as will be seen in 1 Enoch.). Similarly, K. Koch, "Messias und Menschensohn: Die zweistufige Messianologie der jüngeren Apokalyptik," JBT 8 (1993) 73-102. Cf. Coppens, Le Fils d'homme vétéro- et intertestamentaire, 113-15.

12. The seventy years in Jeremiah are reckoned from the first capture of Jerusalem by Nebuchadnezzar (597 B.C.), i.e., a lifetime of a land ruined and laid waste following the capture. See, however, the way the time is reckoned in 2 Chr 36:20-22; Ezra 1:1; Zech 1:12.

uity, and to introduce everlasting righteousness; and to ratify both vision and prophet and to anoint the Holy of Holies. 25 You are to know and to understand (this): From the utterance of a word to rebuild Jerusalem to the coming of an Anointed One, a prince, (there shall be) seven weeks. Then during sixty-two weeks it shall be rebuilt with streets and moats, but in times of trouble. 26 After sixty-two weeks an Anointed One shall be cut down with no one to help him. The people of a prince who comes shall destroy the city and the sanctuary. Its end shall be with a flood, and at the end, war and decreed desolation. 27 He shall make a mighty covenant with many for one week, and for a half of a week he shall put an end to sacrifice and offering. On the temple wing shall be the desolating abomination until the decreed end is poured out on the horror. (Dan 9:24-27)[13]

The prophet Daniel thus gives a new interpretation to Jeremiah's pronouncement about "seventy years," making them "seventy weeks of years," or 490 years.[14] Daniel wishes to show from Jeremiah that Judah would be restored to its previous status. The numbers are only approximations that denote the passage of a long time, from the Edict of Cyrus (538 B.C.), who was indeed מָשִׁיחַ (Isa 45:1), at the end of the Babylonian Captivity, until the persecution of Antiochus IV Epiphanes (175-164), and his "desolating abomination," when "an Anointed One shall be cut down and have nothing," which is probably a covert reference to Onias III, who was removed from his high-priestly office and assassinated in 171 (2 Macc 4:30-38).[15] Antiochus himself is "the prince," whose "people come to de-

---

13. Verses 24-27 are preserved in the MT with a number of variant readings, some of which are corrupt, making the understanding of these four verses very difficult. See M.-J. Lagrange, "La prophétie des soixante-dix semaines de Daniel (Dan. ix, 24-27)," *RB* 39 (1930) 179-98.

14. Cf. 2 Chr 36:21, which speaks of seventy sabbatical years, which interprets Jeremiah's words in light of Lev 26:31-35, 43. For a discussion of the chronology involved, see D. Dimant, "The Seventy Weeks Chronology (Dan 9, 24-27) in the Light of New Qumranic Texts," in *The Book of Daniel in the Light of New Findings*, ed. A. S. Van der Woude. BETL 106 (Louvain: Leuven University Press, 1993) 57-76; B. Z. Wacholder, "Chronomessianism: The Timing of Messianic Movements and the Calendar of Sabbatical Cycles," *HUCA* 46 (1975) 201-18; L. L. Grabbe, "The Seventy-Weeks Prophecy (Daniel 9:24-27) in Early Jewish Interpretation," in *The Quest for Context and Meaning: Studies in Biblical Intertextuality in Honor of James A. Sanders*, ed. C. A. Evans and S. Talmon. Biblical Interpretation 28 (Leiden: Brill, 1997) 595-611; M. J. Gruenthaner, "The Seventy Weeks," *CBQ* 1 (1939) 44-54.

15. See Klausner, *The Messianic Idea in Israel*, 233; Collins, *Daniel*, 356.

stroy the city and the sanctuary" (9:26; cf. 1 Macc 1:54). See further Dan 8:21-25; 11:21-45.

All-important in this passage is the occurrence of the word מָשִׁיחַ in v. 25 with a temporal preposition having a future connotation: מִן־מֹצָא דָבָר לְהָשִׁיב וְלִבְנוֹת יְרוּשָׁלַם עַד־מָשִׁיחַ נָגִיד שָׁבֻעִים שִׁבְעָה, lit., "from the going forth of a word to return and build Jerusalem up until an Anointed One, a Prince, seven weeks." Here one finds the first occurrence in the Old Testament itself of מָשִׁיחַ used for an awaited Anointed One, even though in the context it might refer to one who is or has been already on the scene. It would refer to some sort of Messiah in the narrow sense.[16] This is found, then, in an Old Testament passage dating from the second quarter of the second century B.C. The context of the expectation is the time of the "rebuilding" of the Temple city, Jerusalem, i.e., the reconsecration of the Temple after the desolation wrought in it by the abomination erected there by Antiochus IV Epiphanes, a statue of himself as Olympian Zeus set up near the altar of sacrifice (see Dan 11:31; 12:11; 1 Macc 1:54; 2:7-13; 4:36-59; 2 Macc 6:2; Josephus *Ant.* 12.5.4 §253).

This means that messianism in the narrow sense emerged indeed within late pre-Christian Judaism, and well before the Roman period, the time when messianism was supposed to appear according to H. L. Ginsberg.[17] It emerged also in a piece of apocalyptic writing, which otherwise has no mention of the Davidic dynasty. This lack of mention, however, does not mean that the author has no hope for the restoration of that monarchy, but rather that he is totally preoccupied with the problem caused by Antiochus IV Epiphanes and his efforts to hellenize the Jewish people under his control. The author is concerned above all about the anointing of "the Holy of Holies" (9:24), i.e., the reconsecration of the Jerusalem Temple after the "abomination of desolation." That anointing is almost certainly not a reference to a person.[18]

---

16. See R. T. Beckwith, "Daniel 9 and the Date of Messiah's Coming in Essene, Hellenistic, Pharisaic, Zealot and Early Christian Computation," *RevQ* 10 (1979-81) 521-42; "The Year of the Messiah: Jewish and Early Christian Chronologies, and Their Eschatological Consequences," in *Calendar and Chronology, Jewish and Christian: Biblical, Intertestamental and Patristic Studies.* AGJU 33 (Leiden: Brill, 1996) 217-75.

17. See H. L. Ginsberg, "Messiah," *EncJud* 11:1407 (quoted on p. 3 above).

18. The phrase לִמְשֹׁחַ קֹדֶשׁ קָדָשִׁים, "to anoint the Holy of Holies," has been interpreted as referring to a person (e.g., Vg: *ut ungatur sanctus sanctorum* [a tendentious version, probably coming from a Christian translator]; A. Lacocque, *The Book of Daniel* [At-

A person, however, is clearly envisaged in Dan 9:25, where מָשִׁיחַ נָגִיד occurs. Because נָגִיד, "leader," can mean either a king (as in Ps 76:13[Eng. 12]; 1 Sam 9:16 [Saul]; 13:14 [David]) or a priest (as in Neh 11:11 [three High Priests]; Jer 20:1; 1 Chr 9:11; 2 Chr 35:8), it might seem difficult to say whether this expected Anointed One is a king or a priest, for מָשִׁיחַ has been used for the postexilic "anointed priest" (Lev 4:3, 5, 16; 6:15[22]).[19] It may be preferable, however, to understand מָשִׁיחַ נָגִיד in Dan 9:25 as a kingly Messiah (someone like Zerubbabel), in this second-century context.[20] In any case, the words יִכָּרֵת מָשִׁיחַ וְאֵין לוֹ, "an Anointed One shall be cut down with no one to help him" (9:26a; cf. 11:45), cannot refer to the same Anointed One of 9:25, because the Anointed One of v. 26 appears later, "after sixty-two weeks," and that undoubtedly means the already mentioned Onias III.[21] That he is the one meant by "an Anointed One shall be cut down" (9:26) is commonly admitted by commentators today, but that he should be called a "slain Messiah" in the Old Testament, as R. A. Rosenberg would have it, is a moot question, indeed.[22]

lanta: John Knox, 1979] 193-94). But the accompanying phrases, וְעַל עִיר קׇדְשֶׁךָ, "and for your holy city" (9:24), and לְהָשִׁיב וְלִבְנוֹת יְרוּשָׁלַ͏ִם, "to rebuild Jerusalem" (9:25), show that the most sacred part of the Temple is meant, since the verb מָשַׁח is used elsewhere of the anointing of cultic places or objects (Exod 30:26-29 [the tent, etc.]; 40:9-11 [the tabernacle, altar, and laver]). The LXX renders the last clause thus: καὶ εὐφρᾶναι ἅγιον ἁγίων "and to gladden the Holy of Holies."

For an attempt to identify "the Holy of Holies" with a particular Jewish community, see T. Meadowcroft, "Exploring the Dismal Swamp: The Identity of the Anointed One in Daniel 9:24-27," *JBL* 120 (2001) 429-49.

19. It has been understood as referring to Joshua, ben Jozadak, the High Priest, by many commentators (e.g., A. Bentzen [*Daniel*, 2nd ed. HAT 19 (Tübingen: Mohr [Siebeck], 1952) 74]; L. F. Hartman and A. A. Di Lella [*The Book of Daniel*. AB 23 (Garden City: Doubleday, 1978) 251]; Collins, *Daniel*, 355]). It is taken to be an unnamed priestly figure by S. Mowinckel, *He That Cometh*, 6 n. 8; H. Gressmann, *Der Messias*. FRLANT 43 (Göttingen: Vandenhoeck & Ruprecht, 1929) 3 n. 9; R. Mason, "The Messiah in the Postexilic Old Testament Literature," in J. Day, *King and Messiah in Israel*. JSOTSup 270 (Sheffield: Sheffield Academic, 1998) 358-59; Heaton, *The Book of Daniel*, 213.

20. Zerubbabel himself has been proposed as the kingly Anointed One (Quintus Julius Hilarianus, *Chronologia sive Libellus de mundi duratione* 10.11) and even Cyrus the Persian of Isa 45:1 (Rashi). On נָגִיד, *nāgîd*, and its meanings, see P. K. McCarter, Jr., *1 Samuel*. AB 8 (Garden City: Doubleday, 1980) 179.

21. See p. 61 above.

22. R. A. Rosenberg, "The Slain Messiah in the Old Testament," *ZAW* 99 (1987) 259-61. He adds that Zech 12:10-11 is a "ritualistic mourning for a slain Messiah," which is "analogous to the lamentation for Josiah that in II Chron 35, 25 is styled a 'statute upon Israel' insti-

In any case, even if one cannot determine specifically to whom משיח נגיד refers, this passage in Daniel 9 shows that messianism truly emerged in pre-Christian Palestinian Judaism and was not merely a visionary fore-shadowing of what New Testament writers would predicate of Jesus of Nazareth. Moreover, what is asserted here about a coming Anointed One will be confirmed in the pre-Christian Jewish writings of the Dead Sea Scrolls.[23]

(3) Sometimes interpreters find echoes of the Fourth Servant Song of Isaiah 53 toward the end of the book of Daniel, in 12:1-3, or better in 11:33-35 and 12:1-3. In 11:33-35, there is mention of ומשכילי עם, "the wise among the people," namely, the persecuted Jews, who reappear in 12:3: "those who are wise shall shine like the brightness of the sky" along with "those who lead many to righteousness." These verses have been considered an allusion to Isa 52:13, the opening of the Fourth Song, "Look! My Servant shall act wisely" (הנה ישכיל עבדי), and to 53:11b, "my Servant, the righteous one, shall make many righteous." They have been called "The Oldest Interpre-tation of the Suffering Servant."[24] That may be, but there is no reference in these verses to any "messianic" figure.

---

tuted by Jeremiah." But "Messiah" is a gratuitous title given to the unnamed sufferer of Zechariah 12, which almost certainly has nothing to do with Dan 9:26. That the "suffering Servant" of Isaiah 52–53 came to be applied to a slain Messiah in later Jewish tradition may be admitted, but it says nothing about the meaning of Dan 9:26 in its own setting or context.

23. See further J. Becker, *Messianic Expectation in the Old Testament* (Philadelphia: Fortress, 1980), 93-96.

24. See H. L. Ginsberg, "The Oldest Interpretation of the Suffering Servant," *VT* 3 (1953) 400-404. Cf. M. Hengel, "The Effective History of Isaiah 53 in the Pre-Christian Pe-riod," in *The Suffering Servant: Isaiah 53 in Jewish and Christian Sources,* ed. B. Janowski and P. Stuhlmacher (Grand Rapids: Wm. B. Eerdmans, 2004) 90-98.

CHAPTER 6

The Septuagint's Interpretation
of Some Old Testament Passages

NOTE: *Some of the interpretations in the LXX may antedate the book of Daniel discussed in chapter 5. The reader should consult the first paragraph of that chapter before proceeding here.*

As we begin to discuss this phase of the Davidic dynasty's development, it is important to recall two fundamental things about the Greek translation of the Old Testament: (1) it represents the thinking of Diaspora Judaism that at times differed from that of Palestinian Judaism; and (2) most of the manuscripts of the Greek translation of the Old Testament were produced by Christian scribes of the fourth and later centuries.[1] Consequently, one has to reckon with the possibility that some of the differences in the Greek version(s) cited here may have been influenced by Old Testament passages quoted in the Greek New Testament, or by subconscious Christian theological interpretations, or even other contemporary social or political trends. The evidence for such influence may be minimal, but it has to be reckoned with. We begin with the LXX translation of those Old Testament passages that contain the Hebrew word משיח, distinguishing them from those that do not.

---

1. See M. Hengel, *The Septuagint as Christian Scripture: Its Prehistory and the Problem of Its Canon.* OT Studies (Edinburgh: T. & T. Clark, 2002); Hengel and A. M. Schwemer, eds., *Die Septuaginta zwischen Judentum und Christentum.* WUNT 72 (Tübingen: Mohr Siebeck, 1994) 182-284; M. Harl, G. Dorival, and O. Minnich, *La Bible Grecque des Septante: Du judaïsme hellénistique au christianisme ancien* (Paris: Editions du Cerf, 1988) 219-22; K. H. Jobes and M. Silva, *Invitation to the Septuagint* (Grand Rapids: Baker, 2000) 86-102.

(1) In the vast majority of the instances where מָשִׁיחַ occurs, this word is translated into Greek simply by the verbal adjective χριστός "anointed,"[2] which is often accompanied by the genitive of a personal pronoun (enclitic μου, σου, or αὐτοῦ, "my," "your," "his") or by κυρίου, "of the LORD." When מָשִׁיחַ is used for "the anointed priest" in Lev 4:5, 16; 6:15(22), it is rendered simply as ὁ ἱερεὺς ὁ χριστός, but in Lev 4:3 it appears rather as ὁ ἀρχιερεὺς ὁ κεχρισμένος, "the anointed high priest," with the perfect passive participle instead of the verbal adjective. In 1 Chr 16:22 and Ps 105:15, τῶν χριστῶν μου, "My anointed ones," stands in parallelism to τοῖς προφήταις, "the prophets." None of these instances is surprising, because they all follow the translation that one would expect.[3]

(2) Dan 9:25-26, however, offers some anomalies. In the MT, the crucial part of the Hebrew of v. 25 reads: וְתֵדַע וְתַשְׂכֵּל מִן־מֹצָא דָבָר . . . לְהָשִׁיב וְלִבְנוֹת יְרוּשָׁלַיִם עַד־מָשִׁיחַ נָגִיד שָׁבֻעִים שִׁבְעָה, "you [sing.] are to know and to understand (this): From the going forth of a word to rebuild Jerusalem up until an Anointed One, a Prince, (there shall be) seven weeks . . . ." This becomes in the LXX, καὶ γνώσῃ καὶ διανοηθήσῃ καὶ εὐφρανθήσῃ καὶ εὑρήσεις προστάγματα ἀποκριθῆναι καὶ οἰκοδομήσεις Ἰερουσαλὴμ πόλιν κυρίῳ, "you will know and understand and be gladdened, and you will discover (the) ordinances to reply, and you will build Jerusalem as a city for the LORD."[4] Such a version has misunderstood the preposition עַד, "up until," as the noun עִיר, "city," not only confusing the *daleth* with a *resh*, but interpreting מָשִׁיחַ נָגִיד as a title for God, as κυρίῳ is substituted. The change of what should be the infinitive οἰκοδομῆσαι to οἰκοδομήσεις, "you will build," makes God address Daniel as the one who is to rebuild Jerusalem's Temple. It has thus eliminated all mention of an Anointed One and substitutes for it "as a city for the LORD." Obviously, this version manifests no "messianic" development.

The Hebrew of v. 26 in the MT reads וְאַחֲרֵי הַשָּׁבֻעִים שִׁשִּׁים וּשְׁנַיִם יִכָּרֵת מָשִׁיחַ וְאֵין לוֹ וְהָעִיר וְהַקֹּדֶשׁ יַשְׁחִית עַם נָגִיד הַבָּא וְקִצּוֹ בַשֶּׁטֶף וְעַד קֵץ מִלְחָמָה נֶחֱרֶצֶת שֹׁמֵמוֹת, "and after sixty-two weeks an Anointed One

2. See H. W. Smyth, *Greek Grammar*, rev. ed. (Cambridge, MA: Harvard University Press, 1956) §471-72.

3. Also in Sir 46:19.

4. See J. Ziegler, *Susanna, Daniel, Bel et Draco*. SVTG 16/2 (Göttingen: Vandenhoeck & Ruprecht, 1954) 190. What appears in the MT after עַד־מָשִׁיחַ נָגִיד שָׁבֻעִים שִׁבְעָה, is omitted entirely and found in the LXX as v. 27a. The hiphil of the verb שׁוב is translated often in the LXX by a form of ἀποκρίνομαι.

shall be cut down with no one to help him. The people of a prince who comes shall destroy the city and the sanctuary. Its end shall be with a flood; and at the end, war and decreed desolation." This becomes in the LXX, καὶ μετὰ ἑπτὰ καὶ ἑβδομήκοντα καὶ ἑξήκοντα δύο ἀποσταθήσεται χρῖσμα καὶ οὐκ ἔσται, καὶ βασιλεία ἐθνῶν φθερεῖ τὴν πόλιν καὶ τὸ ἅγιον μετὰ τοῦ χριστοῦ, καὶ ἥξει ἡ συντέλεια αὐτοῦ μετ᾽ ὀργῆς καὶ ἕως καιροῦ συντελείας· ἀπὸ πολέμου πολεμηθήσεται, "and after seventy-seven and sixty-two [weeks?],[5] (the) anointing will be withdrawn, and it will be no more. A kingdom of Gentiles will destroy the city and the holy (place) together with the Anointed One. Then will come the end of it/him with wrath; and up until the time of the end from war war will be made."[6]

In this verse, even though the Greek translation has preserved a mention of χριστός, "Anointed One," it does not appear where it is expected, and the crucial Hebrew words יכרת משיח, "an Anointed One shall be cut down," is rendered as ἀποσταθήσεται χρῖσμα, "(the) anointing will be withdrawn." So an abstraction has been substituted for a personal Anointed One in what appears to be a corruptly transmitted Greek text. As a result, it is not easy to assess the contribution of the LXX, if any, to the emergence of messianism that these important verses of Daniel reveal in the MT.

(3) By contrast, the later version of Theodotion has preserved משיח in a much more literal translation of the verse:[7] καὶ γνώσῃ καὶ συνήσεις· ἀπὸ ἐξόδου λόγου τοῦ ἀποκριθῆναι καὶ τοῦ οἰκοδομῆσαι Ἰερουσαλὴμ ἕως χριστοῦ ἡγουμένου ἑβδομάδες ἑπτὰ . . . , "you will know and understand: from the going forth of a word to reply and to build Jerusalem up until an Anointed One, a Leader, (there will be) seven weeks . . . ."[8] In this case, the

---

5. Ziegler, *Susanna, Daniel, Bel et Draco*, 190-91. The Greek text of v. 26 is obviously corrupt. There is no noun to which the numbers refer, and the number "seventy-seven" is unintelligible. The scribe seems to have written ἑβδομήκοντα, "seventy," when he should have written ἑβδομάδας, "weeks."

6. For a fuller discussion of the problems of this LXX translation, see L. L. Grabbe, "The Seventy-Weeks Prophecy (Daniel 9:24-27) in Early Jewish Interpretation," in *The Quest for Context and Meaning: Studies in Biblical Intertextuality in Honor of James A. Sanders*, ed. C. A. Evans and S. Talmon. Biblical Interpretation 28 (Leiden: Brill, 1997) 595-611, esp. 598-99; also S. P. Jeansonne, *The Old Greek Translation of Daniel 7–12*. CBQMS 19 (Washington: Catholic Biblical Assocation of America, 1988) 125-30.

7. Theodotion's version is usually dated to the second century A.D., and it is usually regarded as an attempt to make the earlier Greek translation conform more to the MT, which it does in the two instances cited here.

8. See Ziegler, *Susanna, Daniel, Bel et Draco*, 190.

only anomaly is the translation of להשיב by ἀποκριθῆναι, "to reply" (as also in the LXX). Here the mention of a future χριστός, who is also called ἡγούμενος (the usual translation of Hebrew נגיד in the LXX), is clearly preserved, but it really adds nothing new to the MT formulation.

Again, the later version of Theodotion is somewhat closer to the meaning of the MT of v. 26: καὶ μετὰ τὰς ἑβδομάδας τὰς ἑξήκοντα δύο ἐξολεθρευθήσεται χρῖσμα, καὶ κρίμα οὐκ ἔστιν ἐν αὐτῷ· καὶ τὴν πόλιν καὶ τὸ ἅγιον διαφθερεῖ σὺν τῷ ἡγουμένῳ τῷ ἐρχομένῳ, καὶ ἐκκοπήσονται ἐν κατακλυσμῷ, καὶ ἕως τέλους πολέμου συντετμημένου τάξει ἀφανισμοῖς, "and after the sixty-two weeks anointing will be utterly done away with, and there is no judgment in it (or him?). It (or He?) will destroy the city and the holy place with the leader that is coming. They will be cut off in a flood, even up to the end of the shortened war, extermination."[9] Here one notes not only the disappearance of χριστός and the use of a similar expression, ἐξολεθρευθήσεται χρῖσμα, "anointing will be withdrawn," but also the lack of a subject for the verb διαφθερεῖ, "will destroy."

So much for the LXX form of the Old Testament passages where the word משׁיח occurs in the MT. There are, however, some passages in the LXX, where χριστός appears, but where the corresponding Hebrew text of the MT lacks משׁיח.

(4) Lev 21:10, where שׁמן המשׁחה, "the oil of anointing," becomes τοῦ ἐπικεχυμένου ἐπὶ τὴν κεφαλὴν τοῦ ἐλαίου τοῦ χριστοῦ "oil poured on the head of the anointed one [the High Priest]."[10] Similarly in 21:12.

(5) 2 Sam 2:5, where τὸν χριστὸν κυρίου, "the Anointed of the LORD," is added to the name of Saul in some MSS.[11]

(6) 2 Sam 23:3, where φόβον χριστοῦ, "fear of the Anointed One," is read in MS B instead of φόβον θεοῦ, "fear of God."[12]

(7) 2 Chr 22:7, where χριστὸν κυρίου, "the LORD's Anointed," as an appositive to "Jehu the son of Nimshi," is substituted for the verb and pronominal suffix, אשׁר משׁחו יהוה, "whom the LORD anointed."[13]

(8) Ezek 16:4, where in MS A τοῦ χριστοῦ μου, "of my Anointed One,"

---

9. Ziegler, *Susanna, Daniel, Bel et Draco*, 190-91.

10. J. W. Wevers, *Leviticus*. SVTG 2/2 (Göttingen: Vandenhoeck & Ruprecht, 1986) 232.

11. A. E. Brooke, N. McLean, and H. St.J. Thackeray, *The Old Testament in Greek* (Cambridge: Cambridge University Press, 1906-40) 2:110.

12. Brooke, McLean, and Thackeray, *The Old Testament in Greek*, 2:191.

13. Brooke, McLean, and Thackeray, *The Old Testament in Greek*, 2/3:519.

follows ἐν ὕδατι οὐκ ἐλούσθης, "you were not washed with water," as a substitute for the unintelligible Hebrew form לְמִשְׁעִי.[14]

(9) Cant 1:7 (in ms S): πρὸς τὸν νυμφίον χριστόν, "for the anointed groom," is added at the end.

(10) Amos 4:13 (where ἀπαγγέλλων εἰς ἀνθρώπους τὸν χριστὸν αὐτοῦ, "announcing His Anointed One to human beings," is substituted for the puzzling Hebrew וּמַגִּיד לְאָדָם מַה־שֵּׂחוֹ, often translated as "declaring to human beings what his thought is."[15]

It is found also in deuterocanonical Greek writings:

(11) Sir 47:11, χριστός in ms B² as a strange variant for κύριος "the LORD took away his sins," where the Hebrew text has [וגם] יִי הֶעֱבִיר פִּשְׁעוֹ, "and Yahweh [also] did away with his transgression."16

(12) 2 Macc 1:10, where ἀπὸ τοῦ τῶν χριστῶν ἱερέων γένους is found for "from the family of anointed priests."[17]

(13) 2 Macc 3:30, where χῦ (= χριστοῦ) appears as a strange variant in ms A for κυρίου in a clause that speaks of the appearance of the Almighty LORD.[18]

Some other Old Testament passages have been discussed already in chapters 2 and 4, but little is found in the Greek version of them that adds anything significantly different to the emerging tradition about the continuation of the Davidic dynasty. A few passages, however, call for some comment.

(14) In Gen 3:15, where the MT reads וְאֵיבָה אָשִׁית בֵּינְךָ וּבֵין הָאִשָּׁה וּבֵין זַרְעֲךָ וּבֵין זַרְעָהּ הוּא יְשׁוּפְךָ רֹאשׁ וְאַתָּה תְּשׁוּפֶנּוּ עָקֵב, "I will put enmity between you and the woman, and between your offspring and hers; it shall trample your head, and you shall snap at its heel." In the MT, the Hebrew masculine pronoun הוּא refers to the masculine noun זֶרַע, "seed, offspring"; hence its translation in English as "it." The LXX, however, has translated the verse thus: καὶ ἔχθραν θήσω ἀνὰ μέσον σου καὶ ἀνὰ μέσον τῆς γυναικὸς καὶ ἀνὰ μέσον τοῦ σπέρματός σου καὶ ἀνὰ μέσον τοῦ σπέρματος

14. J. Ziegler, *Ezechiel*. SVTG 16/1 (Göttingen: Vandenhoeck & Ruprecht, 1967) 146.

15. J. Ziegler, *Duodecim Prophetae*, rev. ed. SVTG 13 (Göttingen: Vandenhoeck & Ruprecht, 1967) 191. Cf. Jobes and Silva, *Invitation to the Septuagint*, 297.

16. J. Ziegler, *Sapientia Iesu Filii Sirach*. SVTG 12/2 (Göttingen: Vandenhoeck & Ruprecht, 1965) 347.

17. W. Kappler and R. Hanhart, *Maccabaeorum Liber II*. SVTG 9/2 (Göttingen: Vandenhoeck & Ruprecht, 1976) 48.

18. Kappler and Hanhart, *Maccabaeorum Liber II*, 58.

αὐτῆς· αὐτός σου τηρήσει κεφαλήν, καὶ σὺ τηρήσεις αὐτοῦ πτέρναν,[19] "I will put enmity between you and the woman, and between your offspring and hers; he shall keep watch for your head, and you shall keep watch for his heel." The pronoun הוא has been translated literally by the Greek masculine nominative pronoun, αὐτός, and so it can no longer refer to "offspring," which in Greek is a neuter noun, σπέρμα. Such a rendering, however, is an interpretative translation, "he," a male offspring, which is not obvious in the MT, where זרע has a collective meaning.[20] R. A. Martin has argued that "the LXX becomes thereby the earliest evidence of an individual messianic interpretation of Gen 3:15, to be dated in the 3rd or 2nd century B.C."[21] He should have spoken of it rather as the earliest Jewish evidence of an individual personal or male interpretation of the "offspring," because there is no indication in this Greek translation that a "Messiah" was already envisaged. Moreover, since the word forms part of the divine curse of the serpent, there cannot be a promise of a future offspring with such a connotation. Eventually a "messianic" sense was read into the masculine pronoun of the LXX, not in the New Testament, but in patristic writings.[22]

(15) In Gen 49:10, Jacob's blessing of Judah reads, שבט לא־יסור מיהודה ומחקק מבין רגליו עד כי־יבא שילה ולו יקהת עמים, "a scepter shall not depart from Judah, nor a mace from between his feet, until tribute comes to him, and his is the obedience of peoples," or more lit., "until there comes šîlōh, and to him (is) the obedience of peoples." This becomes in the LXX: οὐκ ἐκλείψει ἄρχων ἐξ Ἰουδά, καὶ ἡγούμενος ἐκ τῶν μηρῶν αὐτοῦ, ἕως ἂν ἔλθῃ τὰ ἀποκείμενα αὐτῷ, καὶ αὐτὸς προσδοκία ἐθνῶν,[23] "a ruler shall not depart from Judah, nor a guide from his thighs, until what is stored up comes to him, and he is the expectation of nations." The blessing

---

19. J. W. Wevers, *Genesis*. SVTG 1 (Göttingen: Vandenhoeck & Ruprecht, 1974) 92-93.

20. See C. Westermann, *Genesis 1–11* (Minneapolis: Augsburg, 1984) 260.

21. See R. A. Martin, "The Earliest Messianic Interpretation of Genesis 3₁₅," *JBL* 84 (1965) 425-27 (which has a good discussion of the various ways in which הוא is rendered in Greek in its 103 occurrences in Genesis).

22. From the time of Irenaeus, this verse of Genesis has been known as the *Protevangelium*. Cf. J. Chaine, *Le livre de la Genèse*. LD 3 (Paris: Editions du Cerf, 1951) 50. The eisegesis did not stop there, because in time the masculine pronoun הוא (*hû'*) was read as feminine היא (*hî'*), "she," and translated as *ipsa* in the Vg: *ipsa conteret caput tuum et tu insidiaberis calcaneo eius*, "she will trample your head, and you will lie in wait for her heel." Note the extreme to which the eisegesis was carried by F. X. Peirce, "Mary Alone Is 'the Woman' of Genesis 3:15," *CBQ* 2 (1940) 245-52.

23. See Wevers, *Genesis*, 460.

in the LXX has been given a more personal nuance, for "scepter" and "mace" are translated by personal names, ἄρχων, "ruler," and ἡγούμενος, "guide."[24] Given the longstanding misunderstanding of שׁילה, its Greek translation as "what is stored up" is not surprising, but there is nothing "messianic" about it, despite the future nuance of the accompanying προσδοκία ἐθνῶν, "the expectation of nations," which is very vague. Yet L. Monsengwo-Pasinya maintains that v. 10d gives to the whole passage "un sens résolument messianique."[25] Even though the LXX may speak of a person or a "ruler" who is awaited, it is no more "messianic" than the vague αὐτός of Gen 3:15, because there is no indication that this ruler will be an anointed agent of God.[26]

(16) In Num 24:17, the fourth Oracle of Balaam includes the clauses, דרך כוכב מיעקב וקם שבט מישראל ומחץ פאתי מואב וקרקר כל־בני שת, "a star shall stride forth from Jacob, and a scepter shall arise from Israel; it shall smite the brows of Moab and the skulls of all the sons of Sheth." This becomes in the LXX: ἀνατελεῖ ἄστρον ἐξ Ἰακώβ, καὶ ἀναστήσεται ἄνθρωπος ἐξ Ἰσραήλ, καὶ θραύσει τοὺς ἀρχηγοὺς Μωάβ, καὶ προνομεύσει πάντας υἱοὺς Σήθ,[27] "a star shall arise from Jacob, and a man from Israel; he will shatter the leaders of Moab and plunder all the sons of Seth." Now the "scepter" has become a person, ἄνθρωπος, "man," and the "skulls" have become personal too, "leaders." The individual "man," however, is not given any identifiable "messianic" designation, again because that concept has not yet emerged in ancient Judaism.[28]

---

24. The Hebrew form מחקק is problematic. Actually it is a poel participle, "prescribing," which is sometimes substantivized as a person, "prescriber, commander," as in Deut 33:21; Judg 5:14; Isa 33:22, and sometimes as the "commander's staff, mace," as here in Gen 49:10 (par. שבט, "scepter"); cf. Num 21:18; Pss 60:9(Eng. 7); 108:9(8).

25. See L. Monsengwo-Pasinya, "Deux textes messianiques de la Septante: Gn 49,10 et Ez 21,32," *Bib* 61 (1980) 357-76, esp. 365. He goes even further, saying that "la LXX continue la tradition juive qui voyait en Gn 49,10 un texte messianique," and that "le traducteur alexandrin impose au texte une allure messianique plus claire encore que dans le texte hébreu" (p. 366). But he never explains what he means by "la tradition juive," which, as far as I can see, is nonexistent.

26. It is only by reading into the passage details from Zechariah and Micah that Monsengwo-Pasinya can maintain that Ezek 21:31-32, which does give a reverse interpretation of Gen 49:10 (see p. 29 above), "est une prophétie messianique au sens littéral"! (ibid., 376).

27. See J. W. Wevers, *Numeri*. SVTG 3/1 (Göttingen: Vandenhoeck & Ruprecht, 1982) 293.

28. That the LXX has "close points of contact with the later Targum and Palestinian

(17) The minor changes in the Greek translation of such passages as Gen 9:25-27 (Noah's curse of Canaan), 12:3 (blessing of families of the earth through Abraham), Exod 12:42 (night of vigil to be kept for the Lord), and Deut 18:15-18 (God's promise to raise up a prophet like Moses) have no significance and imply nothing more "messianic" than the original Hebrew formulations.[29]

(18) Even the Oracle of Nathan in 2 Samuel 7, which is found in a slightly expanded Greek form, carries basically the same message as the MT, especially in the crucial vv. 11c-14, which do, however, mention a different builder of God's house:

καὶ ἀπαγγελεῖ σοι κύριος ὅτι οἶκον οἰκοδομήσεις αὐτῷ. καὶ ἔσται ἐὰν πληρωθῶσιν αἱ ἡμέραι σου καὶ κοιμηθήσῃ μετὰ τῶν πατέρων σου, καὶ ἀναστήσω τὸ σπέρμα σου μετά σε, ὅς ἔσται ἐκ τῆς κοιλίας σου, καὶ ἑτοιμάσω τὴν βασιλείαν αὐτοῦ. αὐτὸς οἰκοδομήσει μοι οἶκον τῷ ὀνόματί μου, καὶ ἀνορθώσω τὸν θρόνον αὐτοῦ ἕως εἰς τὸν αἰῶνα. ἐγὼ ἔσομαι αὐτῷ εἰς πατέρα, καὶ αὐτὸς ἔσται μοι εἰς υἱόν.[30]

and the LORD shall declare to you that you will build Him a house. 'When your days are complete and you are lulled to sleep with your fathers, I will raise up your offspring after you, which shall come forth from your loins, and I will prepare his kingship. He shall build for me a

---

tradition" may be clear, as M. Hengel claims ("The Effective History of Isaiah 53 in the Pre-Christian Period," in *The Suffering Servant: Isaiah 53 in Jewish and Christian Sources*, ed. B. Janowski and P. Stuhlmacher [Grand Rapids: Wm. B. Eerdmans, 2004] 81), but it does not make ἄνθρωπος into χριστός. See also G. Dorival ("'Un astre se lèvera de Jacob': L'Interprétation ancienne de *Nombres* 24, 17," *ASE* 13 [1996] 295-352) and K. J. Cathcart ("Numbers 24:17 in Ancient Translations and Interpretations," in *The Interpretation of the Bible*, ed. J. Krašovec. JSOTSup 289 [Sheffield: Sheffield Academic, 1998] 511-20), both of whom use later Jewish and Christian interpretations to impose a messianic meaning on ἄνθρωπος of the LXX.

One could also cite Num 24:7, which in the MT reads, יזל־מים מדליו וזרעו במים רבים, "Water shall flow from his buckets, and his seed (shall be) on many waters." This becomes in the LXX, ἐξελεύσεται ἄνθρωπος ἐκ τοῦ σπέρματος αὐτοῦ καὶ κυριεύσει ἐθνῶν πολλῶν, "a man shall come forth from his seed and shall rule over many nations." Again, an unnamed male remains unidentified. The change in the LXX may sound like a "messianic" development, but to call it that is a failure to respect the vague imagery that the LXX is using.

29. See p. 32 above.

30. Brooke, McLean, and Thackeray, *The Old Testament in Greek*, 2/1:128.

house for my name, and I will establish his throne forever. I will be to him a father, and he shall be to Me a son.

The Greek form of the oracle, however, does not really advance the understanding of it much beyond the MT, even though it does change the sense of the oracle radically about who will build the house in the first clause quoted above.

The passages in Isaiah 7, 9, and 11 that deal with the continuation of the Davidic dynasty, as they have been translated in the LXX, shed a little new light on its development.[31] In general, one detects a tendency to consider pronouncements of the prophet as being fulfilled in the translator's time, but sometimes there is a thrust to an even more remote future.

(19) The Greek of the crucial verse in Isa 7:14 reads: διὰ τοῦτο δώσει κύριος αὐτὸς ὑμῖν σημεῖον· ἰδοὺ ἡ παρθένος ἐν γαστρὶ ἕξει καὶ τέξεται υἱόν, καὶ καλέσεις τὸ ὄνομα αὐτοῦ Ἐμμανουήλ,[32] "for this reason the Lord Himself will give you (plur. [= house of David]) a sign. Look, a virgin shall be with child and shall bear a son, and you (sing.) shall call him Immanuel." Three changes from the MT are noteworthy: (a) future indicatives (ἐν γαστρὶ ἕξει, "shall be with child," and τέξεται, "shall bear") replace the present participles of the MT (הרה and ילדת), which thus give a more remote meaning to the sign; (b) העלמה, "young girl," of the MT is given a more specific meaning, ἡ παρθένος, "virgin";[33] and (c) the ambiguous וקראת, which is vocalized in the MT as וְקָרָאת, i.e., fem. 3rd person sing., "and she shall call," can also be read as קָרָאתָ (as in Judg 12:1), i.e., masc. 2nd person sing. This is the way the Greek translator has understood it, writing καλέσεις "you (sing. [Ahaz?]) shall call." In any case, none of these

---

31. The Greek translation of the book of Isaiah is thought to have been made in early Hasmonean times. According to A. van der Kooij (*Die alten Textzeugen des Jesajabuches: Ein Beitrag zur Textgeschichte des Alten Testaments.* OBO 35 [Freiburg-Schweiz: Universitäts-verlag, 1981] 71-72), it was produced shortly after the fall of Carthage in 146 b.c., between 146 and 132 b.c. It would then come from a time later than the final redaction of the book of Daniel, and of the emergence of משיח in the sense of an awaited anointed agent of God. Cf. I. L. Seeligmann, *The Septuagint Version of Isaiah and Cognate Studies.* FAT 40 (Tübingen: Mohr Siebeck, 2004) 222-51.

32. See J. Ziegler, *Isaias.* SVTG 14 (Göttingen: Vandenhoeck & Ruprecht, 1939) 147.

33. ἡ παρθένος is the preferred reading in the critical editions of the LXX of Isaiah, but ἡ νεᾶνις, "a young girl," is read in other Greek versions and in some mss of the LXX. See Hengel, *The Septuagint as Christian Scripture,* 29-30, for the way Justin Martyr defended the translation of the LXX against other versions in his *Dialogue with Trypho.*

differences changes the meaning of the sign into a more pronounced "messianic" connotation. The most important difference is ἡ παρθένος, which affects the woman, whereas the value of the sign is found in the birth and name of the child, as was noted already in the MT.[34]

(20) In Isa 9:5-6(Eng. 6-7), the prophet hails the birth of a royal heir through whom God will bring about a human society marked with justice and righteousness. In the LXX it reads thus:

> A child has been born to us, even a son has been given to us, upon whose shoulder dominion has been laid, and his name is called Messenger of Great Counsel (καὶ καλεῖται τὸ ὄνομα αὐτοῦ Μεγάλης βουλῆς ἄγγελος).[35] For I shall bring peace unto rulers, peace and health for him. His dominion is great, and of his peace there is no limit, upon David's throne and his kingdom, to establish it and to sustain it in righteousness and judgment from now and for ever. The zeal of the LORD of hosts shall do this.

As in the MT, the reference to the Davidic dynasty is clear, even though the context of this passage opened with a reference to the Northern Kingdom (Isa 9:1[2]). The child's four symbolic throne-names (Wonderful Counselor, Warrior God, Everlasting Father, Prince of Peace) have been reduced to one, "Messenger of Great Counsel," which resembles the first of the four. The Greek version speaks more of "peace," which reflects the fourth name. The imperfect verb with *waw* consecutive (ויקרא), "one has named," is now rendered as a present passive, καὶ καλεῖται τὸ ὄνομα αὐτοῦ, "his name is called." But the future sense of the Greek verbs is no more pronounced than that of the MT. Again, they could refer to an ideal future Davidic king, but he is not called χριστός, "Messiah," and J. Lust has rightly recognized that, though these verses contribute to the proper understanding of the eschatological role of God's messenger, they say nothing about a messianic figure.[36]

(21) Similarly a promise of the continuation of the dynasty is made in Isa 11:1-10. The crucial vv. 1-3 run thus in the LXX: "A shoot shall come forth from the root of Jesse, and a blossom shall rise from the root. The

---

34. See p. 36 above.

35. See Ziegler, *Isaias*, 155-56.

36. See J. Lust, "Messianism in the Septuagint: Isaiah 8:23B–9:6 (9:1-7)," in J. Krašovec, *The Interpretation of the Bible*, 147-63.

spirit of the LORD shall rest upon him: a spirit of wisdom and understanding, a spirit of counsel and might, a spirit of knowledge and piety (εὐσεβείας).³⁷ A spirit of the fear of God shall fill him."

The only real difference from the MT is in the qualities of the successor on David's throne: the substitution of "piety" (εὐσέβεια) for "fear of the LORD." This quality is then expressed in the last sentence (instead of which the MT has: "And his delight shall be in the fear of the LORD"). The concluding v. 10 of the passage reads: καὶ ἔσται ἐν τῇ ἡμέρᾳ ἐκείνῃ ἡ ῥίζα τοῦ Ἰεσσαὶ καὶ ὁ ἀνιστάμενος ἄρχειν ἐθνῶν, ἐπ' αὐτῷ ἔθνη ἐλπιοῦσι, καὶ ἔσται ἡ ἀνάπαυσις αὐτοῦ τιμή,³⁸ "on that day the root of Jesse shall even be the one who rises to rule over nations; in him nations shall find hope, and his resting place shall be an honor." Even though the Greek version is not an exact translation of the Hebrew, it ascribes a similar recognition of rule and importance to a coming heir of Jesse's root. It may refer again to a postexilic heir, but nothing "messianic" is even hinted at.

(22) The important verses of the Fourth Servant Song in Isa 52:13–53:12, as they appear in the LXX, also have to be considered:³⁹

καὶ δώσω τοὺς πονηροὺς ἀντὶ τῆς ταφῆς αὐτοῦ καὶ τοὺς πλουσίους ἀντὶ τοῦ θανάτου αὐτοῦ· ὅτι ἀνομίαν οὐκ ἐποίησεν, οὐδὲ εὑρέθη δόλος ἐν τῷ στόματι αὐτοῦ. καὶ κύριος βούλεται καθαρίσαι αὐτὸν τῆς πληγῆς· ἐὰν δῶτε περὶ ἁμαρτίας, ἡ ψυχὴ ὑμῶν ὄψεται σπέρμα μακρόβιον· καὶ βούλεται κύριος ἀφειλεῖν ἀπὸ τοῦ πόνου τῆς ψυχῆς αὐτοῦ, δεῖξαι αὐτῷ φῶς καὶ πλάσαι τῇ συνέσει, δικαιῶσαι δίκαιον εὖ δουλεύοντα πολλοῖς, καὶ τὰς ἁμαρτίας αὐτῶν αὐτὸς ἀνοίσει. διὰ τοῦτο αὐτὸς κληρονομήσει πολλοὺς καὶ τῶν ἰσχυρῶν μεριεῖ σκῦλα, ἀνθ' ὧν παρεδόθη εἰς θάνατον ἡ ψυχὴ αὐτοῦ, καὶ ἐν τοῖς ἀνόμοις ἐλογίσθη· καὶ αὐτὸς ἁμαρτίας πολλῶν ἀνήνεγκε καὶ διὰ τὰς ἁμαρτίας αὐτῶν παρεδόθη. (Isa 53:9-12)⁴⁰

---

37. See Ziegler, *Isaias,* 165.

38. Ziegler, *Isaias,* 167.

39. See E. R. Ekblad, Jr., *Isaiah's Servant Poems According to the Septuagint.* CBET 23 (Leuven: Peeters, 1999) 167-266, esp. 173-77; K. F. Euler, *Die Verkündigung vom leidenden Gottesknecht aus Jes 53 in der griechischen Bibel.* BWANT 66 (Stuttgart: Kohlhammer, 1934); H. Hegermann, *Jesaja 53 in Hexapla, Targum und Peschitta.* BFCT 2/56 (Gütersloh: Bertelsmann, 1954) 34, 46, 54-55; J. Ziegler, *Untersuchungen zur Septuaginta des Buches Isaias.* ATA 12/3 (Münster in W.: Aschendorff, 1934) 175-212.

40. See Ziegler, *Isaias,* 322-23.

And I [the LORD] will set the wicked for his [the Servant's] burial and
the rich for his death; for he has done no wrong, and no deceit has
been found in his mouth. The LORD is pleased to purge him of his mis-
fortune. If you (plur.) give (something) for sin, you yourselves shall see
long-lived offspring. The LORD is pleased to remove (him) from the
anguish of his soul, to show him light, and to mold (him) with understanding; to justify the righteous one who serves many well, for he
shall bear their sins. Therefore he shall inherit many, and he shall share
the spoils of the mighty, because his life has been handed over to
death; he has been reckoned among the lawless. He has borne the sins
of many and was handed over because of their sins.

Although ὁ παῖς μου, "my Servant," is found at the beginning of the
Fourth Song (Isa 52:13) in the LXX, it disappears in 53:11b, where the MT
has צדיק עבדי, "my Servant, the righteous one." The Greek translation is
not always exact, but the general message of the LXX rendering is the
same as that of the difficult MT, which emphasizes the vicarious suffering
of the Servant for others as well as God's reward of him, along with the
misunderstanding of the people (= "we" and "our") and their sinfulness.

One notes, however, some differences from the MT: (a) a change of
tenses: the imperfect with *waw* consecutive (ויתן) in v. 9, "and he set," becomes a future (καὶ δώσω), "and I will set"; the stative perfect (חפץ) in
v. 10a, "was pleased," becomes a present (βούλεται), "is pleased."[41] (b) The
LORD is introduced in v. 9 as the one who changes the situation; this is expressed as a divine promise by the change of person, as the 3rd person
(ויתן) becomes 1st person (καὶ δώσω). Whereas in the MT the Servant is
assigned a grave with the wicked and the rich, now in the LXX God promises to give the wicked and the rich over to judgment. Because of his vicarious suffering, the Servant becomes their judge.[42] The Greek form thus enhances the Servant's reward. (c) The Greek version of 53:10bc is
anomalous, because of the way it renders the peculiar Hebrew, אם־תשים
אשם נפשו יראה זרע יאריך ימים. Literally this would mean, "If you
(sing.) make yourself a sin-offering, he may see offspring, he may prolong
days." The LXX has, however, ἐὰν δῶτε περὶ ἁμαρτίας, ἡ ψυχὴ ὑμῶν ὄψεται
σπέρμα μακρόβιον, lit., "if you (plur.) give (something) for sin, your soul

---

41. The same verbal form is used to translate also the cognate noun חפץ, "good pleasure, will," later in the verse.

42. See M. Hengel, "The Effective History of Isaiah 53," 122-23.

will see long-lived offspring." The change here is strange and hard to interpret. M. Hengel understands the 2nd person plur. to refer to the people
mentioned as "we" in 53:1-7,[43] who will have a share in the rewarded life to
be enjoyed by the Servant. That is possible. (d) In v. 11, where the MT reads
simply יִרְאֶה, "he shall see," the LXX reads the verb as a causative and supplies both a direct and indirect object, δεῖξαι αὐτῷ φῶς, "to show him
light." This is a reading that is attested in some Qumran copies of Isaiah.[44]
(e) Finally, it is again significant that the Servant is nowhere said to be
χριστός, and that is no more implied here than in the MT.[45] The Suffering
Servant of Isaiah is a well-established motif of the Old Testament, and it is
not to be confused or merged, even in its Septuagintal formulation, with
the later messianic idea that emerges in the book of Daniel and is found in
subsequent writings.

(23) Six royal psalms that lack the word מָשִׁיחַ were discussed in
chapter 4 for their contribution to the theme of the continuation of the
Davidic dynasty, Psalms 21, 45, 72, 101, 110, and 144:1-11.[46] They continue to
do that in a Greek form in the LXX, and in no case is there any difference
in the Greek that would suggest a "messianic" connotation. In fact, in most
cases the translation carries the same nuance as the Hebrew of the MT.

In Psalm 110, part of which is poorly transmitted in the MT, there are
a few interpretative differences in the LXX, especially in v. 3. As part of an
enthronement psalm, in which a court poet recites an oracle of Yahweh

43. Hengel, "The Effective History of Isaiah 53," 125.

44. See p. 41 above. Cf. Jobes and Silva, *Invitation to the Septuagint*, 227.

45. In saying this, I find myself in agreement with F. Hahn, who wrote, "A messianic
interpretation cannot be recognized even in the Septuagint version of Isaiah 53"
(*Christologische Hoheitstitel*. FRLANT 83 [Göttingen: Vandenhoeck & Ruprecht, 1964] 154
n. 1). Hengel, however, is not so sure, claiming that "in the second century B.C.E. the concept
of what was 'messianic' was not yet as clearly fixed on the eschatological saving king from
the house of David as it was later to become in the post-Christian rabbinic tradition. We
must not allow the narrow concept of the Messiah in the post-Christian rabbis to regulate
the diverse pre-Christian messianic ideas"; "The Effective History of Isaiah 53," 136). In the
second century B.C, however, shortly after the time of Dan 9:25-26, the concept of a coming
Messiah, either kingly or priestly, was making its appearance, and what is found in the
Septuagintal form of Isaiah 53 makes little contribution to it, or even to what Hengel calls
the later post-Christian rabbinic understanding of the Messiah. It is simply neutral. Even
though the Suffering Servant of Isaiah may resemble conceptually what will be true of an
awaited Messiah, the prophet's formulation uses discrete imagery, which the interpreter
must respect.

46. See pp. 43-46 above.

promising a new king victory over his foes, v. 3 reads: עַמְּךָ נְדָבֹת בְּיוֹם חֵילְךָ בְּהַדְרֵי־קֹדֶשׁ מֵרֶחֶם מִשְׁחָר לְךָ טַל יַלְדֻתֶיךָ, which may be rendered, "Your people offer themselves willingly on the day of your power. In majestic holiness, from the womb of the morning, like dew have I begotten you." In the LXX, however, this verse is translated: μετὰ σοῦ ἡ ἀρχὴ ἐν ἡμέρᾳ τῆς δυνάμεώς σου ἐν ταῖς λαμπρότησιν τῶν ἁγίων· ἐκ γαστρὸς πρὸ ἑωσφόρου ἐξεγέννησά σε,[47] "Dominion is with you on the day of your power in the splendors of the holy ones. From the womb, before the morning star, I have begotten you." The last half of the verse, especially in the LXX, may suggest that the king is one conceived before the earth itself. There are two major problems in the verse. The first is the prepositional phrase בְּהַדְרֵי קֹדֶשׁ, "in majestic holiness" (lit., "in the honors of holiness"), because there is a variant reading in some MSS בְּהַרְרֵי קֹדֶשׁ, "on holy mountains" (so RSV), and the phrase is then taken with what precedes. Those who read בְּהַדְרֵי קֹדֶשׁ, however, usually take the phrase with what follows, as in the translation of the MT given above. The LXX takes the words with the first part and understands קֹדֶשׁ as "holy ones." The second problem is the vocalization of the first two words. In the MT, they are read: עַמְּךָ נְדָבֹת, lit., "your people (are) freewill-offerings," i.e., willing volunteers. In the LXX, μετὰ σοῦ ἡ ἀρχή presupposes the vocalization of the first word to be עִמְּךָ, "with you," and then it is difficult to say how ἀρχή came from נדבת.

The following v. 4 of this psalm runs thus in the LXX: ὤμοσεν κύριος οὐκ μεταμεληθήσεται, Σὺ εἶ ἱερεὺς εἰς τὸν αἰῶνα κατὰ τὴν τάξιν Μελχισεδέκ,[48] "The LORD has sworn and shall not renege, 'You are a priest forever according to the order of Melchizedek.'" These differences, however, do not give the psalm any more of a "messianic" connotation than the MT.

(24) At least six Old Testament passages from the preexilic(?), exilic, and postexilic times speak of a coming David. They represent a development in the theme of the continuation of the Davidic dynasty, and they are likewise preserved in the Greek version of the LXX.

(a) Thus Hos 3:5 tells of Israelites who will "seek for the LORD their God and David their king" (οἱ υἱοὶ Ἰσραὴλ . . . ἐπιζητήσουσιν κύριον τὸν

---

47. A. Rahlfs, *Psalmi cum Odis.* SVTG 10 (Göttingen: Vandenhoeck & Ruprecht, 1967) 277.

48. Rahlfs, *Psalmi cum Odis,* 277.

θεὸν αὐτῶν καὶ Δαυὶδ τὸν βασιλέα αὐτῶν).⁴⁹ Such a pronouncement is similar to others about a coming David in exilic and postexilic prophetic writings.

(b) At the time of the Babylonian deportation, Jeremiah passes on God's message that Israel and Judah will work no longer for foreigners, but for the "LORD their God, and I will raise up for them David their king" (. . . καὶ τὸν Δαυὶδ βασιλέα αὐτῶν ἀναστήσω αὐτοῖς [LXX Jer 37:8-9 (MT 30:8-9)]). This promise of a future David is reformulated in Jer 23:5ff.:

> Look! Days are coming, says the LORD, when I shall raise up for David a righteous growth (ἀναστήσω τῷ Δαυὶδ ἀνατολὴν δικαίαν), and he shall rule as king, be wise, and execute judgment and righteousness on the land. In his days Judah will be saved, and Israel will dwell confidently, and this is his name, which the LORD will call him: Josedek among the prophets (καὶ τοῦτο τὸ ὄνομα αὐτοῦ, ὃ καλέσει αὐτὸν [κύριος] Ἰωσεδὲκ ἐν τοῖς προφήταις).⁵⁰

In this reformulation about the heir for David, he is ἀνατολὴ δίκαια, which renders Hebrew צמח צדיק (*ṣemaḥ ṣaddîq,* "righteous scion"). His new throne-name is now "Josedek,"⁵¹ and it is said to be given to him by "the LORD," which is different from the MT that has יהוה צדקנו (*Yahweh ṣidqēnû,* "the LORD is our righteousness"); it may, however, be merely a different spelling of Zedekiah, the name usually thought to be meant in the MT.⁵² This development is, indeed, building toward the "Messiah" (χριστός) as the kingly heir of David, but significantly that title is not yet given to him, as Lust recognizes.⁵³

(c) When in 3:8 Zechariah addresses Joshua, the postexilic High Priest, who is called ὁ ἱερεὺς ὁ μέγας (lit., "the great priest"), he says,

---

49. J. Ziegler, *Duodecim Prophetae,* 153. For the context and date of this pronouncement of Hosea, see p. 47 above.

50. J. Ziegler, *Jeremias, Baruch, Threni, Epistula Ieremiae.* SVTG 15 (Göttingen: Vandenhoeck & Ruprecht, 1957) 263.

51. The Greek Ἰωσεδέκ seems to be an attempt to transcribe Hebrew יוצדק (see Ezra 3:2, 8).

52. See J. Lust, "Messianism and the Greek Version of Jeremiah," in *VII Congress of the International Organization for Septuagint and Cognate Studies: Leuven 1989,* ed. C. E. Cox. SBLSCS 31 (Atlanta: Scholars, 1991) 87-122, esp. 89-90.

53. Lust, "Messianism and the Greek Version of Jeremiah," 96, 99.

"Look! I am leading in my servant, the Growth (ἰδοὺ ἐγὼ ἄγω τὸν δοῦλόν μου Ἀνατολήν)"; again an allusion is made to Jer 23:5, ἀνατολὴ δίκαια, "righteous growth" (= צמח צדיק, "righteous scion" or "branch"). Moreover, when the prophet speaks about the vision of the lampstand and the two olive trees and identifies the latter as "two sons of oil who stand by the LORD of the whole earth" (Zech 4:14), the LXX renders that expression as οἱ δύο υἱοὶ πιότητος, lit., "the two sons of fatness" (= oil). In neither of these passages is there an allusion to what later came to be called χριστός, or even a use of the verb χρίω, "anoint."

(d) The same has to be said about the Greek version of two passages in the writings of Ezekiel where a future or coming David is again mentioned: 34:23-24 ("I will set over them one shepherd and he will tend them, my servant David, and he will be their shepherd" — almost the same as the MT); and 37:24-25 ("My servant David shall be a leader [ἄρχων] among them, and there shall be one shepherd for all . . . , and David, my servant, shall be their leader [ἄρχων] forever"). Here the leadership of the Davidic heir is promised, but he is not yet called χριστός, "Messiah," but either ποιμήν, "shepherd," or ἄρχων, "leader."

(e) Similarly for the Greek version of Mic 5:1(Eng. 2), "But you, Bethlehem, house of Ephrathah, are the smallest to be among the clans of Judah, from you shall come forth for me one who is to be ruler (ἄρχοντα) in Israel, and his going-forth (ἔξοδοι) is from the beginning, (from) days of old."

(25) The Greek version of Malachi ends with the promise to send Elijah: "Look! I am sending to you Elijah, the Tishbite, before the great and glorious day of the LORD comes, who will restore the heart of a father to (his) son and the heart of a man to his neighbor, lest I come and thoroughly smite the land" (Mal 3:23-24[Eng. 4:5-6]; cf. Sir 48:9-10).

(26) Finally, a passage in Ezekiel calls for comment, not because it contains משיח or because the LXX version of it has χριστός, but because it illustrates how Christian scribes sometimes "christianized" a text that sounded "messianic" to them and that they considered an allusion to the crucified Jesus. In the MT of Ezek 17:22d-23a, God is quoted as saying, ושתלתי אני על הר־גבה ותלול. בהר מרום ישראל אשתלנו, "and I will plant [it] on a high and lofty mountain; on a mountain top in Israel will I plant it." This becomes in the LXX, καὶ καταφυτεύσω ἐγὼ ἐπ' ὄρος ὑψηλόν· καὶ κρεμάσω αὐτὸν ἐν ὄρει μετεώρῳ τοῦ Ἰσραὴλ, "and I will plant on a high mountain; and I will hang him on a mountain top of Israel." The

translator apparently did not understand the *hapax legomenon* Hebrew adjective תלול *(tālûl)*, said to mean "lofty," and took it to be a form of תלה, "hang." So he wrote, καὶ κρεμάσω, "and I will hang," to which he added a masculine sing. pronoun as the direct object, αὐτόν, "him." The LXX has introduced, then, a meaning that sounds like New Testament phrases about the crucified Jesus, such as Acts 5:30 ("you killed by hanging him on a tree"; cf. 10:39). However, Lust has shown that Papyrus 967 omits the pronoun αὐτόν and reads καὶ κρεμαστόν, which would mean "(on) a high and suspended mountain,"[54] which is a version that corresponds to the MT. It shows how the forthright Hebrew text of the MT was given in the LXX a loaded meaning, making Ezekiel's words foreshadow the Christian description of the crucifixion of Jesus.[55]

Apart from the last-mentioned instance, one can see from this survey of the LXX passages, which render the Hebrew texts that develop the theme of the continuation of the Davidic dynasty, that their contribution is really minimal.

---

54. See J. Lust, "And I Shall Hang Him on a Lofty Mountain: Ezek 17:22-23 and Messianism in the Septuagint," in *IX Congress of the International Organization for Septuagint and Cognate Studies: Cambridge 1995*, ed. B. A. Taylor. SBLSCS 45 (Atlanta: Scholars, 1997) 231-50, esp. 242-43. Papyrus 967 was not available to Ziegler in 1952, when he published the first edition of *Ezechiel*, but it now appears in the 1977 revised edition by D. Fraenkel (p. 337).

55. See further Jobes and Silva, *Invitation to the Septuagint*, 298.

CHAPTER 7

Extrabiblical Jewish Writings
of the Second Temple Period

Once the term מָשִׁיחַ has been found in the sense of an awaited anointed
agent of God for the deliverance of His people in some eschatological
sense, it is not surprising that it continues to appear in pre-Christian Jewish writings.[1] Among these writings there are some in which there is no
mention of a "Messiah," e.g., the book of *Jubilees*,[2] *The Testament of Job*,
The Assumption of Moses,[3] *The Biblical Antiquities* of Pseudo-Philo, or
3 Baruch (Greek Apocalypse of Baruch).

    (1) The first of the extrabiblical writings to be considered is the so-

---

1. See G. Dalman, *Messianische Texte aus der nachkanonischen jüdischen Literatur für
den akademischen Gebrauch* (Leipzig: Hinrichs, 1898); D. Flusser, "Messiah, Second Temple
Period," *EncJud*, 11:1408-10; P. Grelot, "Le Messie dans les Apocryphes de l'Ancien Testament:
État de la question," in *La venue du Messie: Messianisme et eschatologie*, ed. E. Massaux.
RechBib 6 (Paris: Desclée de Brouwer, 1962) 19-50; M. A. Knibb, "Messianism in the Pseud-
epigrapha in the Light of the Scrolls," *DSD* 2 (1995) 165-84; H. Lichtenberger, "Messianic Ex-
pectations and Messianic Figures in the Second Temple Period," in *Qumran-Messianism:
Studies on the Messianic Expectations in the Dead Sea Scrolls*, ed. J. H. Charlesworth et al.
(Tübingen: Mohr Siebeck, 1998) 9-20; M. Wittlieb, "Die theologische Bedeutung der
Erwähnung von 'Māšîaḥ/Christos' in den Pseudepigraphen des Alten Testaments
palästinischen Ursprungs," *BN* 50 (1989) 26-33.

2. However, some writers such as J. Klausner find in it what has been called the "messianic idea," esp. in *Jubilees* 23, but that is once again a misuse of the adjective "messianic,"
for he really means "eschatological"; see *The Messianic Idea in Israel* (New York: Macmillan,
1955; London: Allen and Unwin, 1956) 302-9. Similarly, B. Byrne ("Jesus as Messiah in the
Gospel of Luke," *CBQ* 65 [2003] 80 n. 2), who so considers *Jub* 31:18-20; but that is merely a
blessing of Judah and his sons in whom Israel is said to find salvation.

3. See, e.g., Klausner, *The Messianic Idea in Israel*, 325-29.

called Similitudes of *1 Enoch.* In the Sethian genealogy of Gen 5:1-32, Enoch, son of Jared, "walked with God; and he was not, for God took him" (5:18-24). This brief description becomes in the LXX: "and Enoch pleased God very much, and he was not found, because God had transferred him," i.e., Enoch's burial place was unknown, because he had been taken to God's abode (as in Elijah's transfer, 2 Kgs 2:11-12). Later, Enoch is described in *Jubilees* as the first human being who learned to write; he acquired knowledge and wisdom, and wrote a book about the "signs of heaven" and the order of their months. In that book, too, he is said to have warned human beings about their conduct and the inevitable judgment of every generation (4:17-20). Such a writing of Enoch was known to the author of the Epistle of Jude, who attests that "Enoch of the seventh generation from Adam prophesied, saying, 'Look! The Lord has come with ten thousand holy ones'" (14-15), a quotation from what is known today as *1 Enoch* (1:9).

Messianic passages in *1 Enoch* are found only in the Similitudes, which sometimes are called the Parables; they form the second of the five parts of *1 Enoch,* chs. 37–71.[4] The book of *Enoch* is a composite work, which must have been put together at different times in antiquity. Consequently, scholarly opinion is divided about its origin and the dating of its parts. The second part of *1 Enoch,* containing the Similitudes, is extant neither in Aramaic nor in Greek, but is known only in the "granddaughter" version preserved in a fifth-century(?) Ethiopic translation,[5] and preserved in the earliest of the Ethiopic manuscripts.[6] The date given for the Similitudes varies consid-

---

4. Some older interpreters maintained that *1 Enoch* 90:37-38, part of the Book of Dreams, was also messianic. The white "lamb" that "became a great animal" was said to be a clear symbol of a Messiah (R. H. Charles, *APOT,* 2:269; Grelot, "Le Messie dans les Apocryphes," 23; Dalman, *Messianische Texte,* 290). The name "lamb," however, is not certain; Knibb translates it "wild-ox" (*AOT,* 291). The most one can say is that it lords over other sheep and animals and causes the Lord to rejoice over them. That it has the symbolic meaning of a righteous human leader may be granted, but there is nothing "messianic" about it, and nothing is mentioned about its being anointed. The same has to be said about alleged "Messianic conceptions" in the so-called historical section (83-90), *pace* Klausner (*The Messianic Idea in Israel,* 277-89).

5. See M. A. Knibb, *The Ethiopic Book of Enoch* (Oxford: Clarendon, 1978), 1:108-214; 2:125-67; M. Black, *The Book of Enoch or I Enoch.* SVTP 7 (Leiden: Brill, 1985) 42-69, 181-252. See my review of Knibb's book in *JBL* 99 (1980) 631-36 (esp. for his questionable relating of the Ethiopic translation to the Aramaic texts). Both he and Black give abundant references to older publications of *1 Enoch* and to the varied Enochic literature.

6. About forty-seven Ethiopic MSS of *1 Enoch* are known, and the earliest come from

erably among scholars. For R. H. Charles, they come from the first half of the last century B.C. (105-64);[7] for M. Hengel, "between the Parthian invasion of 40 B.C.E. and the Jewish War of 66 C.E.";[8] for M. Black, "around the turn of the millennium, ca. first century B.C.E.-first century C.E.";[9] for M. A. Knibb, "the end of the first century AD";[10] for J. T. Milik, the end of the third century A.D. ("around the year A.D. 270 or shortly afterwards"),[11] which is certainly too late. In any case, the Similitudes belong to the period after the final redaction of the book of Daniel, and thus the items found in them continue to reveal the current messianic belief in Palestinian Judaism.

After an introductory chapter (§37), the second part of 1 Enoch has three parables: I: chs. 38–44; II: chs. 45–57; and III: chs. 58–69; and then two concluding chapters (§70-71).[12] Even though this second part of 1 Enoch is not extant in the Qumran fragments, it is the part of the book that has always been quoted in the interpretation of New Testament passages mentioning the titles predicated of Jesus, such as "Messiah," "Elect One," "Righteous One," and "Son of Man." Each of these titles is of distinct ori-

---

the 15th century, whereas the vast majority date from the 18th-19th century, and about a half-dozen were copied in the 20th century.

7. See *APOT*, 2:164.

8. "The Effective History of Isaiah 53 in the Pre-Christian Period," in *The Suffering Servant: Isaiah 53 in Jewish and Christian Sources*, ed. B. Janowski and P. Stuhlmacher (Grand Rapids: Wm. B. Eerdmans, 2004) 99.

9. M. Black, "The Messianism of the Parables of Enoch: Their Date and Contribution to Christological Origins," in J. H. Charlesworth et al., *The Messiah* (Minneapolis: Fortress, 1987) 162.

10. See *AOT*, 174. Also M. A. Knibb, "The Date of the Parables of Enoch: A Critical Review," *NTS* 25 (1978-79) 345-59, esp. 358.

11. J. T. Milik, *The Books of Enoch: Aramaic Fragments of Qumrân Cave 4* (Oxford: Clarendon, 1976) 96. Milik regards the Similitudes as a Christian Greek composition, which was substituted for the Book of Giants, a part of Enochic literature as found in Qumran Cave 4; see pp. 89-97 for his reasons. Cf. his earlier article, "Problèmes de la littérature hénochique à la lumière des fragments araméens de Qumrân," *HTR* 64 (1971) 333-78. But see J. C. Greenfield and M. E. Stone, "The Enochic Pentateuch and the Date of the Similitudes," *HTR* 70 (1977) 51-65; C. L. Mearns, "The Parables of Enoch — Origin and Date," *ExpTim* 89 (1977-78) 118-19; also J. A. Fitzmyer, "Implications of the New Enoch Literature from Qumran," *TS* 38 (1977) 332-45, esp. 340-41; and Knibb, *NTS* 25 (1978-79) 345-59.

12. The last chapters (§70-71) are sometimes thought not to have been originally part of the Similitudes, but J. C. VanderKam has argued convincingly that "there is every reason to believe that chs. 70-71, therefore, formed the original and organic conclusion to the Similitudes"; see the reasons in his article, "Righteous One, Messiah, Chosen One, and Son of Man in 1 Enoch 37–71," in Charlesworth, *The Messiah*, 169-91, esp. 177-85.

gin and discrete meaning in the Old Testament itself,[13] but in the Similitudes all four titles are predicated of one individual, whose origin is "hidden" and who is depicted as an eschatological judge who will appear along with God on his heavenly throne at the Final Assize.

The four titles are (a) "Righteous One" (Ethiopic *ṣādeq*): 1 En 38:2; 53:6. This title always appears along with one or another of the titles just mentioned.[14] The adjective *ṣādeq* also appears in 1 En 47:1, 4 in a collective sense, "the Righteous."

(b) "Messiah" (Ethiopic *mas/šiḥ*): 1 En 48:10 ("they denied the Lord of Spirits and His Messiah" [an echo of Ps 2:2], who is also called "Son of Man" [48:2] and regarded as preexistent [48:6]); 52:4 ("shall serve the dominion of His Messiah," who is also called "Elect One" in 52:6, 9).

(c) "Elect One" (Ethiopic *ḫ/ḥeruy*): 1 En 39:6; 40:5; 45:3 ("my Elect One shall sit on a throne of glory");[15] 45:4; 48:6 (used as an adjective to describe the Son of Man [48:2]); 49:2 ("the Elect One stands before the Lord of the Spirits"); 49:4; 51:3 (the Elect One "shall sit on his/my throne"); 51:5; 52:6 (mountains will melt like wax before the Elect One); 52:9 (Elect One appears before the Lord of the Spirits); 53:6 (Righteous One and Elect One); 55:4 (Elect One judging Azazel and his minions, who led Israel astray and away from the Torah); 61:5; 61:8; 61:10 (Elect One included in list of angels); 62:1 (acknowledgement of the Elect One, who is called Son of Man in 62:5, 7, 9, 14).

(d) "Son of Man," which is expressed in Ethiopic in three different ways:

(i) *walda sab'* (lit., "son of men," 4 times, only in Parable II): 46:2; 46:3; 46:4; 48:2; he is considered preexistent and called the "Elect One" in 48:6 (with an echo of Dan 7:13).

(ii) *walda be'si* (lit., "son of man," 4 times in Parable III and the conclud-

---

13. For "Messiah," see Dan 9:25-26; for "Elect One," see Ps 89:4(Eng. 3) (David); 106:23 (Moses); Isa 45:4 (Israel); for "Son of Man," see Ps 8:5(4) (Hebrew בן אדם); Dan 7:13 (Aramaic בר אנש); for "Righteous One," see Isa 53:11. All such titles in the Old Testament are distinct in meaning, with connotations different one from the other.

14. In this survey, I am heavily dependent on the analysis of VanderKam in his article, "Righteous One, Messiah," 170-76.

15. See J. C. Collins, *The Scepter and the Star*. ABRL (New York: Doubleday, 1996) 143 for the pertinence of such pre-Christian Jewish passages depicting the Elect One and the Son of Man (see below) seated on heavenly thrones.

ing chapter): 62:5 (pain shall take hold of people when they see the Son of Man sitting on his throne of glory, but there is a variant reading, "Son of Woman" [*walda be'sit*]); 69:29 (twice: the Son of Man has appeared and has sat on the throne of his glory; and word of the Son of Man shall go forth); 71:14 (the angel said to Enoch, "You are the Son of Man, who was born to righteousness" [an identification of Enoch himself as such]).

(iii) *walda 'eg"āla 'emma-ḥeyāw* (lit., "son of the offspring of the mother of the living," 8 times in Parable III and concluding chapters): 62:7 ("from the beginning the Son of Man was hidden" [= preexistent?]); 62:9 (people shall "set their hope on that Son of Man"); 62:14; 63:11; 69:26 (the name of the Son of Man revealed); 69:27 (judgment given over to the Son of Man); 70:1 (the presence of that Son of Man and of the Lord of Spirits); 71:17 (there shall be length of days with that Son of Man).[16]

What is noteworthy in these Similitudes is not only the predication of these four titles of one individual transcendent being, regarded as having a heavenly origin and destined to share in carrying out the eschatological judgment of humanity along with the Lord of Spirits, but the allusion in some of the passages also to the Danielic Son of Man and the Isaian Servant Songs, which they further interpret. The "Son of Man," which some claim stands for a collectivity in Daniel 7 (see vv. 18, 22), but is more likely an angelic figure, now becomes a heavenly individual who will judge humanity (*1 En* 69:27, 29; see the earlier passage in *1 Enoch* 14 for an apocalyptic description of the judgment scene).[17] Furthermore, the phrase "light of the nations" echoes the First Servant Song (Isa 42:6) and the Second Song (Isa 49:6). The "hidden" Son of Man (*1 En* 62:7) also alludes to the Second Song (Isa 49:2), and the title "Righteous One" echoes the Fourth Song (Isa 53:11).[18] The reaction of people when "they see the

16. R. H. Charles (*The Book of Enoch or 1 Enoch* . . . [Oxford: Clarendon, 1912] 86-87) has shown convincingly that the three Ethiopic expressions are minor literary variants of one underlying Greek term. See also M. Black, "Aramaic Barnāshā and the 'Son of Man,'" *ExpTim* 95 (1983-84) 200-6 (for a refutation of the idea that the "apocalyptic Son of Man" in the book of Enoch was a "myth," as B. Lindars has argued); cf. J. Coppens, *Le fils d'homme vétéro- et intertestamentaire*. BETL 61 (Louvain: Peeters, 1983) 128-34.

17. See P. Grelot, "Daniel vii, 9-10 et le livre d'Hénoch," *Sem* 28 (1978) 59-83.

18. For the debate, whether the "hidden" Son of Man means "preexistent" or "premundane," see Knibb, *DSD* 2 (1995) 171-72.

Son of Man sitting on the throne of his glory" (*1 En* 62:5) recalls the Fourth Song (Isa 52:14, 15).[19]

Nevertheless, there is no idea of a suffering Son of Man or a suffering Messiah in *1 Enoch*, as has been noted often by interpreters like E. Sjöberg, J. Theisohn, M. Black.[20] So VanderKam concludes his discussion of the titles:

> 1 Enoch 37-71 is perhaps the most ancient but hardly the only witness to the messianic interpretation of the servant. Moreover, the theme of a *suffering* servant in Isaiah does not form part of the writer's appropriation of motifs from his biblical source. In the Similitudes, the chosen one/son of man does not suffer. Rather, the focus there is upon his exaltation and his extraordinary status at the end of time.[21]

For the purpose of this discussion, two passages in the Similitudes of *1 Enoch* are all-important, because they use explicitly the Ethiopic title *masiḥ* in the narrow sense:

> There shall be no one to take them by the hand and raise them up, for they have denied the Lord of Spirits and His Messiah. Blest be the name of the Lord of Spirits! (48:10)
>
> All these things that you have seen shall serve the dominion of His Messiah, that he may be mighty and powerful on the earth. (52:4)

In these instances the Anointed One is an awaited agent of God for the deliverance of His people at the time of judgment, as the other three titles that are given him make clear. In 48:10 the title recalls the use of מְשִׁיחוֹ in Ps 2:2, "conspire together against the LORD and His Anointed One," but it is now employed in a clearly future context, which was lacking in the psalm itself. In 52:4, "all these things" refers to world-empires that will become subservient to the coming Messiah. There may be an echo of the "kingdom" that the holy ones are to possess in Dan 7:18,[22] but the connotation is

---

19. So Hengel, "The Effective History of Isaiah 53," 100.

20. See E. Sjöberg, *Der Menschensohn im äthiopischen Henochbuch* (Lund: Gleerup, 1946) 128-32; J. Theisohn, *Der auserwählte Richter: Untersuchungen zum traditionsgeschichtlichen Ort der Menschensohngestalt der Bilderreden des äthiopischen Henoch*. SUNT 12 (Göttingen: Vandenhoeck & Ruprecht, 1975) 114-24; M. Black, "The Messianism of the Parables of Enoch," 157-61.

21. "Righteous One, Messiah," 190.

22. As Black sees it (*Book of Enoch*, 215); cf. Klausner, *The Messianic Idea in Israel*, 277-301.

no longer collective; it is rather individual, as the nearby title, "Elect One" (52:6), makes clear. The sense of "Messiah" now is almost certainly kingly or royal, but nothing rules out the possibility of understanding it as a priestly anointed figure.

(2) Various Qumran texts reveal the developing Jewish messianism of the pre-Christian centuries, and first of all those that use the term משיח.[23] It is, however, not easy to date these texts, even if approximate datings can be assigned to some of the copies, because the date of the copy may not say much about the date of the composition of the text. Years ago J. Starcky sought to distinguish four stages in the development of Qumran messianism,[24] but R. E. Brown eventually exposed the weakness of that attempt,[25] and it has not been followed.

I have already treated many of the pertinent Qumran texts in my article "Qumran Messianism,"[26] which I shall not repeat here. I am concentrating rather on the aspects of those texts that are important for this study. Many studies have been devoted to Qumran messianism.[27] So I

23. See M. G. Abegg, Jr. et al., eds., *The Dead Sea Scrolls Concordance*, 1: *The Non-Biblical Texts from Qumran* (Leiden: Brill, 2003), 1:490 (29 instances). Cf. L. T. Stuckenbruck, "'Messias' Texte in den Schriften von Qumran," *Mogilany 1993: Papers on the Dead Sea Scrolls Offered in Memory of Hans Burgmann*, ed. Z. J. Kapera. Qumranica mogilanensia 13 (Kraków: Enigma, 1996) 129-39; M. G. Abegg and C. A. Evans, "Messianic Passages in the Dead Sea Scrolls," in Charlesworth, Lichtenberger, and Oegema, *Qumran-Messianism*, 191-203.

24. J. Starcky, "Les quatres étapes du messianisme à Qumrân," *RB* 70 (1963) 481-505.

25. R. E. Brown, "J. Starcky's Theory of Qumran Messianic Development," *CBQ* 28 (1966) 51-57. See also F. M. Cross, "Some Notes on a Generation of Qumran Studies," in *The Madrid Qumran Congress: Proceedings of the International Congress on the Dead Sea Scrolls, Madrid, 18-21 March, 1991*, ed. J. Trebolle Barrera and L. Vegas Montaner. STDJ 11/1 (Leiden: Brill, 1992) 1-14, esp. 14 n. 34.

26. See J. A. Fitzmyer, *The Dead Sea Scrolls and Christian Origins*. SDSSRL (Grand Rapids: Wm. B. Eerdmans, 2000) 73-110.

27. See M. G. Abegg, C. A. Evans, and G. S. Oegema, "Bibliography of Messianism and the Dead Sea Scrolls," in Charlesworth, Lichtenberger, and Oegema, *Qumran-Messianism*, 204-14.

See R. E. Brown, "The Messianism of Qumran," *CBQ* 19 (1957) 53-82; C. A. Evans, "Messiahs," *EDSS*, 1:537-42; "The Messiah in the Dead Sea Scrolls," in *Israel's Messiah in the Bible and in the Dead Sea Scrolls*, ed. R. S. Hess and M. D. Carroll R. (Grand Rapids: Baker, 2003), 85-101; H. Lichtenberger, "Qumran-Messianism," in *Emanuel: Studies in Hebrew Bible, Septuagint, and Dead Sea Scrolls in Honor of Emanuel Tov*, ed. S. M. Paul et al. VTSup 94/1-2 (Leiden: Brill, 2003) 323-33; W. Loader, "The New Dead Sea Scrolls: New Light on Messianism and the History of the Community," *Colloquium* 25 (1993) 67-85; A. S. Van der Woude, *Die messianischen Vorstellungen der Gemeinde von Qumrân*. SSN 3 (Assen: Van Gorcum, 1957) 75-89.

want to cull from them details that help in the understanding of the messianic expectations among the Jews who composed these writings, or at least made use of them in their thinking and theological conceptions. I consider the sectarian texts among the Qumran writings to have been composed by the Jews that Josephus and Philo called the "Essenes," and regard them as reflecting Palestinian Jewish thinking from the mid-second century B.C. on.

Among these sectarian writings, one finds mainly three kinds of texts that use the word משיח :

(a) *Qumran Texts that Speak of Two Messiahs.* (i) The most important of these texts is 1QS 9:10-11, which runs: ונשפטו במשפטים הרשונים אשר החלו אנשי היחד ל‹ה›תיסר בם עד בוא נביא ומשיחי אהרון וישראל, ". . . but they will be governed by the first regulations, by which the men of the community began to be instructed, until the coming of a prophet and the Messiahs of Aaron and Israel."[28] Here one finds an affirmation of the community's expectation of three coming figures: a *prophet* (undoubtedly a prophet like Moses, an allusion to Deut 18:15, 18),[29] a (priestly) *Messiah of Aaron,* and a (kingly) *Messiah of Israel,* who are all to be God's agents for the deliverance of His people. Such an affirmation has to be seen as a development beyond that of Dan 9:25, where the coming Anointed One was expressed as עד משיח נגיד, "up until an Anointed One, a prince." Not only is the title introduced now by the same preposition (עד) with a future connotation, but its plural object and its collocation with "a prophet" reveal that one must translate משיח no longer as "Anointed One," but as "Messiah" (with a capital M), because the term is now being used in its technical, narrow sense and denoting a role distinct from that of the awaited prophet.[30] As was noted earlier, נגיד, "prince," oc-

28. See M. Burrows, *The Dead Sea Scrolls of St. Mark's Monastery,* 2/2: *Plates and Transcription of the Manual of Discipline* (New Haven: American Schools of Oriental Research, 1951) pl. 9; J. H. Charlesworth et al., eds., *The Dead Sea Scrolls: Hebrew, Aramaic, and Greek Texts with English Translations,* 1: *Rule of the Community and Related Documents.* PTSDSSP 1 (Louisville: Westminster John Knox, 1994) 40.

29. Cf. 4QTestim (4Q175) 1–8, which alludes to Deut 18:18-19, preceded by Deut 5:28-29, a combination already found in the Samaritan Pentateuch of Exod 20:21; cf. 1 Macc 14:41. See further Fitzmyer, "Qumran Messianism," 98; Collins, *The Scepter and the Star,* 116-22.

30. This is said to acknowledge that משיח in such a text has a "narrow" sense, indeed, but to admit that does not deny that the Essenes awaited "other eschatological redeemers," *pace* J. C. Poirier ("The Endtime Return of Elijah and Moses at Qumran," *DSD* 10 [2003] 221-42, esp. 222-23). As the rest of the presentation in this chapter will show, the Essene commu-

curs in the Old Testament meaning both a kingly and a priestly figure.[31] So it is not surprising that one finds in this Palestinian Jewish sectarian text the expectation of both a priestly and a kingly Messiah.[32]

The last clause of 1QS 9:11, however, is completely missing in 4QS[e] (4Q259) 1 iii 6, another copy of the *Rule of the Community*, which has the words of 1QS 9:12 following directly on those of 1QS 8:15, ‏אש[ר צוה‏ ‏ביד משה‏, "which He has ordered through Moses."[33] Such a copy of the *Rule of the Community* may attest to a messianic development at different stages of the community's existence, or else 4QS[e] may be only a defective copy.[34]

(ii) If there be any hesitation about the meaning of 1QS 9:11 because of 4Q259, another text clarifies the expectation of two Messiahs, CD 19:35–

---

nity had varied and wide expectations, even if the figures so awaited do not all fit into what Poirier calls "the messianic scheme."

31. See p. 63 above.

32. Recall also "the anointed priest" of Lev 4:3, 5, 16: 6:15(Eng. 22); the "priest" who accompanies the "scion/branch" in Zech 6:13b; and the "two sons of oil" in Zech 4:14; also pp. 18, 52, above.

See further M. Burrows, "The Messiahs of Aaron and Israel," *ATR* 34 (1952) 202-6; C. T. Fritsch, "The So-called 'Priestly Messiah' of the Essenes," *Jaarbericht ex Oriente Lux* 6 (1959-66) 242-48; F. García Martínez, "Two Messianic Figures in the Qumran Texts," in *Current Research and Technological Developments on the Dead Sea Scrolls: Conference on the Texts from the Judean Desert, Jerusalem, 30 April 1995*, ed. D. W. Parry and S. D. Ricks. STDJ 20 (Leiden: Brill, 1996) 14-40; A. J. B. Higgins, "Priest and Messiah," *VT* 3 (1953) 321-36; "The Priestly Messiah," *NTS* 13 (1966-67) 211-39; K. G. Kuhn, "The Two Messiahs of Aaron and Israel," in *The Scrolls and the New Testament*, ed. K. Stendahl (New York: Harper, 1957; repr. New York: Crossroad, 1992) 54-64; W. S. LaSor, "'The Messiahs of Aaron and Israel,'" *VT* 6 (1956) 425-29; R. B. Laurin, "The Problem of Two Messiahs in the Qumran Scrolls," *RevQ* 4 (1963-64) 39-52; S. Sabugal, "1 Q Regla de la Comunidad ix, 11: Dos ungidos, un mesías," *RevQ* 8 (1972-75) 417-23; M. Smith, "What Is Implied by the Variety of Messianic Figures?" *JBL* 78 (1959) 66-72; J. R. Villalón, "Sources vétéro-testamentaires de la doctrine qumranienne des deux Messies," *RevQ* 8 (1972-75) 53-63; Cross, "Some Notes on a Generation of Qumran Studies," 13-14; "Notes on the Doctrine of the Two Messiahs at Qumran and the Extracanonical *Daniel Apocalypse (4Q246)*," in Parry and Ricks, *Current Research and Technological Developments*, 1-13.

33. See P. S. Alexander and G. Vermes, *Qumran Cave 4: XIX, Serekh ha-yaḥad and Two Related Texts*. DJD 26 (Oxford: Clarendon, 1998) 144 and pl. XV (frg. 3a); Charlesworth et al., *The Dead Sea Scrolls*, 1:86.

34. This has been suggested by J. C. VanderKam, "Messianism in the Scrolls," in *The Community of the Renewed Covenant: The Notre Dame Symposium on the Dead Sea Scrolls*, ed. E. C. Ulrich and VanderKam. Christianity and Judaism in Antiquity 10 (Notre Dame: University of Notre Dame Press, 1994) 211-34, esp. 213.

20:1, which reads: מיום האסף }יור מורה{ }מיום{ מורה היחיד עד עמוד . . .
משיח מאהרן ומישראל, ". . . from the day of the gathering in {erasures} of
the Teacher of the Community until the rising of a Messiah from Aaron
and from Israel."[35] Now משיח is singular, but it refers to a Messiah who is
to come both from Aaron and from Israel, hence one priestly Messiah and
one kingly Messiah.[36]

(iii) A puzzling passage is found in 4QD^e (4Q270) 2 ii 13-15, which
has no counterpart in the medieval copy of CD: או] אשר יגלה את רז
עמו לגואים או יקלל א]ת עמו או ידבר[/ סרה על משיחי רוח הקדש
ותועה ב]חוזי אמתו בהמרותו[/ את פי אל . . . , "[or anyone] who will dis-
close a secret of his people to the Gentiles or will curse [his people or
preach] rebellion against those anointed by the holy Spirit or leads astray
[the seers of His truth in rebelling against] God's word . . . ."[37] The plural
expression משיחי רוח הקדש, "those anointed by the holy Spirit," is different, and it will appear again below. Here it is employed with verbs that express the future. Because of the mention of "the holy Spirit," it is difficult
to translate משיחי as "Messiahs," even though the text must refer to them;
they are mentioned in the plural and seem to denote the Messiahs of
Aaron and Israel. Note too the political connotation of the term that
emerges here and in the next occurrence.

(iv) 4QBer^b (4Q287) 10:13: Only a part of a line remains: ה עׁל[
משיחי רוח קוד]שׁו, "against those anointed by [His] ho[ly] Spirit," where
the final *he* before the preposition may be the end of the word סרה, "rebellion," as in 4QD^e 2 ii 14 (above).[38] Cf. CD 6:1 and 4QD^b (4Q267) 2:6 below.

35. See M. Broshi, *The Damascus Document Reconsidered* (Jerusalem: Israel Exploration Society, 1992) 44-47. The medieval scribe, not understanding the meaning of יחד, "community," changed its spelling to a more common word, יחיד, "only one." Cf. J. H.
Charlesworth et al., *The Dead Sea Scrolls*, 2:32-34.

36. See further G. J. Brooke, "The Messiah of Aaron in the *Damascus Document*,"
RevQ 15 (1991-92) 215-30; C. Hempel, *The Damascus Texts*. Companion to the Qumran
Scrolls 1 (Sheffield: Sheffield Academic, 2000) 75-79. But compare S. Mowinckel, *He That
Cometh*, 289, who regards the interpretation of this text as speaking of two Messiahs to be
"incorrect." That judgment was made, however, before the discovery of the Qumran Scrolls,
which now show that it is not incorrect.

37. See J. M. Baumgarten, *Qumran Cave 4.XIII: The Damascus Document (4Q266-
273)*. DJD 18 (Oxford: Clarendon, 1996) 144 and pl. XXVII.

38. The restoration of it as חה[נ, "The Holy Spirit [sett]led upon His Messiah,"
though possible, is highly unlikely (see R. H. Eisenman and M. Wise, *The Dead Sea Scrolls
Uncovered* [Rockport: Element, 1992] 228, 230).

(v) Perhaps 4Q521 8:9 should be mentioned here, which reads ה[ ] ה וכל משיחיה, "and all its (fem.) Messiahs (*or* Anointed Ones)," in a badly preserved fragment that seems to deal with the Temple.[39] It is impossible to tell in this case whether the Anointed Ones are awaited or not.

(b) *Qumran Texts That Speak of One Messiah.* These are actually more numerous, but it is not easy to explain the relation of them to the texts that mention two Messiahs. In fact, the first three deal with only one of the two Messiahs mentioned in 1QS 9:11, and the second three, though using משיח אהרון וישראל may be trying to say the same thing as CD 19:35–20:1.[40]

(i) 1QSa (1Q28a) 2:11-13: ה[וא [זה מו[שב אנשי השם]קריא[י] מועד[לעצת היחד אם יוליד /]אל[א[ת] המשיח אתם יבוא]הכוהן[רואש כול עדת ישראל וכול / א[חיו בני] אהרון הכוהנים, "[This is the as]sembly of the men of renown [summoned] to a feast for the council of the community, when [God] will beget the Messiah among them. [The priest] will enter [as] the head of all the congregation of Israel, and (then) all [his] bro[thers, the sons of] Aaron, the priests."[41] This passage describes a meal of the community to be eaten when the Messiah appears (2:11-12). Its reading is controverted, because some scholars read יוליך, "will lead," and claim that יוליד is not correct; but it is practically certain.[42] In any case, "the Messiah" is considered to be present "with them," and in the next pas-

39. See E. Puech, *Qumran Cave 4.XVIII: Textes hébreux (4Q521-4Q528, 4Q576-4Q579).* DJD 25 (Oxford: Clarendon, 1998) 28.

40. See Cross, "Some Notes on a Generation of Qumran Studies," 14. Cf. M. G. Abegg, Jr., "The Messiah at Qumran: Are We Still Seeing Double?" *DSD* 2 (1995) 125-44. Abegg thinks that "the dual messiah that we have come to accept as dogma in discussions of the DSS must be tempered" (143). See L. D. Hurst, "Did Qumran Expect Two Messiahs?," *BBR* 9 (1999) 157-80.

41. See J. T. Milik, "28a. Règle de la Congrégation (1QSa)," in *Qumran Cave I,* ed. D. Barthélemy and Milik. DJD 1 (Oxford: Clarendon, 1955) 108-18; J. H. Charlesworth et al., *The Dead Sea Scrolls,* 1:116.

42. See Barthélemy and Milik, *Qumran Cave I,* 110 and pl. XXIV. Cf. J. A. Fitzmyer, *The Dead Sea Scrolls and Christian Origins,* 84 n. 31 (on the reading); also R. Gordis, "The 'Begotten' Messiah in the Qumran Scrolls," *VT* 7 (1957) 191-94.

Cf. M. Smith, "'God's Begetting the Messiah' in 1QSa," *NTS* 5 (1958-59) 218-24; P. Sigal, "Further Reflections on the 'Begotten' Messiah," *HAR* 7 (1983) 221-33. See also 4Q249[f] 1-3:1-2, where a few letters are preserved on fragments of a Cryptic Text, 4Qpap cryptA 4QSerekh ha-ʿEdah[f] published by S. J. Pfann, *Qumran Cave 4.XXVI: Cryptic Texts.* DJD 36 (Oxford: Clarendon, 2000) 562, which may be related to 1QSa 2:11-13.

sage he is identified as the "Messiah of Israel."[43] Even though this passage uses the singular המשיח, it is a reference to one of the two Messiahs mentioned in 1QS 9:11.

(ii) 1QSa 2:14-15: ואחר י]שב מש[יח ישראל וישבו לפניו ראשי א]לפי ישראל אי[ש לפי כבודו, "And afterwards the [Mes]siah of Israel shall ta[ke his seat]. Then there will sit before him the heads of the thou[sands of Israel, ea]ch according to his dignity."[44] The title is partly restored, but with certainty. The first word ואחר, "and afterwards," comes after the mention of [הכוהן], "the priest," restored with certainty, to whom the Messiah of Israel is subordinated. This is a noteworthy development because the text thus gives priority to the priestly Messiah over the kingly Messiah.

(iii) 1QSa 2:20-21: ואח]ר יש[לח משיח ישראל ידיו בלחם, "And afterwards the Messiah of Israel [will p]ut forth his hands to the food."[45] In this instance, the Messiah of Israel is again subordinated to הכוהן, "the priest," who first blesses the bread and the new wine. These three texts come from the Appendix of the *Rule of the Community* (1QSa). The "priest" is considered by many interpreters to be "the Messiah of Aaron," even though he is not so named, and some think that there is an allusion to Zech 4:14, "the two sons of oil."[46] So the three instances of singular משיח may not be different from the dual Messiahs of 1QS 9:11.

(iv) CD 12:23–13:1: המתהלכים באלה בקץ הרשעה עד עמוד משוח

43. See E. Puech, "Préséance sacerdotale et Messie-Roi dans la Règle de la Congrégation (*1QSa* ii 11-22)," *RevQ* 16 (1993-95) 351-65.

44. See Barthélemy and Milik, *Qumran Cave I*, 110, 117-18; J. H. Charlesworth et al., *The Dead Sea Scrolls*, 1:116.

45. See Barthélemy and Milik, *Qumran Cave I*, 111, 117-18; J. H. Charlesworth et al., *The Dead Sea Scrolls*, 1:116.

46. This phrase from Zech 4:14 is quoted in a poorly preserved text, 4QCommGen^c (4Q254) 4:2, [ ]שני בני יצהר אשר[ ], "two sons of oil, which [ ]," but it is impossible to give it any messianic meaning, as the editor, G. J. Brooke, has recognized: "The phrase does not necessarily refer explicitly to messiahs, since שמן rather than יצהר is always used in scriptural designations of anointing"; "254. 4QCommentary on Genesis C," *Qumran Cave 4.XVII: Parabiblical Texts, Part 3*. DJD 22 (Oxford: Clarendon, 1996) 217-32, esp. 224. For an interpretation of the words, based on much later traditions read anachronistically into this text, see C. A. Evans, "'The Two Sons of Oil': Early Evidence of Messianic Interpretation of Zechariah 4:14 in 4Q254 4 2," *The Provo International Conference on the Dead Sea Scrolls: Technological Innovations, New Texts, and Reformulated Issues*, ed. D. W. Parry and E. Ulrich. STDJ 30 (Leiden: Brill, 1999) 566-75. Cf. J. F. Priest, "The Messiah and the Meal in 1QSa," *JBL* 82 (1963) 95-100.

... אנשים עשרה עד וישראל אהרן, "Those who walk according to these (statutes) in the wicked end time until the rising of the Messiah of Aaron and Israel; and (they shall form groups of) up to ten men . . . ."[47] For the medieval scribe's משוח, one should read משיח, even though one might be tempted to read <י>משיח, as in 1QS 9:11. Perhaps the scribe used a singular form to make the text conform to a medieval expectation of a single Messiah. Because, however, וישראל אהרון משיח is a construct chain with a singular *nomen regens* and two *nomina recta*, it is like ועמרה מלך־סדם, "King of Sodom and Gomorrah" (Gen 14:10), which is the subject of plural verbs, "they fled . . . they fell."[48] Hence the construct chain can be read as meaning two Messiahs.

(v) CD 14:18-19: בקץ בהם ישפטו] אשר המשפטים פרוש וזה עונם ויכפר וישראל אהרן[ח משי עמוד עד הרשעה, "This is the exact interpretation of the regulations [by] which [they will be judged in the wicked end time, until the rising of the Mess]iah of Aaron and Israel, and their iniquity will be expiated."[49] Here the singular משיח appears (partly restored, but with certainty), and with a singular verb in the following clause.[50] The same sentence is found in 4QD[a] (4Q266) 10 i 11-13[51] and badly preserved in 4QD[d] (4Q269) 11 i 1-2.[52] In this text, "Messiah of Aaron and Israel" might seem to be a single Messiah, but F. M. Cross translates it "the messiah of Aaron and the one of Israel."[53] Whether the Messiah is said to perform a notably priestly function (of expiation) depends on how the verb is translated.[54]

47. Broshi, *The Damascus Document Reconsidered*, 32-35; J. H. Charlesworth et al., *The Dead Sea Scrolls*, 2:52.

48. Compare 1 Chr 18:10 with 2 Sam 8:10.

49. Broshi, *The Damascus Document Reconsidered*, 36-37; J. H. Charlesworth et al., *The Dead Sea Scrolls*, 2:56.

50. Many scholars have translated the singular verb יכפר as qal imperfect active, "he will expiate," but Cross maintains that it should be "passive, *yĕkuppar*," i.e., pual, as in Isa 22:14 ("Some Notes on a Generation of Qumran Studies," 14), which I have adopted.

51. But it reads ממוד instead of עמוד!

52. See Baumgarten, *Qumran Cave 4.XIII*, 72, 134.

53. "Some Notes on a Generation of Qumran Studies," 14. Cross finds the doctrine of the two Messiahs in CD, 1QS, 1QM, 4Q174, and 4Q175, "with the Balaam Oracle concerning the Star and the Scepter a favorite proof text. . . . The putative single messiah is a phantom of bad philology." Cf. R. Deichgräber, "Zur Messiaserwartung der Damaskusschrift," *ZAW* 78 (1966) 333-43.

54. For discussion of "expiation" carried out by a messianic figure, see J. M. Baum-

(vi) CD 19:10-11: After quoting Zech 13:7 and interpreting its "little ones" as "the poor of the flock" (Zech 11:9), who will escape, the text continues: והנשארים ימסרו לחרב בבוא משיח אהרן וישראל, "And those who are left will be given over to the sword at the coming of the Messiah of Aaron and Israel."[55] In this case, the Messiah is related to a time of eschatological visitation, when wrongdoers will be punished.

(vii) An important instance of a text that mentions one Messiah is found in 4QpGenᵃ (4Q252) 6 (col. 5):3-4 (*olim* 4QPBless): אל[פי ישראל] / המה הדגלים (*vacat*) עד בוא משיח הצדק צמח דויד כי לו ולזרעו נתנה ברית מלכות עמו עד דורות עולם, "[. . . and the thou]sands of Israel are 'the standards,' until the coming of the righteous Messiah, the Scion of David. For to him and to his offspring has been given the covenant of kingship over His people for everlasting generations."[56] Here the biblical term צמח, "branch, scion," is now joined explicitly with "David" and related to a coming Messiah, to whom is attributed the quality of "righteousness," as it was given to the scion in Jer 23:5, והקמתי לדוד צמח צדיק, "I will raise up for David a righteous scion."

Moreover, this instance of משיח occurs in a comment on Gen 49:10, לא יסור שבט מיהודה, "a scepter shall not depart from Judah." This assertion now becomes לו[א] יסור שליט משבט יהודה, "A ruler shall not turn aside from the tribe of Judah," and he has already been said to be, יושב כסא לדויד, "one sitting on the throne of David" (line 2). Whereas the impersonal scepter and mace of Genesis 49 itself became personal in the LXX,[57] the "scepter" now becomes at first a vague "ruler" who "sits on the throne of David," but who is finally named "the righteous Messiah, the scion of David."[58] This text interprets Gen 49:10 to show that Judah will play a kingly and military role in Israel until the Messiah, David's heir,

---

garten, "Messianic Forgiveness of Sin in CD 14:19 (4Q266 10 i 12-13)," in Parry and Ulrich, *The Provo International Conference*, 537-44.

55. Broshi, *The Damascus Document Reconsidered*, 42-43; J. H. Charlesworth et al., *The Dead Sea Scrolls*, 2:30.

56. G. J. Brooke, "252. 4QCommentary on Genesis A," in *Qumran Cave 4.XVII*, 185-207, esp. 205-6. Brooke insists on the correctness of the reading הדגלים, "the standards," and not הרגלים, which might make one think of Gen 49:10b. Cf. Charlesworth et al., *The Dead Sea Scrolls*, 6B:216.

57. See pp. 70-71 above.

58. Cf. the further mention of "the scion of David" in 4QFlor (4Q174) 1-2 i 11; and the restoration in 4QIsaᵃ (4Q161) 8-10:17 [*sic*, read 18], cited below.

comes to take over. It also gives a good example of how titles, which in the Old Testament itself were discrete and nonmessianic, have eventually become messianic in the postbiblical Jewish tradition, precisely by being predicated of a Messiah.[59] This Qumran text joins, then, the evidence from 1 *Enoch* in predicating multiple titles of one individual, again of an awaited anointed agent of God.

(viii) 4Q521 2 ii + 4:1-14: This text, also called 4QMessianic Apocalypse, is important for what it presents as the role of the coming Messiah:

"1 [for the hea]vens and the earth will listen to His Messiah (ישמעו למשיחו), 2 [and all th]at is in them will not swerve from the commandments of the holy ones. 3 Be strengthened in His service, all you who seek the Lord (אדני)! *(vacat)* 4 Shall you not find the Lord (אדני) in this, all those (= you) who hope in their hearts? 5 For the Lord (אדני) shall seek out pious ones, and righteous ones He shall call by name. 6 Over afflicted ones shall His Spirit hover, and faithful ones He shall renew with His power. 7 He shall honor (the) pious on a throne of eternal kingship, 8 freeing prisoners, giving sight to the blind, straightening up those be[nt over]. 9 For[ev]er will I cling [to tho]se who hope, and with His steadfast love He shall [recompense]; 10 the frui[t of a] good [dee]d shall be delayed for no one. 11 Wond<r>ous things, such as have never been (before), will the Lord (אדני) do, just as He s[aid]. 12 For He shall heal (the) wounded, revive the dead, (and) proclaim good news to the afflicted; 13 (the) [po]or He shall satiate, (the) uprooted He shall guide, and on (the) hungry He shall bestow riches; 14 and (the) intel[ligent], and all of them (shall be) like hol[y ones].[60]

---

59. See further G. S. Oegema, "Tradition-Historical Studies on 4Q252," in Charlesworth, Lichtenberger, and Oegema, *Qumran-Messianism,* 154-74 (with good bibliog. on the text).

60. See E. Puech, "521. 4QApocalypse messianique *(4Q521),*" *Qumran Cave 4.XVIII,* 1-38 and pl. I-III, esp. 10-18 and pl. II; also his preliminary publication in "Une apocalypse messianique," *RevQ* 15 (1991-92) 475-522. Cf. his article, "Messianic Apocalypse," *EDSS,* 1:543-44. The title that Puech has given to it, "a messianic apocalypse," is unfortunate, because the text has "none of the formal marks of apocalyptic revelation," as J. J. Collins has rightly noted ("The Works of the Messiah," *DSD* 1 [1994] 98-112, esp. 98). See further Puech, "Some Remarks on 4Q246 and 4Q521 and Qumran Messianism," in Parry and Ulrich, *The Provo International Conference,* 545-65.

The wording of this text is heavily dependent on Psalm 146, one of those in the Psalter that begin with הללו־יה (*hallĕlû-Yāh*, "Praise the LORD"), and it lauds the Lord for the help supplied to the downtrodden in view of their eschatological salvation. But the phrases are considerably modified by the introduction of "His Messiah" (משיחו), a term not found in the psalm itself. There are echoes also of phrases in Isa 34:1; 35:5; and 61:1.

As this passage is interpreted sometimes, the wondrous deeds of freeing prisoners, giving sight to the blind, reviving the dead, and so forth have been ascribed to the Messiah, "as God's agent" or as "an eschatological prophet."[61] That, however, is far from clear, because line 3 ends with *vacat*, and the subject of lines 4-14 is rather "the Lord" (אדני). Hence they are deeds that the Lord will accomplish in the time of His Messiah. Moreover, the words מתים יחיה, "He will revive the dead," has caused some interpreters to speak of "resurrection,"[62] when they should be saying "resuscitation" or "reanimation," which is something quite different from the "resurrection" of Jesus Christ, or even the resurrection of the dead mentioned in Dan 12:2.[63]

(ix) 4Q521 9:3: This is another passage in the same text, but it is poorly preserved and, though it mentions what seems to be a Messiah, there is no way of being sure of its sense: בה תעזוב ב]י[ד משיח] [ ], "[ ]*bh* [ ]you/she shall abandon into the [ha]nd of (your? its?) Messiah."[64]

(x) pap4QparaKings (4Q382) 16:2: Again the context is lost: [משיח [מ ישר[א]ל, "[M]essiah of Isr[a]el."[65]

(xi) Perhaps one should join to the foregoing texts 11QMelch (11Q13) 2:18, which reads: והמבשר הו[אה]משיח הרו[ח] כאשר אמר דנ]יאל עליו עד משיח נגיד שבועים שבעה], ". . . the herald i[s] the Anointed of

---

61. See Collins, *DSD* 1 [1994] 98-99.

62. So the original editor, Puech (*RevQ* 15 [1991-92] 475); Collins (*DSD* 1 [1994] 98); G. Vermes ("Qumran Forum Miscellanea I," *JJS* 43 [1992] 299-305, esp. 303-4); Eisenman and Wise, *The Dead Sea Scrolls Uncovered*, 21.

63. The same has to be said about 4Q521 7+5 ii 6, which reads יקי[ם המחיה את מתי עמו, "(when) the vivifier [sha]ll raise up the dead of His people." In this instance there is no mention of a Messiah.

64. See Puech, "521. 4QApocalypse messianique," 30; M. Becker, "4Q521 und die Gesalbten," *RevQ* 18 (1997-98) 73-96.

65. See S. Olyan, "4QpapparaKings et al.," in *Qumran Cave 4.VIII: Parabiblical Texts, Part 1*, ed. H. Attridge et al. DJD 13 (Oxford: Clarendon, 1994) 363-416, esp. 372.

the Spir[it], [about] whom Dan[iel] said, ['Up until an Anointed One, a prince, seven weeks]."[66] The reading משיח is not certain; Y. Yadin read it as משוח, the passive participle of משח, but the translation would be the same.[67] In any case, the title, derived from Dan 9:25, is being extended to someone called מבשר, "messenger, herald," of good news, which is an echo of Isa 52:7 that is quoted in the foregoing lines 15-16 of this text. It is debated whether המבשר is applied to Melchizedek himself in the text, which has a definite eschatological thrust and in which Melchizedek is conceived of as a heavenly being, an agent of expiation on the Day of Atonement at the end of the tenth jubilee.[68] Still more important is the way this text cites a verse of Daniel, most likely 9:25 (so restored in the official edition of DJD), and makes of it a clear "messianic" usage in the technical sense.

(xii) Another text is 4QFlor (4Q174) 1-2 i 11, which speaks of God establishing forever the throne of a king to whom He will be father and whom He will regard as His son: "He is the scion of David who is to arise with the Interpreter of the Law, who [. . .] in Zion in the last days."[69] The word משיחו is restored (line 18), in the missing end of a quotation of Ps 2:2: ית[יצבו]מלכי ארץ ור[וזנים נוסדו יחד על יהוה ועל/]משיחו פ[שר [ ]הדבר, "['Earthly kings take their stand, and r]ulers take counsel together against the LORD and against [His Anointed One.' The in]terpretation of the passage [is . . .]." Unfortunately, the beginning of the *pesher* is

66. See F. García Martínez et al., eds., *Qumran Cave 11.II: 11Q2-18, 11Q20-31*. DJD 23 (Oxford: Clarendon, 1998) 221-41, esp. 225, 232, and pl. XXVII; Charlesworth et al., *The Dead Sea Scrolls*, 6B:268. Cf. A. S. Van der Woude, "Melchisedek als himmlische Erlösergestalt in den neugefundenen eschatologischen Midraschim aus Qumran Höhle XI," *OtSt* 14 (1965) 354-73; J. A. Fitzmyer, "Further Light on Melchizedek from Qumran Cave 11," *JBL* 86 (1967) 25-41; repr. *ESBNT*, 245-67; *SBNT*, 245-67, App. p. 293. There I first suggested the reading דנ]יאל in line 18.

67. See Y. Yadin, "A Note on Melchizedek and Qumran," *IEJ* 15 (1965) 152-54.

68. See P. Rainbow, "Melchizedek as a Messiah at Qumran," *BBR* 7 (1997) 179-94. He rightly objects to Melchizedek in this text being called an angel, and even the angel Michael, as did van der Woude and others who followed him. In Qumran literature, Melchizedek is known otherwise as a priest-king (1QapGen 22:14-15); here he becomes a heavenly figure, and probably a messianic figure such as Dan 9:25 envisaged, but not necessarily "the Davidic Messiah"!

69. See J. M. Allegro, *Qumran Cave 4.I (4Q158-4Q186)*. DJD 5 (Oxford: Clarendon, 1968) 53-57, esp. 53-55 and pls. XIX-XX; Charlesworth et al., *The Dead Sea Scrolls*, 6B:252. Cf. S. Schreiber, "König JHWH und königlicher Gesalbter: Das Repräsentanzverhältnis in 4Q174," *SNTSU* 26 (2001) 205-19.

lost, and it continues only with "the elect ones of Israel at the end of days." So one will never learn how Psalm 2 was interpreted eschatologically. The "Interpreter of the Law" (דורש התורה) is also said to come in CD 7:18-21, a passage in which Amos 5:26-27 (about the raising up of the fallen booth of David) and then Num 24:17 are quoted. The latter is then interpreted: והכוכב הוא דורש התורה/הבא דמשק כאשר כתוב דרך כוכב מיעקב וקם שבט/מישראל השבט הוא נשיא כל העדה ובעמדו וקרקר/את כל בני שת, "The star is the Interpreter of the Law, who is coming (to) Damascus, as it is written, 'A star shall stride forth from Jacob, and a scepter shall arise from Israel.' The scepter is the Prince of the whole congregation, and at his rising he shall destroy all the sons of Sheth."[70]

Noteworthy is the interpretation of Num 24:17 as two persons, the "star" as the Interpreter of the Law and the "scepter" as the Prince of the whole congregation. The "Interpreter of the Law" is probably another name for the "Messiah of Aaron."[71] The mention of "the scion of David" is similar to 4QIsa[a] (4Q161) 8-10:17 [sic, read 18], which after quoting Isa 10:34 and commenting on various phrases of it, continues: [פשרו על צמח דויד העומד באח]רית הימים, "[The interpretation of it is about the scion of] David, who is to arise at the e[nd of days]."[72] The data of these texts referring to the "the scion of David" in the "last days" support the text of §2 (vii) cited above (4QpGen A [4Q252]), even if they no longer contain the word משיח.

(c) *Qumran Texts That Speak of Prophets as Anointed Ones.* As we have already seen, there are only two passages in the Old Testament where משיח is possibly used of prophets, 1 Chr 16:22; Ps 105:15. The meaning there is not certain, however, because the term may refer to patriarchs, and hence the use of the term is controverted.[73] In some Qumran texts, how-

---

70. See Broshi, *The Damascus Document Reconsidered*, 22-23. The last clause is a paraphrase of the end of Num 24:17, and the form וקרקר should probably be read as יקרקר, pilpel imperfect of קור. Cf. Deichgräber, *ZAW* 78 (1966) 333-43, esp. 336-37; G. J. Brooke, "The Amos-Numbers Midrash (CD 7₁₃ᵦ-8₁ₐ) and Messianic Expectation," *ZAW* 92 (1980) 397-404.

71. As J. J. Collins has interpreted it ("Teacher and Messiah?: The One Who Will Teach Righteousness at the End of Days," in Ulrich and VanderKam, *The Community of the Renewed Covenant*, 193-210, esp. 207.

72. See Allegro, *Qumrân Cave 4.I (4Q158-4Q186)*, 14 and pl. V. Cf. Fitzmyer, "Qumran Messianism," 102 n. 91; R. Bauckham, "The Messianic Interpretation of Isa. 10:34 in the Dead Sea Scrolls, 2 Baruch and the Preaching of John the Baptist," *DSD* 2 (1995) 202-16, esp. 202-6.

73. See p. 18 above.

ever, the term clearly is employed for prophets. In at least four such passages the verb is in the past tense, so that a messianic meaning is excluded.

(i) 1QM 11:7-8: [צי]ק לנו הגדתה תעודות חוזי משיחיכה וביד מלחמות ידיכה, "And through Your Anointed Ones, who perceive (Your) testimonies, You have told us about the ti[mes] of the battles of Your hands. . . ."[74] The sense of these words is difficult to make out. In the immediately preceding context, there is a quotation (not exact) of Num 24:17-18, which recounts the conquest of "the star" and "the scepter," so that it is implied that these are now considered "the Anointed Ones," through whom God has been telling about the battles of His hands, and the verb is in the past tense, which shows that Num 24:17 was not always used in a future sense.[75]

(ii) 6QD (6Q15) 3:4: [ביד מש[ה ו]ג]ם [במשיחי הקודש], "(They preached rebellion against the commandments of God given) [through Mo]ses and also by the holy Anointed Ones."[76] Since the verb in the context is past, it is probably a way of speaking of "Moses and the prophets."

(iii) CD 2:12: <ויודיעם ביד משיחו רוח קדשו וחוזי אמת<ו>, "And He instructed them through (those) anointed with His holy Spirit and those who perceive <His> truth,"[77] if one reads משיחו as משיחי, as in the pre-

---

74. See E. L. Sukenik, אוצר המגילות הגנוזות שבידי האוניברסיטה העברית (Jerusalem: Bialik Institute and Hebrew University, 1954) pl. 26; Charlesworth et al., *The Dead Sea Scrolls*, 2:118.

75. In CD 7:18b-20, where Num 24:17 is quoted again, "the star" is said to be "the Interpreter of the Law (דורש התורה), who will come to Damascus," and "the scepter" is identified as "the Prince of the whole congregation" (נשיא כל העדה), and "at his rising, he shall destroy all the sons of Sheth." Thus a personal identification of the star and the scepter is made, as in the LXX (see p. 99 above), and here the tense of the verbs is future. That, however, is not impossible because of the difference of text and the difference of author, even though one has to regard both 1QM and CD as sectarian texts. After all, Num 24:15-17 is quoted again in 4QTestim (4Q175); see below. Cf. G. Xeravits, "Précisions sur le texte original et le concept messianique de *CD* 7:13-8:1 et 19:5-14," *RevQ* 19 (1999-2000) 47-59; E. Weymann, *Zepter und Stern: Die Erwartung von zwei Messiasgestalten in den Schriftrollen von Qumran* (Stuttgart: Urachhaus, 1993); W. Horbury, "Messianism in the Old Testament Apocrypha and Pseudepigrapha," in J. Day, *King and Messiah in Israel and the Ancient Near East*. JSOTSup 270 (Sheffield: Sheffield Academic, 1998) 402-33.

76. See M. Baillet, J. T. Milik, and R. de Vaux, *Les 'petites grottes' de Qumrân: Exploration de la falaise, les grottes 2Q, 3Q, 5Q, 6Q, 7Q à 10Q; Le rouleau de cuivre*. DJD 3 (Oxford: Clarendon, 1962) 1:128-31, esp. 130; Charlesworth et al., *The Dead Sea Scrolls*, 2:78.

77. See Broshi, *The Damascus Document Reconsidered*, 12-13; Charlesworth et al., PTSDSSP, 2. 14.

ceding text (6QD). It would, however, be possible to understand משיחו as a defective spelling for משיחיו, "And He made known to them His holy Spirit and those who perceive His truth through His Anointed Ones." In either case, the verb is again in a past tense, so the "Anointed Ones" are the prophets of old through whom God communicated messages to His people.

(iv) CD 5:21–6:2: דברו סרה על מצות אל ביד מושה וגם במשיחו הקודש וינבאו שקר להשיב את ישראל מאחר אל כי. The word משיחו should be corrected to read משיחי, as in 6QD above, because this medieval copy bears almost the same text as 4QD^b (4Q267) 5-7, כי דברו עצה סרה על מצות אל ב[י]ד [מוש]ה וגם במשיחי הקודש וינבאו שקר לה[ש]יב את [ישר]אל מאחרי אל, "For they preached rebellion against the commandments of God (given) through [Mos]es and also by His holy Anointed Ones; and they prophesied deceit to m[a]ke [Isra]el turn from following God."[78] Here "His holy Anointed Ones" is clearly a reference to "the prophets," something like the phrase "Moses and the Prophets," a New Testament combination that is not found in the Old Testament.[79] See, however, 4QMMT (4Q397) 14–21:10, 15; Luke 16:29; 24:27.

(v) Related to the four foregoing texts is 4QapPent^b (4Q377) 2 ii 5, where Moses is so entitled: לכול מ.[ ].. בפי מושה משיחו וללכת אחר יהוה אלוהי אבותינו, "to all [ ] through the mouth of Moses, His Anointed One, and to follow Yahweh, the God of our fathers."[80] Moses as משיח is not surprising here, once we have learned that the Essenes extended the use of the title to prophets, because Moses too was regarded as a prophet (Deut 18:15, 18; 34:10).[81]

(d) Finally, there are two Qumran texts in which משיח is fitted with an article and used as an adjective, הכוהן המשיח, "the anointed priest"

78. See Baumgarten, *Qumran Cave 4.XIII*, 97; Charlesworth et al., *The Dead Sea Scrolls*, 2:22.

79. See the Greek prologue of Sirach, where the formulation is similar but not identical.

80. See J. VanderKam and M. Brady, "377. 4QApocryphal Pentateuch B," in *Qumran Cave 4.XXVIII: Miscellanea, Part 2*, ed. E. Schuller et al. DJD 28 (Oxford: Clarendon, 2001) 205-17, esp. 213 and pl. LI.

81. See Poirier, *DSD* 10 (2003) 221-42 (but beware of his "rubber-band concept" of messiah).

82. See J. Strugnell, "4QApocryphon of Moses," in *Qumran Cave 4.XIV: Parabiblical Texts, Part 2*, ed. M. Broshi et al. DJD 19 (Oxford: Clarendon, 1995) 111-19, esp. 113 and 122-36, esp. 123.

(4QapMos[a] [4Q375] 1 i 9; 4QapMos[b] [4Q376] 1 i 1),[82] which is another nonmessianic usage that merely echoes Lev 4:3, 5, 16; 6:15. A further instance of such usage of the title occurs in one of the Qumran noncanonical psalms, in which phrases echo those of canonical Psalms 86 and 89. Thus in 4QNoncanonical Psalms B (4Q381) 15:7, the psalmist speaks in the first person singular and asks God to be gracious to him. He seems to be a kingly figure who says, אתבננתי משיחך ואני הדו תפארת [אתה כי, "[For You are] the splendor of its majesty, and I, your Anointed One, comprehend . . . ."[83] The statement lacks all future connotation, and so it is undoubtedly nonmessianic. Again, in 4QNarrative A (4Q458) 2 ii 6 one finds משיח מלכות[ה בשמן, "anointed with the oil of kingship . . . ."[84] In this case, משיח is being used in its basic meaning, as a verbal adjective or passive participle.[85] Unfortunately, so little is left of the context of this fragment that it is not possible to say how the word is functioning or of whom it is predicated.

These are the main Qumran texts in which the title משיח occurs.[86] The use of it in these pre-Christian Jewish texts is important because they reveal a clear meaning of "Messiah" in the narrow sense of an awaited figure, either a single Messiah or the dual Messiahs of Aaron and Israel, and also several clear instances in which the word still denotes merely "Anointed One" as predicated of the prophets of old or of an anointed priest or king without a messianic connotation.[87] They show the variety of messianic beliefs in this period of Palestinian Judaism. The Qumran use of Messiah in the narrow sense from some time in the late second century B.C. thus indicates that the messianic expectation was indeed already at home in Palestinian Judaism well before the Roman period and that it was not a Christian invention.[88]

---

83. See E. Schuller, "381. 4QNon-Canonical Psalms B," in *Qumran Cave 4.VI: Poetical and Liturgical Texts, Part 1*, ed. E. Eshel et al. DJD 11 (Oxford: Clarendon, 1998) 87-172, esp. 102 and pl. X.

84. See E. Larson, "458. 4QNarrative A," *Cryptic Texts and Miscellanea, Part 1: Qumran Cave 4.XXVI*, ed. S. Pfann and P. Alexander et al. DJD 36 (Oxford: Clarendon, 2000) 353-65 and pl. XXV.

85. See p. 8 above.

86. There are a few badly preserved fragments where interpreters have at times partly restored משיח: 1Q29 5–7:6 ([משיח]); 1Q30 1:2 (הקודש משיח[מ]); see DJD 1, 131-32. Compare CD 6:1; Pseudo-Philo, *LAB* 59:2: *sanctus christus domini* (cf. P. Winter, "The Holy Messiah," *ZNW* 50 [1959] 275).

87. See also 4QapMoses[b] (4Q376) 1 i 1, where one reads: המשיח הכוהן ני.[ ], ". . . the anointed priest," a use similar to Lev 4:3, 5, 16; 6:15 (DJD 19, 123).

88. But see Hurst, *BBR* 9 (1999) 157-80; he not only objects to the translation of משיח

(3) There are also some Qumran texts in which the term משיח does not occur, but which do contribute to the development of the theme of the One Who Is to Come, because they are related, at least indirectly, to some of the foregoing passages.

(a) 4QTestim (4Q175), written on a single sheet of skin, lists biblical and nonbiblical passages: Deut 5:28-29 + 18:18-19 (promising a prophet like Moses); Num 24:15-17 (Oracle of Balaam about the star and scepter); Deut 33:8-11 (Moses' Blessing of Levi); and Josh 6:26 with part of the 4QapJosh[b] (4Q379) 22 ii 7-15 (condemnation of a Man of Belial).[89] J. M. Allegro maintained that the first three quotations "refer clearly to the prophetic, kingly and priestly functions of the Messiah(s),"[90] and many others saw them as three paragraphs that correspond to 1QS 9:11, "until the coming of a prophet and the Messiahs of Aaron and Israel." Whether that analysis is correct is debated,[91] because P. Skehan had shown that the first passage was actually a single paragraph, "a citation from Ex 20,21b, according to the Samaritan recension of the Pentateuch."[92] It uses the Samaritan introductory words, even if it does correspond to the four verses in the MT that Allegro identified (about the prophet like Moses). In any case, the four passages cited follow the order of biblical books (Exodus, Numbers, Deuteronomy, Joshua), and the text deals with some of the Old Testament passages already discussed as messianic.

(b) 4QSefM (4Q285) 7:1-6 quotes Isa 10:34–11:1 (about a "shoot from the stump of Jesse"). It introduces "the scion of David" (צמח דויד ונשפטו [את]), "and they shall pass judgment on" someone (in the lacuna an enemy was probably mentioned).[93] Then in lines 4-5 it says, והמיתו נשיא .[ ]

---

in the Qumran texts as "messiah" or "Messiah" instead of "anointed one," but also to the idea that there are two of them, because "Aaron and Israel" may mean simply "the community from which the Messiah is to spring" (179). Hence for Hurst "the idea at Qumran of two Messiahs — a 'Messiah of Aaron' and a 'Messiah of Israel' — is certainly one of those 'cherished notions'" that have to be tested by his "generation of scholars" (*sic,* 180)!

89. See Allegro, *Qumrân Cave 4: I (4Q158-4Q186),* 57-60 and pl. XXI; also "Further Messianic References in Qumran Literature," *JBL* 75 (1956) 174-87, esp. 182-87.

90. Allegro, *JBL* 75 (1956) 187.

91. See R. E. Brown, "4QTestimonia," *JBC,* 2:550-51; A. Steudel, "Testimonia," *EDSS,* 2:936-38.

92. See P. W. Skehan, "The Period of the Biblical Texts from Khirbet Qumrân," *CBQ* 19 (1957) 435-40, esp. 435. Cf. F. M. Cross, "Testimonia (4Q175 = 4QTestimonia = 4QTestim)," in Charlesworth et al., *The Dead Sea Scrolls,* 6B:308-27.

93. See P. Alexander and G. Vermes, "285. 4QSefer ha-Milḥamah," in *Qumran Cave 4. XXVI,* 228-48, esp. 238-41.

העדה צמ[ח דויד . . . בנגעי[ם ובמחוללות וצוה כוהן [השם . . . על ח[ן]לל[י]
[ ]כתיים, "and the Prince of the congregation, the scio[n of David], shall put him to death[94] [by stroke]s(?) and wounds(?). And a priest [of renown] shall give orders [about . . . the s]lain of the Kittim." This badly preserved war-fragment seems to speak about the final victory of Israel over the Kittim (Romans), when the Prince of the Congregation and the High Priest will sentence the leader of the Kittim to death, and the High Priest will see to the removal of the dead bodies of the Kittim. It is important because it not only gives the titles "scion of David" and "Prince of the congregation" to one and the same person, but thus identifies "the shoot from the stump of Jesse," indirectly giving that passage of Isaiah a messianic connotation, which it did not have in preexilic times. Moreover, this text uses titles that we have already met in 4QFlorilegium and 4QpIsa[d], quoted above in 3a, where משיח itself is not used either.[95] Compare 2 *Baruch* 40:1, where the Messiah is said similarly to put the leader of the enemy to death (see 9d below), and note especially the political connotation that is being given to these titles, especially in the context of the Roman occupation of Judea.

(4) There are a few Qumran texts that have been interpreted as messianic, but are problematic, to say the least.

(a) 4QSon of God (4Q246) is an important Aramaic text, telling about an awaited royal figure, who shall be "great upon the earth" and whom all peoples "shall serve": [והוא קדיש אל ר]בא יתקרא ובשמה, יתכנה / ברה די אל יתאמר ובר עליון יקרונה, "He shall be called [the holy one of] the [G]reat [God], and by His name shall he be named. He

94. Theoretically והמיתו could be taken as a 3rd person plur. form *(wěhēmîtû)*, "and they shall put to death (the Prince of the Congregation)," as Eisenman and Wise understood it (*The Dead Sea Scrolls Uncovered*, 29). Such a reading of the text, however, would normally demand את, the particle marking a definite direct object, which is missing. Yet such a reading does not cope with the context, which calls for the vocalization of והמיתו as a 3rd person sing. form with a pronominal object suffix, *ûhěmîtô*, "and he shall put him to death," as Alexander and Vermes and many other interpreters have taken it, *pace* J. D. Tabor, "A Pierced or Piercing Messiah? — The Verdict Is Still Out," *BAR* 18/6 (1992) 58-59. Cf. M. G. Abegg, Jr., "Messianic Hope and 4Q285: A Reassessment," *JBL* 113 (1994) 81-91; C. Martone, "Un testo qumranico che narra la morte del Messia? A proposito del recente dibattito su 4Q285," *RivB* 42 (1994) 329-36.

95. See also Abegg, *JBL* 113 (1994) 81-91; M. Bockmuehl, "A 'Slain Messiah' in 4Q Serekh Milḥamah (4Q285)," *TynBul* 43 (1992) 155-69; G. Vermes, "The Oxford Forum for Qumran Research: Seminar on the Rule of War from Cave 4 (4Q285)," *JJS* 43 (1992) 85-90.

shall be hailed Son of God, and they shall call him son of the Most High" (1:9–2:1).[96]

This Palestinian Jewish extrabiblical text is clearly apocalyptic in tone and uses the Aramaic titles, ברה די אל, "Son of God," and בר עליון, "Son of the Most High," for the awaited kingly figure, but it does not have משיחא, "Messiah," a title that is otherwise certainly at home in Qumran sectarian writings and would be expected here if that were part of the writer's intention. One may debate whether this text belongs to the class of sectarian texts of the Essene community. If it does not, then it would be all the more important, because it would represent the apocalyptic thinking of Jews not identified merely with that community at Qumran.

At least five different interpretations of "son of God" in this text have been given. (i) Milik claimed that the title referred to the historical Seleucid king Alexander Balas, the pretended son of Antiochus IV Epiphanes (150-145 B.C.), because he was identified on coins as *theopator,* or *Deo patre natus* ("born of God as father"). Such an interpretation is problematic: would a Palestinian Jewish writer admit that a Seleucid pagan king was "son of God"? (ii) D. Flusser maintained that the title referred not to some historical king but to the Antichrist, claiming that such an idea was "surely Jewish and pre-Christian," as a "human exponent of the Satanic forces of evil," comparing 2 Thess 2:1-12; *Ascen. Isa.* 4:2-16; *Oracle of*

---

96. For the full text of this document, see E. Puech, "246. 4QApocryphe de Daniel ar," in Brooke et al., *Qumran Cave 4.XVII,* 165-84 and pl. XI. Cf. J. A. Fitzmyer, "The Aramaic 'Son of God' Text from Qumran Cave 4 (4Q246)," in *The Dead Sea Scrolls and Christian Origins,* 41-61.

See further E. Puech, "Fragment d'une apocalypse en araméen (4Q246 = pseudo-Dan^d) et le 'Royaume de Dieu,'" *RB* 99 (1992) 98-131; "Notes sur le fragment d'apocalypse 4Q246 — 'Le Fils de Dieu,'" *RB* 101 (1994) 533-58; "Some Remarks on 4Q246 and 4Q251 and Qumran Messianism," 545-65; "Le 'Fils de Dieu' en 4Q246," in Levine et al., *Frank Moore Cross Volume,* 143*-52*; J. Zimmermann, "Observations on 4Q246 — The 'Son of God,'" in Charlesworth, Lichtenberger, and Oegema, *Qumran-Messianism,* 175-90; F. M. Cross, "Notes on the Doctrine of Two Messiahs," 1-13; "The Structure of the Apocalypse of 'Son of God' (4Q246)," in Paul et al., *Emanuel,* 151-58; E. M. Cook, "4Q246," *BBR* 5 (1995) 43-66; Collins, *The Scepter and the Star,* 154-72; "The Background of the 'Son of God' Text," *BBR* 7 (1997) 51-61; F. García Martínez, "The Eschatological Figure of 4Q246," in *Qumran and Apocalyptic: Studies on the Aramaic Texts from Qumran.* STDJ 9 (Leiden: Brill, 1992) 162-79; J. D. G. Dunn, "'Son of God' as 'Son of Man' in the Dead Sea Scrolls? A Response to John Collins on 4Q246," in *The Scrolls and the Scriptures: Qumran Fifty Years After,* ed. S. Porter and C. A. Evans. Roehampton Institute London Papers 4. JSPSup 26 (Sheffield: Sheffield Academic, 1997) 198-210.

Hystaspes (in Lactantius, *Divinae Institutiones* 7.17.2-4); and *As. Mos.* 8.[97]
Such an interpretation is equally problematic: practically all of Flusser's alleged evidence comes from Christian texts! (iii) F. García Martínez thinks that the title in this text belongs to an eschatological savior of angelic or heavenly character, like Melchizedek, who is depicted thus in 11QMelchizedek, or like Michael, or like the Prince of Light (1QM 13:10).[98] It too is a problematic interpretation: where does one ever find such titles as "Son of God" or "Son of the Most High" used for such figures? (iv) Hengel has suggested rather that the titles should be understood collectively "of the Jewish people, like the Son of Man in Dan. 7,13."[99] Though not impossible, this understanding is unlikely because the parallels that he cites invariably mean individual persons. (v) E. Puech, who published 4Q246 in the official publication in DJD 22, finally understands the titles to be messianic. In this, he adopts the interpretation of H.-W. Kuhn and is followed by F. M. Cross, J. Collins, et al.[100]

The Aramaic titles used here ascribe sonship to a kingly figure, who may be of Davidic lineage, but not even that is said. At the period of Jewish history to which this text belongs, there were kings (of the Hasmonean dynasty, of which the Essenes did not approve), but the author of this apocalyptic text may be alluding to a hoped-for restoration of the Davidic line, "until there arises the people of God, and everyone rests from the sword" (2:4). Once again the awaited kingly figure appears in a political context.

In the Old Testament, "Son of God" is a title used in ways different from "Messiah," and even from "Anointed One," but there is no passage where it is predicated of a Messiah, despite the fact that historic kings have been considered in a filial relation to God (as in Ps 2:7; 89:26; 2 Sam 7:14). I agree with Collins that "there is no evidence that any king of Israel or Ju-

---

97. See D. Flusser, "The Hubris of the Antichrist in a Fragment from Qumran," in *Judaism and the Origins of Christianity* (Jerusalem: Magnes, 1988) 207-13, esp. 34.

98. See García Martínez, "The Eschatological Figure of 4Q246," esp. 172-79.

99. See M. Hengel, *The Son of God: The Origin of Christology and the History of Jewish-Hellenistic Religion* (Philadelphia: Fortress, 1976) 45.

100. See H.-W. Kuhn, "Rom 1,3f und der davidische Messias als Gottessohn in den Qumrantexten," in *Lesezeichen für Annelies Findeiss . . .* , ed. C. Burchard and G. Theissen (Heidelberg: Wissenschaftlich-theologisches Seminar, 1984) 103-13; Cross, "Notes on the Doctrine of the Two Messiahs," 11-13; Collins, *The Scepter and the Star*, 163-64. Also S. Kim, "*The 'Son of Man'*" *as the Son of God* (Grand Rapids: Wm. B. Eerdmans, 1985) 20-22, esp. n. 33.

dah was not anointed," and that "a future 'successor to the Davidic throne' in an apocalyptic or eschatological context is by definition a Davidic messiah."[101] But Collins still has not given any evidence of the use of the title "Son of God," for a Davidic Messiah either in the Old Testament or in Qumran literature. His reference to 4Q174 rightly builds on 2 Sam 7:14, but that text is not yet "messianic," as used in Qumran literature. The double predication of "Son of God" and "Messiah" for one individual is still first attested in Christian usage, as we shall see. It is not to be foisted on a pre-Christian Jewish writing.

Even in Psalm 2, where an enthroned historical Davidic "king" (v. 6) is called "His Anointed" (v. 2) and eventually "My son" (v. 7), מְשִׁיחוֹ is not yet meant as "Messiah,"[102] because that psalm is a prayer for some historical king on David's throne, and it provides no justification for the messianic interpretation of this Qumran text. Psalm 2:2 is given a messianic interpretation in *1 En.* 48:10, as we have seen; yet even such an interpretation in one text does not mean that one can therefore extend it to all contemporary and later texts indiscriminately.[103]

(b) 1QSb (1Q28b) is an appendix to the *Rule of the Community* of Cave 1, which is said to contain a collection of blessings: for faithful members of the congregation (1:1-20), for the High Priest (1:21–3:21), for the Sons of Zadok, the priests (3:21–5:19), and for the Prince of the congrega-

---

101. Collins, *The Scepter and the Star*, 164.

102. As we have seen, pp. 19-20 above; cf. J. A. Fitzmyer, "The Background of 'Son of God' as a Title for Jesus," *The Dead Sea Scrolls and Christian Origins*, 63-72.

103. *Pace* Puech, to whom the official publication of the 4QSon of God text was entrusted for DJD 22, and who maintains that 2 Sam 7:8-16; Pss 2:7; 89:27-30[Eng. 26-29]; 110:3 "had certainly been given a messianic interpretation about the middle of the second century" (B.C. [Brooke, *Qumran Cave 4.XVII*, 181]). With that general judgment I have no difficulty; for the present survey of Qumran texts shows how that can be said. When, however, Puech says that I have refused to admit "même une lecture messianique de Ps 2:2 dans le Judaisme préchrétien," he continues, "voir cependant *Psaumes de Salomon* 17" (DJD 22, n. 40). Yet when one looks at *Ps. Sol.* 17, one finds in it no use of canonical Ps 2:2, 7. That *Psalm of Solomon* acknowledges God as "our king" (βασιλεὺς ἡμῶν), His choice of David as a human king over Israel, and His promise of an everlasting Davidic dynasty (17:4). It even asks God to raise up a son of David as their king (ἀνάστησον αὐτοῖς τὸν βασιλέα αὐτῶν υἱὸν Δαυίδ 17:21). Of him it says, καὶ αὐτὸς βασιλεὺς δίκαιος διδακτὸς ὑπὸ θεοῦ . . . καὶ βασιλεὺς αὐτῶν χριστὸς κυρίου, "And he will be a righteous king, taught by God . . . and their king (will be) the Anointed of the Lord" (17:32; cf. 18:7). The last phrase is an echo of the commonly used מְשִׁיחַ יהוה or χριστὸς κυρίου (e.g., 1 Sam 12:3,5; 24:7-11[6-10]); it is not an echo of a phrase from Psalm 2.

tion (5:20-29[?]).[104] Milik regarded this appendix as "bénédictions de la Congrégation *eschatologique*,"[105] but it is far from clear that the blessings were meant only for the eschatological future, because the phrase, "at the end of days" (באחרית הימים), is not used in it, and the temporal noun עולם, which occurs in several places, simply means "everlasting" (ברית עולם, "everlasting covenant" [2:25] or אמת עולם, "everlasting truth" [2:28]). Moreover, the so-called blessing of the High Priest is not certainly a blessing of the "Messiah of Aaron" (1QS 9:11). Into his translation of 1:21, Milik introduced the words, "Pour bénir *le Grand Prêtre*," in square brackets, which means that this title is not extant in the fragments,[106] and then argued that such a figure represented the Messiah of Aaron.[107] Nothing, however, in the text suggests that הכוהן הגדול or כוהן הראש, as the High Priest is called elsewhere in these texts, is the figure to be blessed, even though the second blessing has to do, indeed, with a priest. It is simply a blessing of whoever might be the priestly head of the congregation at a given time, as distinct from the Prince of the congregation, who is the one to be blessed in the fourth blessing. Recall the title given to the Teacher of Righteousness in 4QpPs[a] 1,3-4 iii 15: [. . . צדק]הכוהן מורה ה, "the priest, the Teacher of [Righteousness . . .]."[108] The text is simply a collection of blessings used at various times in the community's liturgical services to bless all of them or certain individuals.

(c) CD 6:10-11 is also a problematic text, which runs: וזולתם לא ישיגו עד עמד יורה הצדק באחרית הימים, "and without them they will not attain (it [instruction]) until there arises at the end of days one who teaches righteousness."[109] In the last clause, יורה הצדק, "one who teaches righteousness," is an allusion to Hos 10:12, ועת לדרוש את־יהוה עד־יבוא וירה צדק לכם, "It is time to seek Yahweh that He may come and rain

104. See Barthélemy and Milik, *Qumran Cave 1*, 118-30; Charlesworth et al., *The Dead Sea Scrolls*, 1:119-31.

105. Barthélemy and Milik, *Qumran Cave 1*, 121 (my italics). Milik was followed by G. Vermes, who also interpreted the text as messianic (*The Dead Sea Scrolls in English* [Baltimore: Penguin, 1962], 235).

106. See Barthélemy and Milik, *Qumran Cave 1*, plate XXV, frg. 5.

107. Barthélemy and Milik, *Qumran Cave 1*, 120-22.

108. See Allegro, *Qumrân Cave 4: I (4Q158-4Q186)*, 44. Others too have queried Milik's interpretation of 1QSb: J. Licht, מגילת הסרכים, 274-75; J. C. VanderKam, "Messianism in the Scrolls," 224-25; cf. M. G. Abegg, Jr., "1QSb and the Elusive High Priest," in Paul et al., *Emanuel*, 3-16.

109. See Broshi, *The Damascus Document Reconsidered*, 20-21.

down upon [*or* teach] you righteousness." This may imply an expected figure like the community's Teacher of Righteousness, but it does not say that
the latter himself would return as "their resurrected Teacher who would
lead the theocratic community of the New Israel in the Last Days," as Allegro once interpreted the words.[110] That is reading far too much into the
text, because the most it says is that someone is expected who will "teach
righteousness" at the end of days. The verbal form יורה is not the noun
מורה, "teacher," i.e., *the* Teacher (of Righteousness).

(d) 4QPrEnosh (4Q369) 1 ii 1-12 contains an address to God by some
early patriarch who speaks about a place (probably Jerusalem), for which
God has brought on the scene "a first-born son" (בן בכו[ר]) and set him
up as "a prince and ruler in all your earthly land" (לשר ומושל בכול
תבל ארצכה [1 ii 6-7]). Because of the fragmentary character of the text, it
is impossible to say, whether the words refer to Abraham, David, or "an eschatological messianic figure."[111] In any case, the text does not use the title
משיח, and there is no reason to think that the "first-born son," "a prince
and ruler," who has been set up (past tense) is meant to be an eschatological anointed figure. This has to be stressed because of attempts to argue
that "first-born" and "prince and ruler in all your earthly land" in this text
are echoes of Ps 89:21, 27-28(Eng. 20, 26-27), which does use משיח of the
historical David. Such echoes do not make 4Q369 a "Qumran Messianic"
text, *pace* C. A. Evans.[112]

(e) We saw above how the Servant Songs of Isaiah are reflected in
the Similitudes of *1 Enoch*, but it is a matter of debate whether one finds
any echo of them elsewhere in the Qumran literature. O. Betz has noted
that there are no quotations or explicit references to the Songs, but he

---

110. See J. M. Allegro, *The Dead Sea Scrolls: A Reappraisal* (2d ed.; Harmondsworth,
Middlesex: Penguin, 1964) 167. Cf. Collins, "Teacher and Messiah?," 193-210; M. A. Knibb,
"The Teacher of Righteousness — A Messianic Title?" in *A Tribute to Geza Vermes: Essays on
Jewish and Christian Literature and History*, ed. P. R. Davies and R. T. White. JSOTSup 100
(Sheffield: JSOT, 1990) 51-65. Both write against the interpretation given by Davies, "The
Teacher of Righteousness and the 'End of Days,'" *RevQ* 13 (1988-89) 313-17.

111. As the editors of the text themselves admit. See H. Attridge and J. Strugnell, "369.
4QPrayer of Enosh," *Qumran Cave 4.VIII*, 353-62, esp. 356-58.

112. See C. A. Evans, "Are the 'Son' Texts at Qumran Messianic? Reflections on 4Q369
and Related Scrolls," in Charlesworth, Lichtenberger, and Oegema, *Qumran-Messianism*,
135-53, esp. 145-52; "A Note on the 'First-born Son' of 4Q369," *DSD* 2 (1995) 185-201. Evans is
oh! so right when he says towards the end of the first-mentioned article that he doubts "that
4Q369 will cause Fitzmyer to change his mind" (152).

finds echoes of them in the description of the Teacher of Righteousness and the priestly Messiah passages.[113] However, Hengel maintains that there are many allusions to the Songs in the Aramaic Apocryphon of Levi[a-b] (4Q540–4Q541), texts that have been named and renamed and published in various forms.[114] Hengel agrees with Puech that these texts contain "the first and oldest midrashic exploitation of the Servant Songs of Isaiah interpreted in terms of an individual, in a current of Palestinian Judaism which more or less dates from the second century B.C.E. at the latest."[115]

Hengel also finds echoes of the Third and Fourth Servant Songs in 4QM[a] (4Q491) 11 i 11-18, a text that the original editor, M. Baillet, called "a Canticle of Michael," but which, as subsequent studies of it have determined, has to do rather with a human being who has been enthroned in the heavens with God and His angels.[116] Today this passage is recognized as a fragmentary text that really has nothing to do with the War Scroll and is often called 4Q491C or 4QSelf-Glorification Hymn[a]. The problem is to say who the person is, who speaks in the 1st person sing., אני עם אלים אתחשב ומכוני בעדת קודש , "I am reckoned with gods, and my residence in the holy assembly" (line 14), and again, [כ]יא אניא עם אלים אחשב[ב ו,]כבודיא עם בני המלך, "[F]or I shall be reckon[ed] with gods, [and] my glory is with royal heirs" (line 18). Is an individual meant, or what does he represent, if he is meant to stand for a collectivity? Baillet took the individual to mean the archangel Michael (apparently on the basis of 1QM 17:7, where Michael is said to rule over אלים, "gods," understood as "angels"), whereas Hengel leaves it vague. Collins understands it as either "the one who would 'teach righteousness at the end of days' (CD 6:11) or the eschatological 'Interpreter of the Law' of the Florilegium (4Q174),"[117] but M. G.

---

113. See O. Betz, "The Servant Tradition of Isaiah in the Dead Sea Scrolls," *Journal for Semitics* 7 (1995) 40-56.

114. See M. Hengel, "The Effective History of Isaiah 53," 106-18, for an attempt to sort out the confusion. The official publication of them is found in E. Puech, "4Q540-541. 4QApocryphe de Lévi[a-b]? ar," *Qumran Cave 4: XXII, Textes araméens, Première partie 4Q529-549* (DJD 31; Oxford: Clarendon, 2001) 213-23, 225-56. Cf. Fitzmyer, "The Aramaic Levi Document," *The Dead Sea Scrolls and Christian Origins*, 237-48.

115. Hengel, "The Effective History of Isaiah 53," 118.

116. See M. Baillet, *Qumrân Grotte 4.III (4Q482-4Q520)*. DJD 7 (Oxford: Clarendon, 1982) 12-44, esp. 26-30. Cf. Hengel, "The Effective History of Isaiah 53," 140-45.

117. Collins, *The Scepter and the Star*, 148.

Abegg cites parallels to lines 14 and 18 in 4Q427 7 i 6-17; 1QH 15(old 7):28; and 1QH 18(old 10):8 and on the basis of them identifies the individual with the author of some Thanksgiving Psalms, namely, the Teacher of Righteousness.[118] In any case, there is no indication in this fragmentary text that the individual might be a "Messiah," or even that he is thought of as anointed.

This brings the discussion of the varied Qumran texts to a close, both those that mention משיח and those that do not but have often been claimed to be "messianic." Some of them do testify to a vivid messianic expectation current among Essene Jews, but it is important to realize that it may not have been current in all the same details among all their Jewish contemporaries.

In any case, the foregoing Qumran texts provide an important background against which the previously known pseudepigraphic writings with the mention of a Messiah can now be judged.

(5) Before leaving the messianic data in the Qumran literature, I have to discuss two recent books that interpret some of the Qumran texts (along with other ancient writings) and relate them to Jesus of Nazareth. Because the main texts used in these books come from Qumran, they are treated here better than in the next chapter, which will be devoted to the use of the messianic title in the New Testament. The first book is *The First Messiah: Investigating the Savior before Jesus,* written by Michael O. Wise.[119] The second is *The Messiah before Jesus: The Suffering Servant of the Dead Sea Scrolls,* written by Israel Knohl.[120] Even though the two books utilize some of the same Qumran texts and have Jesus of Nazareth as an object of their discussion, they are similar only in an extrinsic way, because the messianic figures said to precede Jesus are not identical in the two works, and they are supposed to have lived at different times.

118. M. G. Abegg, Jr., "Who Ascended to Heaven? 4Q491, 4Q427, and the Teacher of Righteousness," in C. A. Evans and P. W. Flint, *Eschatology, Messianism, and the Dead Sea Scrolls.* SDSSRL (Grand Rapids: Wm. B. Eerdmans, 1997) 61-73, esp. 70-73. Moreover, there is no evidence of a messianic interpretation of Zech 4:14 in 4Q254 4:2, which does quote the words "two sons of oil," *pace* C. A. Evans, "'The Two Sons of Oil,'" 566-75.

119. M. O. Wise, *The First Messiah: Investigating the Savior before Jesus* (San Francisco: HarperSanFrancisco, 1999).

120. I. Knohl, *The Messiah before Jesus: The Suffering Servant of the Dead Sea Scrolls* (Berkeley: University of California Press, 2000).

I shall begin with the smaller book that is intended for a general readership, Knohl's *The Messiah before Jesus*. The thesis of his book is that "Jesus was the heir and successor of the Messiah of Qumran."[121] By the latter Knohl means the "Messiah of Israel," mentioned in 1QSa 2:14-20,[122] to whom he maintains several hymns allude (4QH^e, 4QH^a 7, 1QH^a 26, 4Q491 11 i) and who was understood as the Suffering Servant of Isa 53:4-13. This Messiah was the leader of the Essene sect but was killed by Roman soldiers in the revolt that followed the death of Herod the Great (4 b.c.). His body was left unburied, and after three days his followers believed that he had been vindicated and exalted to heaven. The story of this Messiah, reconstructed from the hymns, the *Oracle of Hystaspes*, Revelation 13, details from the life of Caesar Augustus, and Virgil's *Fourth Eclogue*, shows that he is none other than Menaḥem the Essene, known from Josephus as a friend of Herod.[123] All of this story would thus provide a historical Judean background for the messianic consciousness of Jesus of Nazareth, for his awareness of himself as Son of God, and for the emergence of Christianity from Palestinian Judaism, because the death of Jesus was interpreted later according to this paradigm.

This bold thesis does not lack originality; in fact, it is ingenious in the way in which it derives and mingles details from texts that are *per se* unrelated: details from Hebrew Old Testament books (Isaiah, Daniel, and Zechariah), the Greek New Testament (Revelation 11 and 13), the Latin of Virgil's *Fourth Eclogue*, the Christian *Oracle of Hystaspes* (known to modern readers only in the early fourth-century Latin patristic writer Lactantius,[124] and usually reckoned to be of Persian origin),[125] and the Latin *Assumption of Moses*. A veritable hodgepodge indeed!

Knohl's interpretation of the Qumran and other texts, however, leaves much to be desired.[126] Knohl admits that he has given an "imaginary reconstruction" of the Messiah's life, and he cites many passages from Qumran texts and from Josephus's writings in support of that reconstruction, but

---

121. Knohl, *The Messiah before Jesus*, 71.

122. See p. 93 above.

123. See Josephus *Ant.* 15.10.5 §372-79.

124. See Lactantius *Divinae Institutiones* 7.16.4; 7.17.4; CSEL 19.635, 638-39.

125. Knohl unfortunately follows the idiosyncratic view of D. Flusser that the oracle is a Jewish composition — for which view neither has offered any real evidence.

126. See the review of Knohl's book written by J. J. Collins in *JQR* 91 (2000-2001) 185-90.

when one checks the references, they do not always say what he claims they do. For instance, the difficult text, often called now the 4QSelf-Glorification Hymn (4Q491 11 i),[127] is claimed by Knohl to be messianic and the basis of the exaltation of the Essene Messiah to heaven. The one who speaks in this hymn uses the first person singular and says that he is "reckoned with the angels." He even exclaims, "Who is like me among the angels? [I] am the beloved of the king, a companion of the ho[ly ones]."[128] But nowhere in the text does he claim to be an anointed figure, and מָשִׁיחַ does not appear in it, even though some commentators admit that "Messianic identity may be implied," but then of the priestly sort.[129] Yet Knohl claims that the text speaks of a royal Messiah, who also "views himself in the image of the 'suffering servant' in Isaiah 53."[130] "The unique character of the hymn [4Q491 11 i] causes us to think that it is the original expression of a historical personality active in the Qumran community. In my opinion, there is evidence that the speaker in the hymn was a leader of the Qumran sect who saw himself as the Messiah and was so regarded by his community."[131] Knohl concludes, "I believe that the figure of the Qumranic Messiah and the messianic ideology connected with him had a profound influence on Jesus and the development of Christian messianism."[132]

Although such an interpretation may be possible, little of it is probable, and none of it is certain; and Knohl has not supplied the "evidence" that he claims to have for such an "opinion," at least as far as influence on Jesus of Nazareth is concerned. He may be right, however, about the influence of Qumran messianism on the "development of Christian messianism," because the material quoted earlier in this chapter has revealed that already.

127. It was frg. 11, col. i of what was called originally 4QM[a] (4Q491), part of the War Scroll texts from Cave 4 (see Baillet, *Qumrân Grotte 4.III*, 12-44, esp. 26-30). With further study, it is now apparent that it is an important fragment related to other texts (4QH[a] [4Q427] 7 i and 12; 1QM 25–26; and possibly 4QH[e] [4Q431] 1). It has been re-edited by E. Eshel as 4QSelfGH[a] (4Q471b) in *Qumran Cave 4: XX, Poetical and Liturgical Texts, Part 2*, ed. E. Chazon et al. DJD 29 (Oxford: Clarendon, 1999) 421-32.

128. As quoted by Knohl, *Messiah before Jesus*, 15.

129. So Collins, *JQR* 91 (2000-2001) 185.

130. Knohl, *Messiah before Jesus*, 16, 42.

131. Knohl, *Messiah before Jesus*, 19-20.

132. Knohl, *Messiah before Jesus*, 46. Equally problematic is Knohl's interpretation of 4QSon of God (4Q246), which he relates to the Roman rulers Julius Caesar and Augustus. See Collins, *JQR* 91 (2000-2001) 189-90.

Quite different is the book of Michael Wise, *The First Messiah,* not only in the identity of the figure whom he regards as the messianic predecessor of Jesus, but also in the treatment of the texts that he uses. His discussion is intended also for popular readership, as is evident in the comparisons that he makes continually with so-called messianic figures of the nineteenth and twentieth centuries and other movements that he introduces, such as David Koresh and the Branch Davidians. For Wise, the "archetypal messiah" was none other than the Teacher of Righteousness, the leader of the Qumran community, whom he thinks can be called "Judah," a name suggested by certain clues that Wise finds in the texts.[133] "Judah stepped forth from the highest ranks of the Jerusalem priesthood, a man well acquainted with the corridors of power and the politics of the royal court."[134] He summoned contemporary Jews to enter a "covenant of repentance, a New Covenant," and issued for them at least Ten Commandments, among which they were to avoid participation in Temple sacrifices, contaminated by the priests who served there and the Pharisees who held power there, because they were following the wrong calendar and not celebrating the feasts on proper dates.

Wise insists that Judah, the Teacher of Righteousness, was really the first Messiah, with none before him, and many after him, because "Jewish [messianism] exploded into the history of ideas in the early first century [B.C.E.] and not before."[135] As already noted, I would put its emergence earlier, in the second century,[136] but I would not fault Wise for this dating, because he still situates the emergence in pre-Christian times.

The difficulty that I have with Wise's presentation is somewhat similar to that of Knohl in that I know of no passage in the Qumran texts where the unnamed Teacher of Righteousness is ever called משיח or is ever said to have been "anointed" (using the verb משח).[137] In fact, the fragmentary text of CD 20:1 clearly distinguishes him from the Messiah: מורה ... היחיד עד עמוד משיח מאהרון ומישראל, ". . . the unique Teacher (*or* the

133. *The First Messiah,* 41.

134. *The First Messiah,* 41.

135. *The First Messiah,* 131 (his bracketed words). Wise is actually quoting J. H. Charlesworth.

136. See p. 62 above.

137. Forms of the verb משח are used in 4Q365 9b ii 2; 12a-b ii 6; 11Q5 (11QPsª) 28:8, 11, 13; but none of them refers to an anointing of the Teacher of Righteousness.

Teacher of the community[138]) until the rising of a Messiah from Aaron and from Israel."

What both Knohl and Wise have written about a figure they call a Messiah describes well a community founder or leader, who may indeed be a sort of precursor of Jesus of Nazareth, but they should not have called him a Messiah. They have undoubtedly forgotten or been unaware of a similar claim that was made in France shortly after the announcement of the discovery of the Dead Sea Scrolls and the first publication of some of them by no less a scholar than André Dupont-Sommer. He was quoted in the important weekend edition of *Le Figaro Littéraire* as posing the question, "A-t-il existé, soixante ans avant le Christ, un Maître de Justice qui prêcha la doctrine de Jésus et fut crucifié comme lui?" (Did there exist, sixty years before Christ, a Teacher of Righteousness who preached Jesus' doctrine and was crucified as he was?).[139] Later on, Dupont-Sommer changed his view and published many articles on the Scrolls and an excellent French translation of the texts that had been published at that time.[140]

With this we can pass on to the discussion of other texts.

(6) *Psalms of Solomon,* which were composed originally in Hebrew and date from the last half of the first century B.C., are extant in Greek and Syriac.[141] The background from which these *Psalms* are derived is debated, whether it be Pharisaic, Essene, or Ḥasidic Judaism.[142] In any case, it is clear that these *Psalms* reflect the hostility of Jews to the Roman occupiers ever since the time of Pompey and their contempt for the Hasmonean priest-kings.[143] The *Psalms* have no obviously Christian traits or interpolations, but they contain two passages that manifest some messianic development; they are dated between 63 B.C. (Pompey's taking of Jerusalem)

138. The word היחיד may be a misspelling of היחד. See p. 91 above and n. 35.

139. *Le Figaro Littéraire,* 24 February 1951, p. 3.

140. It was translated into English under the title *The Essene Writings from Qumran* (Oxford: Blackwell, 1961), and was often reprinted.

141. The Greek text of these *Psalms* can be found in the LXX; cf. Dalman, *Messianische Texte,* 284-86. For the Syriac, see W. Baars, "Psalms of Solomon," *Vetus Testamentum Syriace iuxta simplicem syrorum versionem,* IV/6 (Leiden: Brill, 1972) 1-27.

142. See Klausner, *The Messianic Idea in Israel,* 317 ("Pharisaic book"); Dupont-Sommer, *The Essene Writings from Qumran,* 296, 337; J. O'Dell, "The Religious Background of the Psalms of Solomon (Re-evaluated in the Light of the Qumran Texts)," *RevQ* 3 (1961-62) 241-57 (Ḥasidic); Grelot, "Le Messie dans les Apocryphes," 24-26 (Pharisaic).

143. See K. E. Pomykala, *The Davidic Dynasty Tradition in Early Judaism: Its History and Significance for Messianism.* SBLEJIL 7 (Atlanta: Scholars, 1995) 169.

and 48 B.C. (death of Pompey). They are similar to the Thanksgiving Psalms (*Hôdāyôt*) of Qumran in that they too utilize words and phrases from the canonical Psalter.

(a) *Ps. Sol.* 17:21-35 is part of a psalm "of Solomon" that praises God and acknowledges Him as "our king" (βασιλεὺς ἡμῶν), His choice of "David as king over Israel," and His promise of an everlasting Davidic dynasty (17:4) despite the sins of Israel and the rule usurped by impostors. It also asks God to raise up a son of David as their king (ἀνάστησον αὐτοῖς τὸν βασιλέα αὐτῶν υἱὸν Δαυίδ 17:21; Syriac: *'qym lhwn lmlkhwn lbrh ddwyd*, 17:23). Of him it says, καὶ αὐτὸς βασιλεὺς δίκαιος διδακτὸς ὑπὸ θεοῦ . . . καὶ βασιλεὺς αὐτῶν χριστὸς κύριον, "And he (will be) a righteous king, taught by God . . ., and their king (will be) the Lord's Messiah" (17:32). The last phrase is an echo of the commonly used מָשִׁיחַ יהוה or χριστὸς κυρίου (e.g., 1 Sam 24:7-11[Eng. 6-10]),[144] now understood as the anointed agent of God in His eschatological deliverance. The same title appears again in 18:7 (see next instance). The author is usually thought to be speaking of the restoration of the Davidic dynasty in his hostility to the Hasmonean dynasty that has been in power in Judea and that has been unfaithful to the Davidic heritage. So χριστός is simply continuing the sense of the kingly Messiah of Davidic lineage that has already been attested in other pre-Christian Palestinian Jewish extrabiblical writings, but now in a context that is distinctly national and political and with a description of the investiture of the Messiah for his militant mission.[145]

(b) *Ps. Sol.* 18:5-9 is part of another psalm "of Solomon," which bears the title ἐπὶ τοῦ χριστοῦ κυρίου, "for the Lord's Messiah," and which lauds God for what He has done for "Abraham's offspring, the children of Israel" (18:3). It asks that God "may purify Israel for a day of mercy," and εἰς

---

144. The corresponding Syriac of 17:35, 37 reads *whw mlk' zdyq' mlp mn 'lh' 'lyhwn* / . . . *wmlkhwn mšyḥ mry'*, "and he (will be) a righteous king, taught by God, over them / . . . and their king (will be) the Anointed Lord," which introduces an idea quite different from the Greek, unless one should read *mšyḥ mry'* as a construct chain, which would have the same meaning as the Greek version, "the Lord's Messiah." Such a construction, however, may have been valid in earlier Aramaic, but is highly unusual in Late Aramaic or Syriac.

145. See Klausner, *The Messianic Idea in Israel*, 318-24; Mowinckel, *He That Cometh*, 308-11; M. de Jonge, "The Expectation of the Future in the Psalms of Solomon," *Neotestamentica* 23 (1989) 93-117; C. K. Reggiani, "I Salmi di Salomone, una testimonianza storica," *ASE* 15 (1998) 417-40; K. Atkinson, "On the Herodian Origin of Militant Davidic Messianism at Qumran: New Light from *Psalm of Solomon* 17," *JBL* 118 (1999) 435-60.

ἡμέραν ἐκλογῆς ἐν ἀνάξει χριστοῦ αὐτοῦ, "for a day of election at the raising up of His Messiah" (18:5). It continues with a beatitude that blesses those who will exist in those days, ὑπὸ ῥάβδον παιδείας χριστοῦ κυρίου ἐν φόβῳ θεοῦ αὐτοῦ, "under the disciplinary rod of the Lord's Messiah in the fear of his God" (18:7).[146] Again, χριστός continues the idea of an awaited Messiah, but now without any explicit mention of his Davidic lineage, in this pre-Christian Jewish writing.[147]

(7) *The Sibylline Oracles* contain a few passages that older interpreters often considered to be "messianic." The *Oracles* are preserved in Greek, but their composition and date are complicated and debated.[148] The alleged messianic passages are found in Book 3 (§652-72) and in Book 5 (§414-33).

(a) The first of these passages (3:652-72) belongs to the main corpus of Book 3, which was most likely composed in Alexandria, Egypt, ca. 163-145 B.C.[149] "The eschatology of Sibylline Oracles 3 centers on the expectation of an ideal king or kingdom. The enemies of that king will be killed or subdued by oaths (654). The state of salvation is envisaged in political earthly terms, as a transformation of the earth and exaltation of the Temple . . . ."[150] The main lines (653-56) run thus: "Then God shall send a king from the sun(rise) (καὶ τοτ᾽ ἀπ᾽ ἠελίοιο θεὸς πέμψει βασιλῆα), who will bring the whole earth to cease from the evil of war; some he will kill; on others he will impose oaths of loyalty. He will not do any of these things on his own initiative, but in obedience to the noble teachings of the mighty God." H. C. O. Lanchester claimed that these lines had to do with "the

---

146. Or "of the Anointed Lord," since the genitive case of χριστοῦ is now ambiguous, and this meaning cannot be excluded, because of the way the Syriac renders the phrase in 17:37. The Syriac equivalent of 18:7, however, is not extant.

147. In writing that, I do not share the conviction of J. H. Charlesworth that "the passages in the *Psalms of Solomon* may indicate a reaction against full blown messianism" or that they indicate that "there may have been some diminution of messianism at Qumran"; "Challenging the *Consensus Communis* Regarding Qumran Messianism (1QS, 4QS MSS)," in Charlesworth, Lichtenberger, and Oegema, *Qumran-Messianism*, 120-34, esp. 125-26.

148. The Greek text can be found in J. Geffcken, *Die Oracula Sibyllina*. GCS 8 (Leipzig: Hinrichs, 1902); or A. Rzach, Χρησμοὶ Σιβυλλιακοί: *Oracula Sibyllina* (Leipzig: Freytag, 1891). Cf. J. J. Collins, "Sibylline Oracles (Second Century B.C. — Seventh Century A.D.)," *OTP*, 1:317-472.

149. For the Greek text, see Geffcken, *Oracula Sibyllina*, 82; cf. Dalman, *Messianische Texte*, 283; Collins, "Sibylline Oracles," 354-56.

150. Collins, "Sibylline Oracles," 357.

coming of the Messiah,"[151] but Collins more correctly notes that the king from the sun(rise) is "an Egyptian king,"[152] because in lines 611-15 a king is said to come "from Asia, the traditional threat to Egypt."[153] The following lines recount the final assault that will be made in his days on the (Jerusalem) Temple by abominable kings, and how God will address all empty-minded people and pass judgment on them, "and all will perish at the hand of the Immortal One" (671-72). Clearly, the passage deals with a coming Deliverer, but there is nothing in it that reveals that he is anointed or that the Egyptian author is thinking of a "Messiah."

(b) 5:414-33 is a passage from a different book of the *Sibylline Oracles*, which consists of six oracles against nations, Egypt and Asiatic countries (Babylonia, Media, Persia), and envisages an eventual return of Nero ("a man who is a matricide will come from the end of the earth") as an end-time enemy, and a final destruction of all by fire. It too tells of the coming of a Deliverer. The references to Nero show that Book 5 must have been composed ca. A.D. 70-80, and it is usually said to be of Egyptian origin. The main lines that tell of the coming Deliverer (414-22) run thus:

> For a blessed man has come from the expanse of heaven with a scepter in his hand that God has given him (ἦλθε γὰρ οὐρανίων νώτων ἀνὴρ μακερίτης σκῆπτρον ἔχων ἐν χερσίν, ὅ ὁ θεὸς ἐγγυάλιξεν), and he attained dominion over all and restored to all the good the wealth that earlier men had taken away. He has razed every city to its foundations with sheets of fire, but the city that God loved he has made more radiant than the sun, the stars, and the moon. He provided (for it) adornment and made a holy temple. (5:414-22)[154]

Even though the verbs are in the past tense, they are meant to be understood as expressing now what is still to come. Again, Lanchester understands the lines to describe "the coming of the Messiah,"[155] but there is no evidence of that motif. The upshot is that there is no solid reason for considering such passages of the *Sibylline Oracles* as messianic, even though they

---

151. "The Sibylline Oracles," *APOT*, 2:390.

152. Collins, "Sibylline Oracles," 376.

153. Collins, "Sibylline Oracles," 357.

154. For the Greek text, see Geffcken, *Oracula Sibyllina*, 124; cf. Dalman, *Messianische Texte*, 283-84.

155. Lanchester, *APOT*, 2:405.

may sound like Palestinian Jewish messianic texts. As E. Schürer has called them, they are really "Jewish writings which masquerade as gentile."[156]

(8) *4 Ezra* is a Jewish apocalyptic writing, containing seven revelations that formulate a message of theodicy and seek to explain God's way of dealing with human wickedness. In the course of its description of divine providence, it introduces ideas about the coming Messiah, the Day of Judgment, and retribution on human beings. It was composed originally in either Aramaic or Hebrew, but is extant only in versions (Latin, Syriac, Coptic, Ethiopic, Arabic, Armenian, and Georgian). It undoubtedly dates from the end of the first century A.D., probably after A.D. 70.[157] Its Latin form has a Christian introduction of two chapters (often called *5 Ezra*) and a Christian conclusion of two chapters (often called *6 Ezra*); all together they are called *2 Esdras* in English Bibles with the Apocrypha, of which chs. 3-14 have the seven revelations, called *4 Ezra*. The Latin form is somewhat christianized, and so its messianic verses are not easily interpreted.

(a) *4 Ezra* 7:26-44 is part of the third revelatory vision (6:35–9:25), which, after recounting God's work in creation, instructs Ezra about the wonders of the coming kingdom and the end of the world. Verses 28-29 read thus: *Reuelabitur enim filius meus Iesus cum his qui cum eo, et iocundabit qui relicti sunt annis quadringentis. Et erit post annos hos et morietur filius meus Christus et omnes qui spiramentum habent hominis,* "For my son Jesus shall be revealed with those who are with him, and he shall make those happy who are left [with him] for four hundred years;/ and after these years even my son, the Messiah, shall die and all who draw the breath of human life."[158] Instead of the Latin *filius meus Iesus,* the Syriac version has *bry mšyḥ'*, "my Son, the Messiah,"[159] and other versions have "my Messiah" or "God's Messiah." There is an echo here of Ps 2:2, 7, but the

---

156. E. Schürer, *The History of the Jewish People in the Age of Jesus Christ (175 B.C.–A.D. 135,* rev. G. Vermes, F. Millar, and M. Black (Edinburgh: T. & T. Clark, 1986), 3/1:617. Cf. Klausner, *The Messianic Idea in Israel,* 370-81, who thinks that the *Oracles* tell of "the birth pangs of Messiah" (370-71).

157. F. Zimmerman would date *4 Ezra* as late as A.D. 150, because he thinks the reference to "the star" alludes to Haley's Comet, which appeared A.D. 140; "The Language, the Date, and the Portrayal of the Messiah in IV Ezra," *Hebrew Studies* 26 [1985] 203-18, esp. 214-15.

158. See R. L. Bensly and J. A. Robinson, *The Fourth Book of Ezra.* Texts and Studies 3/2 (Cambridge: Cambridge University Press, 1895) 27.

159. See R. J. Bidawid, "4 Esdras," *Vetus Testamentum Syriace iuxta simplicem syrorum versionem,* IV/3 (Leiden: Brill, 1973) 16.

new details are the charm of the Messiah and his death. The last detail is surprising, and it is not easy to assess the mention of the Messiah's death, whether that was indeed part of the original Jewish writing or a detail derived from the death of the Christian Messiah.[160]

(b) *4 Ezra* 12:31-32 is part of the fifth revelatory vision (11:1–12:51), which is that of an eagle coming from the sea, a symbol of the Roman Empire. The vision is interpreted (12:33-39) as the fourth kingdom (the Greeks) as in Daniel 7, but now applied to the Romans. When it comes to its end in the last days, a lion (the Lion of Judah?) shall come and reprove the eagle for its wickedness: *et leonem quem uidisti de silua euigilantem mugientem et loquentem ad aquilam et arguentem eam iniustitias ipsius et omnes sermones eius, sicut audisti: Hic est unctus, quem reseruauit Altissimus in finem,* "and as for the lion that you saw rousing itself from the forest and roaring and addressing the eagle and reproving it of its injustice, and its utterances that you heard: That is the Messiah, whom the Most High has kept until the end [of days, who will arise from the offspring of David]" (7:31-32).[161] As משיח was rendered χριστός in Greek, so now *unctus,* "anointed," in Latin, and *mšyḥ'* in Syriac. The exact meaning of *reseruauit,* "kept, preserved," is not easy to explain; perhaps it refers to the idea of the hidden or preexistent Messiah of heaven, as in *1 En.* 48:6, 10. In any case, he is probably the one to whom "my Son" in 13:32, 37 refers; cf. *4 Ezra* 7:28-29 above.

(c) *4 Ezra* 13:1-56 contains the sixth vision given to Ezra in a dream about the eschatological woes that will precede the end time and the Day of Judgment: the vision of "the likeness of a son of man (13:3, Syriac: *'yk dmwt'*

160. See further Grelot, "Le Messie dans les Apocryphes," 30; S. Gero, "'My Son the Messiah': A Note on 4 Esr 7₂₈₋₂₉," *ZNW* 66 (1975) 264-67; L. Gry, "La 'mort du Messie' en IV Esdras vii, 29 [III, V, 4]," *Mémorial Lagrange* (Paris: Gabalda, 1940) 133-39; *Les dires prophétiques d'Esdras (IV. Esdras)* (Paris: Geuthner, 1938) 1:146-49; M. E. Stone, "The Concept of the Messiah in 4 Ezra," *Religions in Antiquity: Essays in Memory of Erwin Ramsdell Goodenough,* ed. J. Neusner. Studies in the History of Religions. NumenSup 14 (Leiden: Brill, 1968) 295-312; "The Question of the Messiah in 4 Ezra," *Judaisms and Their Messiahs at the Turn of the Christian Era,* ed. J. Neusner, W. S. Green, and E. S. Frerichs (Cambridge: Cambridge University Press, 1987) 209-24. Mowinckel (*He That Cometh,* 325-26) understands this text as telling of a suffering Messiah who will rise; but he again equates discrete titles, saying that *filius meus* ("my son") = *'abdî* ("my servant"; 325 n. 3).

161. The last clause is missing in the Latin, but found in the Syriac version: *hwyw mšyḥ' hw dnṭr mrym' lšwlmhwn dywmt'. hw ddnḥ mn zr'h ddwyd* (see Bidawid, "4 Esdras," 39; cf. Bensly and Robinson, *The Fourth Book of Ezra,* 61; Dalman, *Messianische Texte,* 295-96).

dbrnš') coming up out of the heart of the sea," who "flies with the clouds of heaven" (an echo of Dan 7:13), before whom all tremble, because his voice is like fire that melts wax.[162] He is confronted by crowds of human beings gathered from the four winds to make war on him. Unarmed, the man from the sea sends forth from his mouth a stream of fire that falls on the crowds and burns them all up. When he descends from the mountain of battle, he is confronted by another crowd of peaceful people. When Ezra awakens, he seeks an explanation of the dream and is told that the man from the sea is "he whom the Most High has been keeping for many ages, who by Himself shall deliver His creation, and he shall direct those who are left" (13:26: *Ipse est quem conseruat Altissimus multis temporibus, qui per semetipsum liberabit creaturam suam, et ipse disponet qui relicti sunt;* Syriac: *hwyw hwdnṭr mrym' lzbn' sgy''. hw db'ydh nprqyh lbryth. whw n'br l'ylyn d'šthrw*). For "days are coming when the Most High will deliver those who are on earth" (13:29: *ecce dies veniunt quando incipiet Altissimus liberare eos qui super terram sunt;* Syriac: *h' ywmy' 'tyn 'mty dn'bd mrym' dnprwq l'ylyn d'l 'r'*). When these things come to pass, "my Son will be revealed whom you saw as a man coming up (from the sea)" (13:32: *tunc reuelabitur filius meus quem uidisti uirum ascendentem;* Syriac: *hydyn ntgl' bry dḥzyt 'yk gbr' dslq*). "My Son will reprove the assembled nations for their ungodliness" (13:37: (*ipse autem filius meus arguet quae aduenerunt gentes impietates eorum;* Syriac: *hw dyn bry nks l'mm' hlyn d'tw 'l rwš'hwn*).[163] The "man from the sea" who "flies with the clouds of heaven" is undoubtedly an allusion to Dan 7:13, "with the clouds of heaven there came one like a son of man," who is now interpreted as an individual whom God has been preserving in order to reveal him as "my Son," perhaps an allusion also to Ps 2:7. The titles, however, of King or Messiah are not mentioned, as P. Grelot recognizes.[164] At any rate, the expected one in this passage becomes a transcendent hidden (= preexistent?) figure, as we have already noted above.[165]

---

162. Zimmerman (*Hebrew Studies* 26 [1985] 212) maintains that the Messiah's origin "from the sea" is a misunderstanding of *miyyam*, which should have been translated as "from the West," i.e., from Palestine, because 4 Ezra was composed in Babylon.

163. See Bidawid, "4 Esdras," 40-43; cf. Dalman, *Messianische Texte*, 296-98.

164. Grelot, "Le Messie dans les Apocryphes," 30. Mowinckel (*He That Cometh*, 305) claims that the idea of "the Messiah (here called the Son of Man) will come up from the sea" is "certainly traditional" and "undoubtedly the pre-existent being, the Son of Man, who will be revealed by a miracle." Yet he gives no evidence for such a "traditional" interpretation.

165. See further Klausner, *The Messianic Idea in Israel*, 349-65, who stresses "the *spiri-*

(9) *2 Baruch (Syriac Apocalypse of Baruch)* was composed originally in Hebrew, which is now lost, but which was translated eventually into Greek, a bit of which is preserved in P. Oxyrhynchus 3.37. The Syriac text was translated from Greek, as the Syriac title indicates. In content, it is similar to *4 Ezra*, and it is dated roughly to the same period after the destruction of Jerusalem (32:2-3), i.e., ca. A.D. 90.[166] It seems to have been composed by a Palestinian Jew who records the grief of his people over the destruction of the Jerusalem Temple. Like *4 Ezra*, it is a writing made up of a series of visions accorded to Baruch, and in it there are six passages where a "Messiah" is mentioned. He will be revealed after the troubles that are often called "the birth pangs of the Messiah."[167]

(a) After a description of twelve periods of troubles that will precede the predetermined end of the ages (27:2-13), it is revealed to Baruch what will then happen to all the earth (29:1): ". . . when all is accomplished that was to come to pass in those parts, the Messiah shall then begin to be revealed" (*mn btr dšlm mdm dʿtyd dnhwh bhlyn mnwtʾ hydyn nšrʾ dntglʾ mšyḥʾ* [29:3]).[168] Then Behemoth shall appear after him, and Leviathan shall arise from the sea, and the two of them together shall serve as food for all who survive, . . . and the earth shall give forth its blessings" (*wntglʾ bhmwt mn ʾtrh wlwytn nsq mn ymʾ tryhwn tnynʾ . . . whydyn nhwwn lmʾkwltʾ lkwlhwn ʾylyn dmštḥryn/ʾp ʾrʿʾ ttl pʾrys ḥd brbw* [29:4-5]). Here the Messiah is God's anointed agent on earth during a period that precedes the final consummation.

(b) After a description of the blessings that will come to the earth in those days, the revelation continues, "when the time of the advent of the Messiah is fulfilled, he shall return in glory (to heaven), and then all of those who have fallen asleep in the hope of him (shall be) rising" (*ʾmty dntmlʾ zbnʾ dmʾtyth dmšyḥʾ, wnhpwk btšbwḥtʾ, hydyn kwlhwn ʾylyn ddmkw bsbrh qymyn* [30:1]).[169] Here the Messiah is said to return to heaven, and his return is related to the resurrection of the dead. These are new elements in the developing messianic tradition.

---

tual bliss of the Days of the Messiah" (his emphasis) in this writing and the lofty conception of its messianism.

166. See S. Dedering, "Apocalypse of Baruch," *Vetus Testamentum syriace iuxta simplicem syrorum versionem*, IV/3 (Leiden: Brill, 1973) 1-50.

167. See Klausner, *The Messianic Idea in Israel*, 332-39.

168. See Dedering, "Apocalypse of Baruch," 15.

169. Dedering, "Apocalypse of Baruch," 16.

(c) Baruch is told about the four ruthless kingdoms that will subdue the earth and its inhabitants, each one worse than the preceding one. When the time comes for the last kingdom to fall, "then my Messiah's beginning shall be revealed . . . , and it shall uproot the hosts that gather against him" (*hydyn ttgl' tyšyth dmšyḥy . . . , t'qwr swg" dknšh* [39:7]).[170]

(d) The leader of the last kingdom will be captured and brought to Zion, where "my Messiah shall charge him with all his iniquities . . . and afterwards shall put him to death; and he shall preserve the remnant of my people" (*wmšyḥy mkh lh 'l kwlhwn rwš'why . . . wmn btr kn nqṭlywhy wngn 'l šrkh d'my hw* [40:1-2]).[171] The Messiah is God's anointed agent for Zion on earth, and a judicial and executory role is described for him.

(e) Through yet another vision Baruch learns about the wars, earthquakes, and fire that will come upon the earth, "and whoever, either of the victors or the conquered, escapes from all these things and comes safely through them, shall be delivered into the hands of my servant, the Messiah" for salvation (*wnhwh dkl mn dmtpṣ' w'rq mn klhyn 'ylyn dmqdmn 'myrn mn 'ylyn dzkw w'zdkyw nštlmwn l'ydwhy d'bdy mšyḥ'* [70:9]).[172]

(f) Finally the recompense is recounted: "After the signs come, about which you were told already, peoples will be in confusion, and there shall come the time of my Messiah; he shall summon all the peoples, and some of them he shall let live, and others he shall kill" (*mn btr d'tyn 'twt' d't'mr lk mn qdym kd nštgšwn 'mm' wn't' zbnh dmšyḥy wnqr' lklhwn 'mm' wmnhwn n'ḥ' wmnhwn nqṭwl* [72:2]).[173] Then he shall sit down in peace on his throne forever. See further 82:2-9.

In these six texts one learns more about the activity of the awaited kingly Messiah who is now expected to play a more militant role on earth.[174]

(10) *Testaments of the Twelve Patriarchs.* These testaments preserve exhortations for good conduct and admonitions about evil behavior (impurity, envy, pride, greed, fornication, etc.). The admonitions are uttered

---

170. Dedering, "Apocalypse of Baruch," 19. The Syriac word for "beginning" probably represents a misunderstood Greek word, ἀρχή, which can mean "beginning," but can mean also "rule, kingdom," which is what should have been used in the translation.

171. Dedering, "Apocalypse of Baruch," 20. Cf. 4QSefM (4Q285) 7:1-6, where the scion of David is said similarly to put an enemy to death.

172. Dedering, "Apocalypse of Baruch," 40.

173. Dedering, "Apocalypse of Baruch," 40.

174. See Klausner, *The Messianic Idea in Israel*, 330-48.

by each of the twelve sons of Jacob. They are difficult to interpret because there is little consensus about their origin, composition, and date, or whether they are a Jewish composition dating from the end of the second century B.C. (Hasmonean period), which was reworked by a Christian at a later date, or a thoroughly Christian work that has incorporated some traditional Jewish material, which would date then from ca. A.D. 200.[175] Forms of two of the *Testaments*, Levi and Naphtali, are known, respectively, in a late Aramaic and a Hebrew version (from different periods of time), but the main and best form of the *Testaments* is preserved in Greek, with versions in Armenian and Old Slavonic. This situation complicates the interpretation of the alleged messianic passages in them: whether they represent pre-Christian Jewish ideas or later Jewish Christian notions. Noteworthy in them is the mention of Levi and Judah together, which seems to many interpreters to reflect the dual messiahship encountered in some of the Qumran texts. In some of the passages usually cited, however, the messianic references are at most indirect, with little use of the title itself.[176] In the next seven passages χριστός occurs only once, in *T. Reu.* 6:8, "the anointed High Priest."[177]

(a) *T. Reu.* 6:7-8: τῷ γὰρ Λευὶ ἔδωκε κύριος τὴν ἀρχὴν καὶ τῷ Ἰούδᾳ, μετ᾽ αὐτῶν κἀμοὶ καὶ Δὰν καὶ Ἰωσήφ, τοῦ εἶναι εἰς ἄρχοντας./διὰ τοῦτο ἐντέλλομαι ὑμῖν ἀκούειν τοῦ Λευί, ὅτι αὐτὸς γνώσεται νόμον κυρίου, καὶ διαστελεῖ εἰς κρίσιν καὶ θυσίας ὑπὲρ παντὸς Ἰσραήλ, μέχρι τελειώσεως χρόνων ἀρχιερέως χριστοῦ ὃν εἶπε κύριος, "For the Lord granted sovereignty to Levi and to Judah — and with them to me, Dan, and Joseph — to be sovereigns. For this reason I order you to listen to Levi, because he will

---

175. See further H. F. D. Sparks, *AOT*, 508-12; L. Rost, *Judaism Outside the Hebrew Canon: An Introduction to the Documents* (Nashville: Abingdon, 1976) 140-46; and esp. M. de Jonge, "Christian Influence in the Testaments of the Twelve Patriarchs," in *Studies on the Testaments of the Twelve Patriarchs: Text and Interpretation.* SVTP 3 (Leiden: Brill, 1975) 193-246; H. D. Slingerland, *The Testaments of the Twelve Patriarchs: A Critical History of Research.* SBLMS 21 (Missoula: Scholars, 1977); Grelot, "Le Messie dans les Apocryphes," 34-41; Klausner, *The Messianic Idea in Israel*, 310-11.

176. See G. R. Beasley-Murray, "The Two Messiahs in the Testaments of the Twelve Patriarchs," *JTS* 48 (1947) 1-12. Cf. M. de Jonge, "Two Messiahs in the Testaments of the Twelve Patriarchs?" in *Tradition and Re-interpretation in Jewish and Early Christian Literature: Essays in Honour of Jürgen C. H. Lebram,* ed. J. W. Van Henten et al. StPB 36 (Leiden: Brill, 1986) 150-62.

177. In *T. Levi* 10:2 χριστόν is added in one MS to "savior of the world," but critical editions regard it as a Christian interpolation.

know the Lord's law and will define (it) expressly for judgment and sacrifices on behalf of all Israel, until the consummation of the times of the anointed High Priest, of whom the Lord has spoken."[178]

This mention of the "anointed priest" echoes Lev 4:3, 5, and possibly also the "Messiah of Aaron," the awaited priestly Messiah of 1QS 9:11, if it could be shown that the author of the *Testament* knew of that literature. M. de Jonge has noted that ἀρχιερέως χριστοῦ could also be translated "of Christ, the high priest,"[179] which might be a christianization of the text. Moreover, the sovereignty acknowledged for Levi and Judah may be hinting at dual messiahship, but it is complicated by the following phrase, "and with them to me, Dan, and Joseph." Even though they make one think of the dual messiahship of the Qumran texts, one has to note also the differences.

(b) *T. Sim.* 7:1-2: καὶ νῦν, τεκνία μου, ὑπακούετε Λευὶ καὶ ἐν Ἰούδᾳ λυτρωθήσεσθε· καὶ μὴ ἐπαίρεσθε ἐπὶ τὰς δύο φυλὰς ταύτας, ὅτι ἐξ αὐτῶν ἀνατελεῖ ὑμῖν τὸ σωτήριον τοῦ θεοῦ./ἀναστήσει γὰρ κύριος ἐκ τοῦ Λευὶ ὡς ἀρχιερέα καὶ ἐκ τοῦ Ἰούδα ὡς βασιλέα, θεὸν καὶ ἄνθρωπον. οὗτος σώσει πάντα τὰ ἔθνη καὶ τὸ γένος τοῦ Ἰσραήλ, "And now, my children, obey Levi, and in Judah you will find redemption. Do not set yourselves up against these two tribes, because from them shall spring God's salvation. For the Lord shall raise up from Levi one like a High Priest and from Judah one like a king, God and man. He will save all the Gentiles and the race of Israel."[180]

Here one reads about dual messiahship only by indirection, but again one suspects a christianization of the text in the appositive to the kingly figure, "God and man." See also *T. Sim.* 6:5: "Then Shem shall be glorified, for the Lord, the great God of Israel, shall appear on earth as man and save Adam in him." These words clearly complicate the interpretation

---

178. See M. de Jonge, *The Testaments of the Twelve Patriarchs: A Critical Edition of the Greek Text.* PVTG 1/2 (Leiden: Brill, 1978) 11-12. This critical text of de Jonge is to be preferred to that of R. H. Charles, *The Greek Versions of the Testaments of the Twelve Patriarchs: Edited from Nine MSS together with the Variants of the Armenian and Slavonic Versions and Some Hebrew Fragments* (Oxford: Clarendon, 1908; repr. Hildesheim: Olms, 1960) 13. The latter has been found wanting in light of more recent discoveries.

179. See his translation in *AOT,* 520 n. 7.

180. See de Jonge, *The Testaments of the Twelve Patriarchs,* 22; cf. Charles, *The Greek Versions,* 25-26. Cf. *T. Jos.* 19:11, which paraphrases and christianizes still more what is said here: "So, my children, observe the Lord's commandments and honor Judah and Levi, for from them shall come to you the Lamb of God, who by grace shall save all the Gentiles and Israel."

of 7:2, because "a king, God and man" might be merely another way of saying what has already been said in 6:5.

(c) *T. Levi* 8:11-15: εἶπαν δὲ πρός με· Λευί, εἰς τρεῖς ἀρχὰς διαιρεθήσεται τὸ σπέρμα σου, εἰς σημεῖον δόξης κυρίου ἐπερχομένου·/καὶ ὁ πιστεύσας πρῶτος ἔσται· κλῆρος μέγας ὑπὲρ αὐτὸν οὐ γενήσεται./ὁ δεύτερος ἔσται ἐν ἱερωσύνῃ./ὁ τρίτος, ἐπικληθήσεται αὐτῷ ὄνομα καινόν, ὅτι βασιλεὺς ἐκ τοῦ Ἰουδὰ ἀναστήσεται, καὶ ποιήσει ἱερατείαν νέαν, κατὰ τὸν τύπον τῶν ἐθνῶν, εἰς πάντα τὰ ἔθνη./ ἡ δὲ παρουσία αὐτοῦ ἄφραστος, ὡς προφήτου ὑψηλοῦ ἐκ σπέρματος Ἀβραὰμ πατρὸς ἡμῶν, "They said to me, 'Levi, your offspring shall be divided for three functions, as a sign of the glory of the Lord who is to come. He who believes shall be the first; no heritage shall be greater than his. The second shall be in the priesthood. As for the third, he shall be called by a new name, because a king shall rise from Judah, and he shall set up a new priesthood, according to the model of the Gentiles, for all the Gentiles. And his coming shall be remarkable, as of a prophet of the (Most) High from among the offspring of Abraham, our father.'"[181] This "new priesthood" is mentioned again in 18:1-2, where it is said that ἐκλείψει ἡ ἱερατεία. τότε ἐγειρεῖ κύριος ἱερέα καινόν, ᾧ πάντες οἱ λόγοι κυρίου ἀποκαλυφθήσονται, "the priesthood will fail; then the Lord shall raise up a new priest, to whom all the words of the Lord shall be revealed." The problem is whether this passage is meant in a messianic sense. It has been so interpreted.[182] The fact that it mentions the failure of the priesthood and the Lord raising up "a new priest" only echoes the discontent of some Palestinian Jews with the priests serving in the Jerusalem Temple, as we have learned from some of the Qumran writings.[183] Moreover, the mention of the three ἀρχαί, "functions," within the tribe of Levi is puzzling. The second clearly refers to the Aaronitic priesthood, but the first, if it means Moses as distinct from Aaron, is strange as a "function" within the tribe of Levi; and so also the third, when it is explained as "a

181. See de Jonge, *The Testaments of the Twelve Patriarchs,* 34; Charles, *The Greek Versions,* 44-45.

182. See M. Black, "The Messiah in the Testament of Levi xviii," *ExpTim* 61 (1949-1950) 157-58; M. Philonenko ("Les interprétations chrétiennes des *Testaments des Douze Patriarches* et les manuscrits de Qumrân," *RHPR* 38 [1958] 309-43; 39 [1959] 14-38) believes that these passages echo Essene ideas, and he goes so far as to identify the "new priest" with the Teacher of Righteousness of the Essene community (20); see Grelot, "Le Messie dans les Apocryphes," 39-41.

183. See 1QpHab 9:4-7.

king" with a new name, who shall "rise from Judah" and as "a prophet" from the offspring of Abraham. De Jonge regards *T. Levi* 18 to be "Christian in its present form" and shows that it is very difficult to sort out "the pre-Christian and possibly Essene elements" in it.[184]

(d) *T. Jud.* 21:2-3, "The Lord has granted me the kingship and him [Levi] the priesthood, and He subjected the kingship to the priesthood. He granted me what is on earth, but him what is in heaven." Why this passage is even brought into the discussion of messianism is puzzling, because the contrast is expressed in the past tense, and there is nothing about an awaited figure. It is simply an exhortation to respect the two Jewish leaders, one kingly, the other priestly, but the kingly figure is subjected to the priestly, which is similar to a characteristic of the Messiahs in the Qumran texts.

(e) *T. Jud.* 24:1: καὶ μετὰ ταῦτα ἀνατελεῖ ὑμῖν ἄστρον ἐξ Ἰακὼβ ἐν εἰρήνῃ, καὶ ἀναστήσεται ἄνθρωπος ἐκ τοῦ σπέρματός μου ὡς ὁ ἥλιος τῆς δικαιοσύνης, συμπορευόμενος τοῖς υἱοῖς τῶν ἀνθρώπων ἐν πραότητι καὶ δικαιοσύνῃ, καὶ πᾶσα ἁμαρτία οὐχ εὑρεθήσεται ἐν αὐτῷ, "And after this a star shall come forth for you in peace out of Jacob, and a man shall arise from my offspring like the sun of righteousness, consorting with other sons of man in meekness and righteousness, and no sin shall be found in him."[185]

This passage follows upon a description of the evil conduct of the people of Judah (their witchcraft, idolatry, prostitution, theft, arson) and a call for repentance. Then it opens with an allusion to Num 24:17, "a star shall stride forth from Jacob," identifying it as an offspring of Judah, who is further said to be like "the sun of righteousness," an echo of Mal 3:20(Eng. 4:2), "for you who fear my name the sun of righteousness shall rise, with healing in its wings." The Greek text here agrees with the LXX of Num 24:17, which has ἄνθρωπος, "a man," as a way of rendering שֵׁבֶט, "scepter" (*or* "comet") of the MT. If this passage is to be considered messianic, it is such only by indirection, for χριστός nowhere appears in it,[186] and there is

184. "Christian Influence," 219; see also Klausner, *The Messianic Idea in Israel*, 313-14.

185. See de Jonge, *The Testaments of the Twelve Patriarchs*, 76-77; cf. Charles, *The Greek Versions*, 101. The end of the text echoes Prov 8:31.

186. *Pace* de Jonge, "Christian Influence," 214 (who imports the name and italicizes it in his translation of 24:2-3). His article, esp. pp. 211-16, is otherwise a good discussion of the problems that this passage of *T. Jud.* raises. He concludes, "Consequently there is little in this chapter that can elucidate the messianology of Qumran" (216). See §2 (xii) above, where Num 24:17 is used also in CD 7:8-12.

no evidence that "sun of righteousness" was anointed or interpreted messianically in pre-Christian Judaism and even in Christianity before the patristic period.[187]

(f) *T. Dan* 5:10-11: καὶ ἀνατελεῖ ὑμῖν ἐκ τῆς φύλης Ἰουδὰ καὶ Λευὶ τὸ σωτήριον κυρίου· καὶ αὐτὸς ποιήσει πρὸς τὸν Βελιὰρ πόλεμον, καὶ τὴν ἐκδίκησιν τοῦ νίκους δώσει πατράσιν ἡμῶν./καὶ τὴν αἰχμαλωσίαν λάβῃ ἀπὸ τοῦ Βελιάρ, ψυχὰς ἁγίων, καὶ ἐπιστρέψει καρδίας ἀπειθεῖς πρὸς κύριον, καὶ δώσει τοῖς ἐπικαλουμένοις αὐτὸν εἰρήνην αἰώνιον, "The Lord's salvation shall arise for you from the tribe of Judah and (from) Levi. He shall make war on Beliar and grant to our fathers a victorious revenge. He shall set free from Beliar the prisoners, the souls of the saints. He shall turn disobedient hearts back to the Lord and accord those who call upon Him everlasting peace."[188]

In this passage, which begins with "salvation" (neuter σωτήριον) arising from Judah and Levi, it is immediately personified in the following masculine singular αὐτός, "he," which amounts to a personification of "salvation." In the next quotation "salvation" is mentioned again, but in a more usual way. If, however, that personification is to be understood as "Messiah," it is again only by indirection.

(g) *T. Naph.* 8:2-3: ὑμεῖς οὖν ἐντείλασθε τοῖς τέκνοις ὑμῶν ἵνα ἑνοῦνται τῷ Λευὶ καὶ τῷ Ἰούδᾳ. διὰ γὰρ τοῦ Ἰουδὰ ἀνατελεῖ σωτηρία τῷ Ἰσραὴλ καὶ ἐν αὐτῷ εὐλογηθήσεται Ἰακώβ./διὰ γὰρ τοῦ σκήπτρου αὐτοῦ ὀφθήσεται ὁ θεὸς κατοικῶν ἐν ἀνθρώποις ἐπὶ τῆς γῆς, σῶσαι τὸ γένος Ἰσραήλ, "Therefore, instruct your children that they stay united with Levi and Judah. For through Judah shall arise salvation for Israel, and in him shall Jacob be blessed. For through his scepter God shall be seen dwelling among human beings on the earth, to save the race of Israel."[189]

Once again, there is no mention of a Messiah, but the promise of salvation coming from Levi and Judah sounds like the "Messiah of Aaron and Israel" of the Qumran texts, and the promised salvation is again personified, when the masculine singular pronoun (ἐν αὐτῷ "in him," and διὰ τοῦ σκήπτρου αὐτοῦ, "through his scepter") is used in reference to it.

In these *Testaments* one finds many passages that are often read as

---

187. See J. P. Lewis, "'Sun of Righteousness' (Malachi 4:2): A History of Interpretation," *Stone-Campbell Journal* 2 (1999) 89-110.

188. See de Jonge, *The Testaments of the Twelve Patriarchs*, 108-9; cf. Charles, *The Greek Versions*, 138-39.

189. See de Jonge, *The Testaments of the Twelve Patriarchs*, 122; cf. Charles, *The Greek Versions*, 155-56.

messianic, because the awaited "Messiah" was already part of contemporary Palestinian Jewish ideas and culture; but, apart from the *Testament of Reuben*, where "Messiah" is found, these passages are more implicitly messianic than they are explicit; and so they differ from other writings that we have considered in this chapter.[190]

(11) There are a few other pre-Christian Jewish writings coming from this period that some have interpreted as messianic (such as the *Apocalypse of Abraham*), but it is hard to take such views seriously (for many reasons, even apart from the lack of the mention of a Messiah). I shall end this survey with comments about two Jewish writers who wrote in Greek, Philo of Alexandria and Flavius Josephus.

(a) The writings of Philo of Alexandria would not reflect Palestinian Jewish thinking, but some scholars have raised the question about his Diaspora understanding of a Messiah and his "messianic" ideas.[191] The Greek title χριστός is not found in his writings; nor is the Greek transcription, μεσσίας, which is otherwise known from the New Testament. Mainly two passages in his writings, however, have been considered in this regard:

(i) In *Conf.* 14 §62-64, Philo speaks of having heard of an oracle of one of Moses' disciples and then quotes Zech 6:12: ἰδοὺ ἄνθρωπος ᾧ ὄνομα ἀνατολή, "Here is a man whose name is scion/branch" (lit., "rising," the way the LXX renders צֶמַח). This name Philo considers the "strangest of titles" for someone composed of body and soul; but it is a good description of "that Incorporeal One who differs not from the divine image" (τὸν ἀσώματον ἐκεῖνον, θείας ἀδιαφοροῦντα εἰκόνος), because he is the eldest son whom the Father of all has raised up (ἀνέτειλε) and has named him elsewhere "First-born" (πρωτόγονον). The son, so begotten, is an imitator of the Father's ways and has shaped forms according to His archetypal pat-

---

190. The same has to be said about *T. Jos.* 19:8, 11; see Grelot, "Le Messie dans les Apocryphes," 33-34.

191. See, e.g., J. de Savignac, "Le messianisme de Philon d'Alexandrie," *NovT* 4 (1960) 319-24. (He claims that Philo "mentions explicitly" a personal Messiah in *De praemiis et poenis* 16 §95, but what he means is a vague allusion to Num 24:17.) Similarly, R. D. Hecht, "Philo and Messiah," in Neusner, Green, and Frerichs, *Judaisms and Their Messiahs*, 139-68. (He shows that neither Wolfson nor Goodenough understood Philo's messianic ideas correctly, and ends by claiming that "Philo's messianism might be understood as a 'realized eschatology' in which exegetical elements that might be naturalized and identified with specific mythical or historical figures in other systems of Jewish thought or in other Jewish communities became allegorical designators for the Logos in Philo" [162]. A new form of the rubber-band concept!)

terns. Philo then compares him to "a worse kind of rising" (τοῦ χείρονος ἀνατολῆς εἴδους), namely, Balak, who in Num 23:7 is said to have come "from the rising of the sun" (ἀπ' ἀνατολῶν) and whom Philo proceeds to interpret in his usual allegorical fashion. Unfortunately, one never learns who "that Incorporeal One" is for Philo because of his allegory, or whom he means by "eldest son" and "First-born." To say that Philo is speaking of a Messiah in such terms is gratuitous eisegesis.

(ii) In *Praem.* 29 §162-65, Philo explains why those who disregard the holy laws of justice and piety suffer curses and penalties as divine chastisements meant to bring sinners to acknowledge their sin and so set themselves free of such slavery.[192] He then says that those diaspora Jews who have gained this unexpected liberty will hasten to return home from exile, "guided by a certain divine and superhuman vision, not clear to others, but manifest only to those who are rescued" (ξεναγούμενοι πρός τινος θειοτέρας ἢ κατὰ φύσιν ἀνθρωπίνην ὄψεως, ἀδήλου μὲν ἑτέροις, μόνοις δὲ τοῖς ἀνασῳζομένοις, §165). The quoted words were interpreted by L. Cohn, the editor of the critical edition of Philo's writings, as a "somewhat obscure allusion to the Jewish expectation of a personal Messiah" (similarly J. Klausner[193]); but F. H. Colson more correctly understands them as "a belief that in the second deliverance the nation would be guided as they were in the first by the Cloud in which was a θεία ὄψις flashing rays of fire, *Mos.* ii.254."[194]

Unfortunately, neither of these passages reveals that Philo of Alexandria had any awareness of an expected messianic figure. He does use χρίω, "anoint," and χρῖσμα, "ointment," when speaking of the anointed High Priest (*Mos.* 2.29-30 §146, 150, 152; *Fug.* 20 §110) or of the anointing of the horns of the altar with blood (*Spec.* 1.42 §231, 233), but never of any kingly figure in Israel's history. So once again it is a misuse of the term "messianic" to describe such passages, where Philo is undoubtedly thinking only about some blessed future status for his people.[195]

---

192. Philo is using motifs drawn from Deut 30:1-10.

193. Klausner, *The Messianic Idea in Israel*, 523.

194. See F. H. Colson, *Philo, with an English Translation.* LCL 8 (Cambridge, MA: Harvard University Press, 1960) 418. He quotes Cohn and means the way Philo interprets the cloud guiding the Israelites in the desert in *Mos.* 2.46 §254.

195. The same has to be said about *Praem.* 16 §95, where Philo cites Num 24:17 as in the LXX and speaks of ἄνθρωπος, "a man," who will subdue great and populous nations (see M. de Jonge, "χρίω," *TDNT* 9:520). Similarly, *Praem.* 15 §88-92; 17 §100-104; 29 §165-72, passages often said to describe Philo's "messianic age." See S. Sandmel, *Philo of Alexandria: An*

(b) It is striking that the only time that χριστός, "Messiah," occurs in the writings of the Jewish historian Flavius Josephus is the two instances where he mentions Jesus of Nazareth.[196] In *Ant.* 20.9.1 §200, Josephus tells of the stoning of "James, the brother of Jesus who was called the Messiah" (τὸν ἀδελφὸν Ἰησοῦ τοῦ λεγομένου Χριστοῦ, Ἰάκωβος ὄνομα αὐτῷ).[197] This passage has usually been regarded as a genuine composition of Josephus, whereas that in *Ant.* 18.3.3 §63-64, where he also speaks of Jesus and acknowledges that "he was the Messiah" (ὁ χριστὸς οὗτος ἦν), is highly suspected of being a Christian interpolation.[198] In any case, Josephus never uses the Greek word μεσσίας (known from the New Testament) and otherwise speaks of a belief in an expected leader among his people only in a rather disparaging way. Thus in the *Jewish War* he writes:

> That which most incited them [i.e., the Jews of Judea] to war was an ambiguous oracle, similarly found in the sacred writings, that some-

---

Introduction (New York: Oxford University Press, 1979), who says, "The absence of a personal Messiah is the greatest distinction between Philo's messianic thought and the attendant range of views which became part of Rabbinic Judaism. There is no echo in Philo of the messiah as a son of David, of a great universal judgment day, or of resurrection. One might put it that Philo has a vision of a future messianic age, but completely without a messiah" (109-10). But then why call it a "messianic age"?

196. He does use χριστός once as a verbal adjective about a "painted" wall (*Ant.* 8.5.2 §137).

197. The translation of χριστός in these passages of Josephus is problematic, because we do not know for sure how he understood the Greek word, whether as "Messiah" or as Jesus' second name, "Christ." The problem is compounded because the manuscripts of Josephus's writings were preserved and copied by Christians. I have used "Messiah" in the translation because that seems to be the sense called for in *Antiquities* 18, despite its authenticity-problem.

198. Josephus never uses χριστός in this sense in any of the passages where he describes many other upstart leaders of popular movements against the Romans after the death of Herod the Great (e.g., *J.W.* 2.4.1-4 §56-65; *Ant.* 17.10.5 §271-84) or during the war of A.D. 66-70 (*J.W.* 2.17.9 §442-48).

Cf. P. Winter, "Bibliography to Josephus, *Antiquitates Judaicae*, XVIII, 63, 64," *Journal of Historical Studies* 2 (1968-1970) 292-96; A.-M. Dubarle, "Le témoignage de Josèphe sur Jésus d'après des publications récentes," *RB* 84 (1977) 38-58; P. A. Gramaglia, "Il *Testimonium Flavianum* — Analisi linguistica," *Henoch* 20 (1998) 153-77; H. Lichtenberger, "Josephus über Johannes den Täufer, Jesus und Jakobus," *BK* 53 (1998) 67-71; J. P. Meier, "Jesus in Josephus: A Modest Proposal," *CBQ* 52 (1990) 76-103; K. A. Olson, "Eusebius and the *Testimonium Flavianum*," *CBQ* 61 (1999) 305-22; S. Pines, *An Arabic Version of the Testimonium Flavianum and Its Implications* (Jerusalem: Israel Academy of Sciences and Humanities, 1971).

one from their land would become the ruler of the inhabited world (ἀπὸ τῆς χώρας αὐτῶν τις ἄρξει τῆς οἰκουμένης). This they took to mean someone of their race, and many of the sages were led astray in judging about it, whereas the saying really meant Vespasian, who was acclaimed emperor in Judea. (*J.W.* 6.5.4 §312-13)

Josephus, however, never tells us where in the "sacred writings" (ἐν τοῖς ἱεροῖς γράμμασιν) such an oracle is found, or whose sacred writings were meant.[199]

The texts that I have surveyed in this chapter show how the promise of a future David and of the continuation of the Davidic dynasty developed in extrabiblical Jewish writings in the last two pre-Christian centuries and even in the first century A.D. so that one can perceive what the expectation of a Messiah or Messiahs was in Judea at the time when Jesus of Nazareth appeared on the scene. Not all of them are clear testimonies to that expectation, but if they do not directly contribute to the understanding of it, most at least do so indirectly. They also bear witness to the variety of the hopes and expectations of the different kinds of Jews from which these testimonies spring. They also reveal that, though the messianic expectation or hope was widespread among Jews in Palestine, it was not uniform in its conception or formulation and not universally held, even in the Diaspora.

Most of these texts are treated by S. Mowinckel in the chapter in which he discusses "the National Messiah."[200] There he treats them under fifteen topical headings (such as "The Messiah as a Historical Person,"

---

199. He may be referring to a view otherwise mentioned by Roman historians. E.g., Tacitus, *Hist.* 5.13: *Pluribus persuasio inerat antiquis sacerdotum litteris contineri eo ipso tempore fore ut valesceret Oriens profectique Iudaea rerum potirentur. Quae ambages Vespasianum ac Titum praedixerat, sed vulgus more humanae cupidinis sibi tantam fatorum magnitudinem interpretati ne adversis quidem ad vera mutabantur,* "Many were convinced that an oracle was preserved in ancient priestly writings, that this was the very time when the East would grow strong and men coming from Judea would take control of matters. This enigmatic oracle really foretold of Vespasian and Titus, but the ordinary people with wishful thinking interpreted such great destinies in reference to themselves and were not turned to face the truth even by adversity." Also Suetonius, *Divus Vespasianus* 4.5. See further F. J. Foakes Jackson, *Josephus and the Jews: The Religion and History of the Jews as Explained by Flavius Josephus* (1930; repr. Grand Rapids: Baker, 1977) 83-85; S. Mason, *Josephus and the New Testament* (Peabody: Hendrickson, 1992) 163-81.

200. Mowinckel, *He That Cometh,* 280-345.

"The Names and Titles of the Messiah," "The Suffering and Death of the Messiah"). In so treating the national Messiah, he unfortunately mixes up the data from these important texts with interpretations from much later sources (e.g., from the Christian New Testament, the Targums, and later rabbinic literature).

I end this chapter with a quotation from S. E. Gillingham, which makes a good point, even if it is restricted to the canonical Psalms; what she says about them can be extended easily to other Old Testament passages as well:

> The development of Messianic expectation in the first century BCE also explains how and why the psalms were used in this way by Christians. They simply continued a tradition that had been set before them. Furthermore, it explains why this approach to psalmody continued after the Christian era within the Jewish tradition: the *Christian* Messianic adaptation of the psalms was a small part of a much larger Jewish process which preceded it and continued alongside it.[201]

---

201. S. E. Gillingham, "The Messiah in the Psalms," in J. Day, *King and Messiah in Israel and the Ancient Near East*, 237.

CHAPTER 8

The Use of Messiah
in the New Testament

The preceding chapter has shown how the belief in the duration of the Davidic dynasty eventually burgeoned into a vivid messianism of different forms, which was current in various types of Palestinian Judaism at the time when Jesus of Nazareth appeared on the scene in the days of Herod the Great and his successors.[1]

This is acknowledged by Paul, when, almost six decades later, in his Letter to the Romans he recounts the seven prerogatives of his former coreligionists, the Jewish people: "They are Israelites, and to them belong the sonship, the glory, the covenants, the giving of the law, the cult, and the promises; to them belong the patriarchs." To these seven he adds another, "and from them by natural descent comes the Messiah" (καὶ ἐξ ὧν ὁ χριστὸς τὸ κατὰ σάρκα, Rom 9:4-5). Paul, however, implicitly identifies him as Jesus, when he adds, "who is God over all, blest forever."[2] Paul thus uses χριστός in Rom 9:5 in its proper titular sense and shows that he understood Jesus' ministry to have taken place in a setting where messianic hopes or ex-

1. See G. Baumbach, "Messias/Messianische Bewegungen: III. Neues Testament," *TRE* 22 (1992) 630-35; D. Juel, *Messianic Exegesis: Christological Interpretation of the Old Testament in Early Christianity* (Philadelphia: Fortress, 1988).

2. For this reading of the end of v. 5 and its controverted character, see J. A. Fitzmyer, *Romans*. AB 33 (New York: Doubleday, 1993) 547-49. In translating ὁ χριστός in Rom 9:5 as "the Messiah," I am disagreeing with N. A. Dahl, who has written that "in no case in Paul can *Christos* be translated with 'Messiah'" ("The Messiahship of Jesus in Paul," in *The Crucified Messiah and Other Essays* [Minneapolis: Augsburg, 1974] 171n.11), because this instance is the rare one when Paul uses the word differently from other passages.

pectations were alive. Moreover, in Rom 1:3, he affirms Jesus' Davidic relationship: "born of David's stock by natural descent" (cf. 2 Tim 2:8).

(1) As we have already seen, this identification of Jesus as χριστός is recognized even by the Jewish historian Flavius Josephus, who composed his *Jewish Antiquities* ca. A.D. 93-94 and referred to James of Jerusalem as τὸν ἀδελφὸν Ἰησοῦ τοῦ λεγομένου Χριστοῦ, "the brother of Jesus, who was called the Messiah" (*Ant.* 20.9.1 §200). By the time the Roman historian Tacitus (A.D. 65-116) writes and tells how Christians were related to the burning of Rome in the time of Emperor Nero, he says of them, *auctor nominis eius [Christianorum] Christus Tiberio imperitante per procuratorem Pontium Pilatum supplicio adfectus erat; repressaque in praesens exitiabilis superstitio rursum erumpebat,* "the inspirer of that name [Christians] was Christ, who had been put to death by the procurator Pontius Pilate, while Tiberius was emperor; though it was suppressed, that pernicious superstition again broke out (and exists) until today" (*Ann.* 15.44.3). These two non-Christian testimonies thus acknowledge the influence that Jesus of Nazareth had among his contemporaries and associate it with a messianic role, as they use of him the name either χριστός or *Christus.* In doing so, they are simply echoing the identification of Jesus of Nazareth as "the Messiah," the belief that his followers recorded about him in the writings that eventually became the Christian Scriptures or the New Testament.

(2) The most succinct formulation of that Christian belief about Jesus in the New Testament is found in the latest of the Gospels, when early in his narrative the evangelist depicts Andrew seeking out his brother, Simon Peter, and saying to him, "We have found the Messiah" (εὑρήκαμεν τὸν Μεσσίαν, John 1:41). The evangelist explains the title, as he continues for his Greek-speaking readers, "which is interpreted 'Anointed One' (*or* 'Christ')." Then Andrew brings Simon Peter to Jesus.

There is also the parallel incident of Philip, who tells Nathanael about finding him "of whom Moses in the Law and also the Prophets wrote, Jesus of Nazareth," and whom Nathanael then addresses as "Rabbi, you are the Son of God! You are the King of Israel" (ῥαββί, σὺ εἶ ὁ υἱὸς τοῦ θεοῦ. σὺ βασιλεὺς εἶ τοῦ Ἰσραήλ, John 1:45, 49). Even though Nathanael's address does not use χριστός, it applies to him who has just been so identified two further titles that are associated with χριστός elsewhere in the New Testament.

In any case, this succinct formulation is found in an early section of the Fourth Gospel in which the evangelist is concerned to present the identity of Jesus as the fulfillment of Jewish messianic expectations (John 1:19-51). In these verses, John the Baptist is depicted denying that he himself is the Messiah and pointing to the one "who comes after me" (1:20-27), whom he eventually identifies as "the Son of God" (1:34) and "the Lamb of God" (1:36). Then the first disciples understand him in Andrew's words as "the Messiah" (1:41) and in Nathanael's triple address as "Rabbi, Son of God, and the King of Israel" (1:49).[3] The whole episode ends with Jesus referring to himself rather as "the Son of Man" (ὁ υἱὸς τοῦ ἀνθρώπου, John 1:51), a title which has been used of a Messiah-figure in *1 Enoch*, as we have seen. Now, however, it is clearly used also as a title of one coming from heaven, the descending (and ascending) revealer.[4]

Perhaps one should include here also John 4:25, where a Samaritan woman says that she knows about the Jewish belief in a coming Messiah: οἶδα ὅτι Μεσσίας ἔρχεται ὁ λεγόμενος χριστός, "I know that the Messiah is coming, who is called Christ [in Greek]."[5] The evangelist reports Jesus' reply, "I who am speaking to you am he" (ἐγώ εἰμι, ὁ λαλῶν σοι, 4:26). Cf. John 4:29b. Note also the implications of the remarks of Jerusalem Jews who use χριστός about Jesus or object to his being so called in John 7:25-31, 41-42; 10:24; 12:34.[6]

Whereas this elaborate identification of Jesus of Nazareth comes at the very beginning of the Fourth Gospel, the gradual recognition of him as Messiah is rather the way he is presented in the earlier Synoptic Gospels, which undoubtedly better reflect the historical situation and its gradual perception of Jesus as a Messiah among his followers. In any case, all four Gospels formulate the primitive belief in Jesus as the embodiment of Jewish messianic expectations.

The title Χριστόν is not often translated as "Messiah" in English Bibles, although it perhaps should be at least sometimes (e.g., Matt 1:16;

---

3. See R. Schnackenburg, *The Gospel According to St. John* (New York: Crossroad, 1980-82) 1:282-85.

4. See W. A. Meeks, "The Man from Heaven in Johannine Sectarianism," *JBL* 91 (1972) 44-72.

5. So the Greek-writing evangelist phrases it. Perhaps he did not know the difference between Jewish and Samaritan expectations of a Coming One, and that is why he presents her speaking of a coming "Messiah," whereas, if she were formulating the expectation according to Samaritan convictions, she would have said, "Returning One." See 11n.24 above.

6. See further M. de Jonge, "Jewish Expectations about the 'Messiah' According to the Fourth Gospel," *NTS* 19 (1972-73) 246-70.

22:42; Luke 20:41; John 1:20; 3:28; Acts 2:36). Shortly after Jesus' death and long before the time that the New Testament writings were composed, Χριστός had become the title par excellence for Jesus of Nazareth among Greek-speaking Christians, and even his *cognomen* or second name, "Jesus Christ," which is often preserved in these writings (e.g., Gal 1:1; 1 Cor 3:11; Rom 1:4; Mark 1:1; Matt 1:1; Acts 2:38). Sometimes it is used alone as his only name, "Christ" (e.g., 1 Thess 2:6; 1 Cor 1:23 [χριστὸν ἐσταυρωμένον, "Christ crucified"]; Rom 5:6, 8; 6:4; Luke 4:41; 23:2). It is almost an exclusively Pauline trait to invert the names on occasion, "Christ Jesus" (e.g., 1 Thess 2:14; Gal 2:4; Rom 6:3, 11; 8:1, 39).[7] In thus coupling the names Jesus and Christ, the New Testament writers declare that the Messiah, for whom Israel had been waiting (in some form) for so long, has now come, and they proclaim Jesus of Nazareth to be such.

In Acts 2:36, Luke sums up early Christian preaching, when he depicts Peter proclaiming to the Jews assembled in Jerusalem on the first Pentecost after Jesus' death, "Let all the house of Israel know for sure, then, that God has made him both Lord and Messiah, this Jesus whom you crucified" (καὶ κύριον καὶ χριστόν). With the title κύριος, "Lord," New Testament writers thus affirm Jesus' risen and exalted status, and with χριστός they assert his messianic role. Moreover, just prior to that summary, Peter announces the relationship of Jesus to David, when he says to the assembled Jews,

> My brothers, one can speak frankly to you about the patriarch David: he died and was buried, and his tomb is here in our midst to this very day. But because he was a prophet and knew that God *had sworn an oath* to him that he *would set one of his descendants upon his throne,*[8] he foresaw and spoke of the resurrection of the Messiah, saying that he was *neither abandoned to the netherworld nor has* his flesh *seen decay.*[9] (Acts 2:29-31)

See further Acts 5:42; 8:5; 9:22; 17:3b; 18:5, 28. So Paul and Luke have summed up the early Christian belief in Jesus of Nazareth as the crucified Messiah, whom God raised from the dead; and other New Testament writers have echoed it in their own way (see 1 Pet 2:21; 3:18; 1 John 2:22).

7. The inverted names are found also in Acts 3:20; 5:42; 17:3; 18:5, 28; 24:24, but then usually as variant readings, probably introduced by copyists familiar with the Pauline usage.

8. Alluding to Ps 132:11.

9. Alluding to Ps 16:10.

The Fourth Gospel eventually makes the issue of acknowledging Jesus as the Messiah the cause of division between Jews and Christians: "for the Jews had already agreed that, if anyone would acknowledge him to be the Messiah, he would be put out of the synagogue" (ἵνα ἐάν τις αὐτὸν ὁμολογήσῃ χριστόν, ἀποσυνάγωγος γένηται, John 9:22b). Cf. Luke 23:2, where "the whole assembly" of the Sanhedrin bring Jesus to Pilate and accuse him, "This man we have found subverting our nation, obstructing the payment of taxes to Caesar, and even claiming to be an anointed king" (λέγοντα ἑαυτὸν χριστὸν βασιλέα εἶναι).

(3) What led early Christians to regard their crucified leader as Χριστός? Although one may never be able to answer that question with certainty, it is possible to suggest some reasons for their conviction and belief.

(a) One might be tempted to say that Jesus regarded himself as "Messiah," but such an explanation is far from clear. The earliest Gospel depicts Jesus being asked by the High Priest at his trial before the Sanhedrin, "Are you the Messiah, the son of the Blessed One?" (σὺ εἶ ὁ χριστός, ὁ υἱὸς τοῦ εὐλογητοῦ; Mark 14:61), and Jesus answering, "I am (ἐγώ εἰμι); and you will see the Son of Man seated at the right hand of Power, and coming with the clouds of heaven."[10] At that, the High Priest tears his garments and accuses Jesus of blasphemy. Jesus' reply sounds like a forthright answer, meaning that he was conscious of his messianic role.

When, however, one compares his reply to the High Priest in the parallel passages of the Matthean and Lukan Gospels one gets a different impression. In Matt 26:64, Jesus answers, σὺ εἶπας, "You have said so" (RSV), i.e., that is your way of putting it. In Luke 22:67-68, Jesus, when asked whether he is the Messiah, retorts, "If I tell you, you will not believe me; and if I ask you a question, you will not answer," which is an evasive response. When they persist, asking "You are, then, the Son of God?" Jesus' reply is, "It is you who say that I am."[11] Neither of these answers is as forth-

---

10. For the allusions in the latter part of Jesus' answer, see §6d below.

11. The two questions asked of the Lukan Jesus mark a genuine christological progression, *pace* B. Byrne ("Jesus as Messiah in the Gospel of Luke," *CBQ* 65 [2003] 80-95, esp. 91), because there would be no point in asking the two questions if the titles did not have a different connotation. Luke has introduced the two questions, differently from the tradition that preceded him, precisely in order to make the point that Jesus is not only the Messiah but also the Son of God in a transcendent sense. Failure to comprehend the difference comes from the tendency to see the latter title as saying no more than the former, repeating the error that interpreters of the Qumran Son of God text (4Q246) have made in calling it "messi-

right as that in the Markan Gospel, and consequently they raise the question, "What really was Jesus' answer?"[12]

Moreover, in the well-known scene at Caesarea Philippi, when Jesus asks his disciples, "Who do people say that I am?" Peter eventually replies, "You are the Messiah" (Mark 8:29);[13] or "God's Messiah" (Luke 9:20); or "You are the Messiah, the Son of the living God" (Matt 16:16).[14] Thus in the Synoptic Gospels, Peter acknowledges Jesus to be "the Messiah," in contrast to what others have been saying about him.[15] However, in all three of those Gospels Jesus immediately forbids his disciples to use that title of him: "He charged them to tell no one about him" (Mark 8:30); "So he gave them strict orders not to say this to anyone" (Luke 9:21); "Then he ordered the disciples expressly to tell no one that he was the Messiah" (Matt 16:20).[16] This prohibition may have stemmed from Jesus' awareness of the political or militant overtones that "Messiah" had acquired in Roman-occupied Judea of his time (as we have seen in some instances in the previous chapter).

---

anic." Certainly, "it is Jesus who determines what messiahship means" (C. Tuckett, "The Christology of Luke-Acts," in *The Unity of Luke-Acts,* ed. J. Verheyden. BETL 142 [Leuven: Leuven University Press, 1999] 164, quoted in Byrne, 95), and that is why the two titles, born of discrete Old Testament origin, have been predicated of one individual (namely, Jesus of Nazareth) for the first time in the *Christian* Scriptures. One has to respect the history of ideas.

12. John 18:19 further complicates the question, "So the High Priest asked Jesus about his disciples and about his teaching." There nothing is asked about his being Χριστός.

13. This acknowledgement of Peter is an important passage in the Markan Gospel, where Χριστός occurs only seven times, for this is the first occurrence of it since the introductory verse (1:1), where it functions as part of the title of the Gospel as a whole, "The beginning of the gospel of Jesus Christ, the Son of God."

14. Contrast the form of Peter's acknowledgement in John 6:69, "We have believed and have come to know that you are the Holy One of God." For a discussion of the implications of these different forms of Peter's response, see R. E. Brown, K. P. Donfried, and J. Reumann, eds., *Peter in the New Testament: A Collaborative Assessment by Protestant and Roman Catholic Scholars* (Minneapolis: Augsburg; and New York: Paulist, 1973) 64-69, 83-89, 131-32.

15. In this scene Peter's confession is not yet an admission of full Christian faith, which would only come with his recognition of the resurrection of Christ. It is an acknowledgement of Jesus as God's Messiah (in the Jewish sense), after Peter has witnessed some of Jesus' ministry as a preacher, teacher, and healer. Eventually, Peter's confession will develop into the Christian belief in "Christ" as the Anointed One who was crucified, raised, and exalted to heavenly glory.

16. This is what Byrne calls "a clear qualification," added in the Gospels to their statement that Jesus is the Messiah (*CBQ* 65 [2003] 80, 82).

So the episode at Caesarea Philippi, while revealing that some of Jesus' contemporaries were thinking of him as a messianic figure, may suggest that he himself did not regard his role or mission as messianic.[17] There is, however, no reason to regard the Gospel accounts as wholly devoid of historical accuracy in this question, even if there is no way of assessing with certainty whether a messianic role would have been part of the consciousness of the Jesus of history.[18] This problem, however, complicates the way one tries to answer the question of what Jesus actually said to the High Priest.[19]

(b) N. A. Dahl and E. Dinkler have plausibly suggested, however, that early Christians were led to regard their crucified leader as Χριστός because of the inscription that was used on the cross on which Jesus died, ὁ βασιλεὺς τῶν Ἰουδαίων, "the King of the Jews" (Mark 15:26).[20]

---

17. Note, however, that in Mark 9:41 Jesus uses Χριστός as a self-reference, "Whoever gives you a drink of water because you bear the name of Christ will not lose his reward." Whether that Markan formulation is what the Jesus of history actually said is also problematic, because in the same saying as recorded in Matt 10:42 Jesus says rather, ". . . because he is a disciple." Moreover, the formulation in the Markan clause, "because you bear the name of Christ," may betray its origin in a time after "the disciples were first called Christians" (Acts 11:26).

18. One has to remember that the Gospels, passages of which have just been considered, were composed about a generation after Jesus' death, and none of them purports to be a stenographic record of his sayings or a cinematic reproduction of his activity. Nevertheless, many attempts have been made to explain his consciousness merely on the basis of them: W. Baldensperger, *Das Selbstbewusstsein Jesu im Lichte der messianischen Hoffnungen seiner Zeit,* 2nd ed. (Strassburg: Heitz, 1892); W. Mundle, "Die Geschichtlichkeit des messianischen Bewusstseins Jesu," *ZNW* 21 (1922) 299-311; A. H. I. Lee, *From Messiah to Preexistent Son: Jesus' Self-Consciousness and Early Christian Exegesis of Messianic Psalms.* WUNT 2/192 (Tübingen: Mohr Siebeck, 2005). But cf. M. de Jonge, "The Earliest Christian Use of *Christos:* Some Suggestions," *NTS* 32 (1986) 321-43, esp. 323; M. Hengel, "Jesus, the Messiah of Israel: The Debate about the 'Messianic Mission' of Jesus," in *Crisis in Christology: Essays in Quest of Resolution,* ed. W. R. Farmer (Livonia: Dove, 1995) 217-40.

19. See further R. E. Brown, *An Introduction to New Testament Christology* (New York: Paulist, 1994) 71-102.

20. See N. A. Dahl, "The Crucified Messiah," in *The Crucified Messiah and Other Essays,* 10-36 (the German original appeared in 1960); E. Dinkler, "Peter's Confession and the Satan Saying: The Problem of Jesus' Messiahship," in *The Future of Our Religious Past: Essays in Honour of Rudolf Bultmann,* ed. J. M. Robinson (New York: Harper & Row, 1971) 169-202 (the German original appeared in 1964). See also Byrne, *CBQ* 65 (2003) 81-82.

This inscription is the only thing that was written about Jesus during his earthly ministry that has come down to us. Although a form of it is preserved in all four Gospels, its

The regal status attributed to him by the Roman prefect, Pontius Pilate, would have led to the association of him with the messianic expectation of Palestinian Judaism. It said in effect, "This crucified man is the kingly leader that you have been awaiting." Crucified as King, he quickly became for his followers "the Messiah," and the title, colored by resurrection-faith, ceased to be a mere appellation and became an honorific designation that suited him alone. "Christ" eventually became part of the primitive kerygma, as 1 Cor 15:3 shows: "*Christ* died for our sins according to the scriptures."

Because that inscription was a Roman formulation, which was contemptuous of the Jewish people, its historicity is scarcely to be contested. If it had been invented by Christians, they may have used Χριστός, but they would scarcely have called their leader "the King of the Jews."

(4) There is a further Christian use of the title that calls for special consideration, namely, the suffering Messiah, which appears in the Lukan Gospel and Acts. In the Old Testament one reads about the Suffering Servant in the Fourth Servant Song (Isa 52:13–53:12), which *per se* has no messianic connotation, even though subsequent references to the Song in the developing Jewish tradition so interpret it, but nothing is read about a suffering Messiah.[21] Even in the Similitudes of *1 Enoch*, where there is the oldest messianic interpretation of the Servant, no mention is made of a suffering Son of Man or a suffering Messiah.[22] In Lukan theology, however, Jesus is presented as a suffering Messiah: "Was not the Messiah bound to suffer all this before entering his glory?" So the risen Christ asks the disciples on the road to Emmaus on the evening of the day of the discovery of his empty tomb (Luke 24:26). Again, "this is what stands written, 'the Messiah shall suffer and rise from the dead'" (Luke 24:46).[23] Moreover, during one of his Temple discourses, Peter announces that God raised Jesus from the dead and "has thus brought to fulfillment what he announced long ago

---

wording differs slightly in each: Matt 27:37; Luke 23:38; John 19:19. The quoted Markan form preserves the essence of the ἐπιγραφή, but the differences, though slight, should caution us about would-be "historical" judgments.

21. *Pace* R. A. Rosenberg, "The Slain Messiah in the Old Testament," *ZAW* 99 (1987) 259-61, who claims that the doctrine is found in Dan 9:26 and Zech 12:10-11. See p. 63 above.

22. See p. 87 above.

23. Luke, however, never tells us where it so "stands written," as he uses a standard introductory formula when citing Old Testament passages. See J. A. Fitzmyer, *The Gospel According to Luke (X-XXIV)*. AB 28A (Garden City: Doubleday, 1985) 1583-84.

through all the prophets, that his Messiah would suffer" (Acts 3:18). See further Acts 17:3a; 26:23. The idea of a suffering Messiah, however, is found nowhere in the Old Testament or in any Jewish literature prior to or contemporaneous with the New Testament. It is a Christian conception that goes beyond the Jewish messianic tradition.[24] This is true despite what Luke writes in 24:27, 46 about "Moses," "all the prophets," and "all the scriptures." These passages are examples of Luke's global christological understanding of the message of the Old Testament and of his favorite hyperbole ("all" the prophets, "all" the scriptures).

Luke undoubtedly developed his idea of Jesus as the "suffering Messiah" from the early gospel tradition that is attested in passages such as Mark 8:31, where, immediately after Peter's confession of Jesus as "the Messiah," he "began to teach them that the *Son of Man* had to *suffer* many things . . . ." From such a pre-Lukan tradition about a suffering Son of Man, Luke developed his own theologoumenon of the suffering Messiah (παθητὸς ὁ χριστός, Acts 26:23). It is, moreover, important to note that it is only Luke in the New Testament that has such a messianic conception.

(5) In the New Testament Χριστός is predicated of Jesus along with other titles, as we have seen in some of the quotations already used above:

(a) Along with Κύριος, "Lord," as in Acts 2:36 (quoted above), so that he becomes "Christ the Lord" (Luke 2:11), "(the/our) Lord Jesus Christ" (e.g., 1 Thess 5:9; Rom 1:7; 5:1; 1 Cor 1:2; 8:6; 2 Cor 1:2; Gal 1:3; Acts 11:17; 15:26); "Jesus Christ our Lord" (e.g., Rom 1:4; 1 Cor 1:9); or "Christ Jesus our Lord" (Rom 6:23; 1 Cor 15:31); "reverence Christ as Lord" (1 Pet 3:15). Cf. Jude 4, 17, 25.

(b) Along with ὁ υἱὸς τοῦ θεοῦ, "Son of God" (Matt 16:16 [cited above]; John 11:27: Martha's expression of belief, "I have believed that you are the Messiah, the Son of God, he who is coming into the world"; John 20:31: "These things have been written that you may believe that Jesus is the Messiah, the Son of God"). Also 2 Cor 1:19; 1 John 4:15.[25] This is the *distinctively Christian collocation* of the two titles, because ὁ υἱὸς τοῦ θεοῦ is not found predicated of anyone called משיח or χριστός in the narrow sense earlier than these New Testament instances, despite the Old Testa-

---

24. See Str-B, 2:273-99, who cite only Jewish sources that come from several centuries later than the Lukan writings, when they speak of "die alte Synagoge."

25. See also the variant reading in Codex Bezae (D) of Luke 23:35: "Save yourself if you are the Son of God, if you are the Messiah."

ment and LXX background that one might cite for this use of this title (e.g., Ps 2:2, 7). Moreover, even in the Qumran text that uses the title "Son of God" (4Q246), there is no accompanying mention of "Messiah."[26]

(c) Along with ἐκλεκτός, "Elect One, Chosen One" (Luke 23:35, 37: "God's Messiah, His Chosen One . . . the King of the Jews" [part of the mockery of the leaders and Roman soldiers]).

(d) Along with ὁ βασιλεὺς Ἰσραήλ, "King of Israel" (Mark 15:32: "Let the Messiah, the King of Israel, come down from the cross!").[27]

(e) Along with ὁ δίκαιος, "the Righteous One" (1 John 2:1: "we have an advocate with the Father, Jesus Christ, the Righteous One"; Acts 3:14; cf. 7:52; 22:14; 1 Pet 3:18: "Christ also died for sins once for all, the righteous for the unrighteous").[28]

(f) Along with σωτήρ, "Savior" (Luke 2:11: "A Savior has been born to you today in the town of David; he is the Messiah, the Lord!"). Cf. 2 Tim 1:10; Titus 1:4; 2 Pet 1:1, 11; 2:20; 3:18.

The Christian predication of multiple titles of the individual, Jesus of Nazareth, has a precedent in the use of four titles in the Similitudes of *1 Enoch* for the figure who will judge humanity along with the Lord of Spirits,[29] and one of them is "Messiah" in the narrow sense.

(6) Christian writers apply to Jesus a number of Old Testament sayings that speak either of a coming or future David or of the everlasting duration of his dynasty, but now they use them explicitly of the Messiah, which was not so in the Old Testament. This is a Christian interpretation of such Old Testament passages. For example:

(a) Ezek 37:25 speaks of a coming "David my servant as their prince forever," without calling him מָשִׁיחַ, and Ps 89:37(Eng. 36) tells of David's "offspring (that) shall endure forever, and his throne as long as the sun before Me." Now the Fourth Evangelist depicts a crowd saying to Jesus, "We have heard from the law that the Messiah remains for ever" (John 12:34). Thus the Christian evangelist predicates explicitly of the Messiah what was only affirmed of a future David or his dynasty, ironically enough, putting the predication on the lips of Jews who object to what Jesus has been saying to them.

---

26. See pp. 104-5 above.

27. See also John 1:49 (in close proximity to John 1:41).

28. See H. Dechent, "Der 'Gerechte' — eine Bezeichnung für den Messias," *TSK* 100 (1928) 439-43.

29. See p. 86 above.

(b) Ps 2:2 speaks of "kings of the earth (that) have drawn up in hostile array, and rulers (that) have gathered together against the LORD and His Anointed," referring to an unnamed historical king on David's throne, but in Acts 4:26-27 Jerusalem Christians pray to God and apply the words of the psalm to Herod, Pilate, Gentiles, and peoples of Israel who have reacted "against your holy servant Jesus, whom You anointed." This Christian application thus gives an explicit messianic connotation to the words of the psalm. See also Heb 1:5; Rev 11:15b.

(c) Ps 45:8(Eng. 7), which is a royal psalm composed as nuptial ode for the marriage of some Davidic king, recognizes that God has blessed the king: "Therefore God, your God, has anointed you with the oil of gladness above your peers." This verse is quoted explicitly in Heb 1:9 as part of the author's argument to show the privileged status of Jesus as God's "Son," who ranks above the prophets of old and even the angels. It thus gives to that psalm a new messianic referent.

(d) Ps 110:1 is part of a "Psalm of David," which promises victory to an enthroned king: "The LORD says to my Lord, 'Sit at my right hand.'" The last part of Jesus' answer to the High Priest in Mark 14:62 alludes to this verse when he says, "You will see the Son of Man seated at the right hand of Power, and coming with the clouds of heaven." Jesus has just admitted that he is "the Messiah, the Son of the Blessed," and so he gives a Christian messianic meaning to this verse of Psalm 110. He also alludes to Dan 7:13, "with the clouds of heaven there came one like a son of man, and he came to the Ancient of Days," giving to "son of man" likewise a Christian messianic sense. Moreover, recall the debate of Jesus with Pharisees (or Scribes) about the Messiah and the meaning of Ps 110:1 in Matt 22:41-45; Mark 12:35-37; Luke 20:41-44; and the way Peter uses it in Acts 2:34.

(e) Isa 61:1, where Trito-Isaiah speaks of "the Spirit of the LORD" anointing the prophet and sending him to preach the good news to the poor, etc., becomes in the Lukan Gospel part of the programmatic scene of Jesus' ministry, as he begins it in the synagogue of Nazareth on a Sabbath (Luke 4:18). Despite what some commentators say about the use of Isa 61:1-2 there, it does not depict Jesus as the Isaian Servant (because that passage in Isaiah is not part of a Servant Song) or as a Davidic Messiah (despite the anointing of the LORD's Spirit). It is rather a prophetic anointing and falls in line with the use in the Old Testament and the Qumran texts of מָשִׁיחַ for prophets. Even though מָשִׁיחַ in Ps 105:15 and 1 Chr 16:22 is not a certain title for prophets, its use for them in Qumran literature is clear, as we have seen.[30] Recall also 11QMelch (11Q13) 1-4 ii 18, which mentions והמבשר [ח]הרו[ן] משיח [אה]הו, "and the herald i[s] the one anointed of the Spirit,"[31] which likewise shows that the term could be used for others than kings and priests. Cf. Acts 10:38.

(f) See §2 above, where Pss 132:11 and 16:10 are used similarly in Acts 2:29-31.

(7) Such New Testament passages thus give an added Christian meaning to the verses of the Old Testament that they quote or allude to, as the verses are applied to him whom Christians acknowledge as the Messiah of Jewish expectation. They are merely part of the varied allusions to Old Testament passages that add a Christian nuance even beyond the messianic connotation. This added meaning is what traditionally has been called "the spiritual sense," which differs from the literal religious sense of Old Testament passages in that it gives them a "plus" meaning, a christological meaning which they do not have in the Hebrew Scriptures.

It is also the sense that reckons with the Christian canon of Scripture. Such a recognition is important, because it assures not only the literal meaning of the Hebrew Scriptures, which Christians have to acknowledge in the same way that Jewish readers do, but then reckons also with the meaning that has been given to such Scriptures by the Christ-event, which Jewish readers might understand but with which they would not agree.

---

30. See pp. 99-101 above.

31. See F. García Martínez et al., *Qumran Cave 11.II: 11Q2-18, 11Q20-31.* DJD 23 (Oxford: Clarendon, 1998) 225 + pl. XXVII.

CHAPTER 9

The Use of Messiah in the Mishnah, Targums, and Other Rabbinic Writings

Expressions of Jewish expectation of the coming of a Messiah continued along with the emergence of the Christian belief in Jesus of Nazareth as the Messiah. In the Jewish literature that dates from the period after the destruction of the Second Temple (A.D. 70) and especially from the second Christian century and later, one finds a continuation of that expectation in multiple forms. In the time of the Tanna'im (A.D. 1-200) and that of the Amora'im (A.D. 200-500) and Ge'onim (A.D. 500–), it continues not only in a political sense (in which the Messiah is thought of as a king, who would subdue the enemies of Israel and restore its kingship and rebuild the Temple), but also in a spiritual sense (in which he would do away with idolatry and sin and establish righteousness and justice). These notions were found at times in the earlier writings that have been discussed in chapter 7. Striking indeed about the development in these latter periods is the absence of any recorded saying about a Messiah from one of the Tanna'im, as J. Klausner has noted.[1] This does not mean that these Sages rejected all messianism, but rather, as Klausner continues, that the Scribes and the early Tanna'im, like the disciples of Hillel, who had no love of the Roman occupiers, "were so convinced of the great importance of the study of the Law that by comparison all political ambitions seemed to them of small significance — especially since these could not possibly be achieved to the extent pictured by the bold Messianic imagination."[2]

1. See J. Klausner, *The Messianic Idea in Israel* (New York: Macmillan, 1955; London: Allen and Unwin, 1956) 392.
2. Klausner, *The Messianic Idea in Israel*, 393.

Grief over the destruction of Jerusalem and its Temple in A.D. 70, however, gave rise to a new hope, not only in a political sense (of vengeance against the Romans, which manifested itself momentarily in the Second Revolt of the Jews against Rome under Simon ben Kosiba, who was regarded as Messiah by Rabbi Aqiba, even though Simon was not of Davidic descent), but also in a spiritual sense (of rebuilding Jerusalem and its Temple and of the restoration and redemption of its people).

(1) One of the oldest expressions of this hope in such Jewish literature occurs in an ancient prayer that every Jew was expected to recite three times a day, the התפלה (hat-Tĕphillāh), "The Prayer," or עמידה ('Amîdāh), or שמונה עשרה (Šĕmôneh 'Eśrēh), "Eighteen (Blessings)," which is extant in two forms (Babylonian and Palestinian) and dates from *ca.* A.D. 80-120. Blessing 14 of the Palestinian form prays that God will show His mercy to Israel in the Messiah of the house of David:

> Be gracious, O LORD, our God, in Your great mercy, to Israel, Your people, and to Jerusalem, Your city; to Zion, the abode of Your glory; to Your Temple and Your habitation; and to the monarchy of the house of David, Your righteous Messiah (מלכות בית דוד משיחך צדקך). Blessed are You, LORD, God of David, who built Jerusalem![3]

Although the Prayer mentions the Messiah, its major blessing is invoked on the people of Israel, the house of David, and Jerusalem.[4]

(2) *The Mishnah and the Tosephtah.* The Hebrew word משנה, *mišnāh*, means "repetition" and denotes the repeating of the unwritten law that was handed down in Judaism over the centuries to be "a fence around the Law" (*m. 'Abot* 1:1), i.e., around the written Law of Moses. This unwritten law or oral tradition of interpreting the written law was ascribed to the *Tannā'îm* ("Repeaters"). It was codified or put in writing eventually under Rabbi Judah the Prince ca. A.D. 200-220. The Mishnah

---

3. See S. Schechter, "Genizah Specimens," *JQR* 10 (1897-98) 654-59, esp. 656-57; G. Dalman, *Messianische Texte aus der nachkanonischen jüdischen Literatur für den akademischen Gebrauch* (Leipzig: Hinrichs, 1898) 300. Cf. R. Kimelman, "The Messiah of the Amidah: A Study in Comparative Messianism," *JBL* 116 (1997) 313-20.

4. For other ancient Jewish prayers that mention the expected Messiah, see A. S. van der Woude, "χρίω" *TDNT* 9:521-22; also the prayer of R. Aqiba recorded in *m. Pesaḥ.* 10:6, which sums up the hopes of restoration and redemption, but does not mention a Messiah. R. Aqiba himself died as a martyr in the persecution of emperor Hadrian, who put an end to the Second Revolt (*b. Sanh.* 12a; *b. Ber.* 61b).

serves as the fundamental document of a postbiblical Judaism that grew out of the Pharisaism of pre-70, being a collection of interpretive legal opinions that on occasion also records something historical or apocalyptic.

Related to the Mishnah is תוספתא, *tôsephtāh*, "addition, supplement," which has gathered other items of the oral tradition that were not included in the Mishnah by Rabbi Judah the Prince, but are closely related to it. These additional traditions were codified ca. A.D. 300.

(a) The legal character and concern of the Mishnah, however, may explain, in part at least, why there are only two occurrences of the title "Messiah" in all of its sixty-three tractates,[5] and in the first it is not ascribed to anyone in particular, but is only mentioned by "the Sages." In *m. Ber.* 1:5 one reads: "It is written, 'That you may remember the day that you came out of the land of Egypt all the days of your life.' . . . The Sages say, 'The days of your life' [means] this world only, but 'all the days of your life' includes the Days of the Messiah" (וחכמים אומרים ימי חייך העולם הזה כל ימי חייך להביא לימות המשיחה).[6] This is an isolated reference to an awaited Messiah of the eschaton, which does not tell us much about what the expectation meant at this time.

(b) In *m. Soṭah* 9:15 one reads: "With the footprints of the Messiah (בעקבות המשיח), presumption increases, and dearth reaches its height; the vine yields its fruit, but wine becomes expensive; the kingdom falls into heresy, and there is none to utter reproof."[7] This is meant to describe the wretched collapse of the social and economic order in Israel prior to the coming of the eschatological Messiah. From these two instances one can see that messianism has played only a minor role in the early postbiblical tradition found in the Mishnah.[8] *"In the whole Jewish Messianic literature of the Tannaitic period there is no trace of the 'suffering Messiah.'"*[9]

---

5. The Hebrew word משיח is used, however, also as an adjective: of the "anointed" High Priest in *m. Meg.* 1:9; *m. Mak.* 2:6; *m. Hor.* 2:1, 2, 3, 7; 3:4; or of one "anointed" to lead Israel in battle in *m. Soṭah* 7:2; 8:1; *m. Mak.* 2:6.

6. O. Holtzmann, *Die Mischna* I/1: *Berakot* (Giessen: Töpelmann, 1912) 44-45.

7. H. Bietenhard, *Die Mischna* III/6: *Soṭa* (Giessen: Töpelmann, 1956) 178-79. Cf. J. Neusner, *Messiah in Context: Israel's History and Destiny in Formative Judaism* (Philadelphia: Fortress, 1984) 25-30.

8. S. Mowinckel does not even mention these two Mishnaic passages.

9. Klausner, *Messianic Idea*, 405 (his emphasis). Klausner refers for support to D. Castelli, *Il Messia secondo gli Ebrei*, 220-24.

(c) The same minor role of messianism is noted also in the related body of writings called the Tosephtah. The Messiah is mentioned occasionally in it, e.g., as it speaks of "the days of the Messiah." Thus in *t. Ber.* 1:10 it adds to *m. Ber.* 1:5 a comment on Deut 16:3:

> Ben Zoma said to the Sages, "But does one mention the exodus from Egypt in the days of the Messiah? For has it not already been said, 'Therefore, look! Days are coming,' says the LORD, 'when men shall no longer say, "As the LORD lives who brought the Israelites up out of the land of Egypt," but rather, "As the LORD lives who brought up and led the descendants of the house of Israel out of the north country [and out of all the countries where he had driven them]"'" (Jer 23:7-8).[10]

These few messianic references in the Mishnah and Tosephtah stand in stark contrast to the numerous instances in the targums where the Messiah has been introduced, i.e., in writings that begin to develop almost at the same time. It is, however, wrong to use such targumic evidence to explain Mishnaic passages, as does C. A. Evans in his criticism of Neusner.[11] The targums, being Aramaic translations of most of the books of the Hebrew Scriptures, are an entirely different literary genre, which developed separately in ancient Judaism and have little connection with the rabbinic legal tradition that is preserved in the Mishnah, Tosephtah, and the subsequent Talmuds that developed from them. Although it is a debatable issue, the targums may even have emerged from different forms of Judaism, because

---

10. K. H. Rengstorf, *Die Tosefta, Seder I: Zeraim.* Rabbinische Texte I/1 (Stuttgart: Kohlhammer, 1983) 7; E. Lohse und G. Mayer, *Die Tosefta, Seder I: Zeraim übersetzt und erklärt.* Rabbinische Texte I/1.1 (Stuttgart: Kohlhammer, 1999) 13-14. Cf. Neusner, *Messiah in Context,* 54-55.

11. See C. A. Evans, "Mishna and Messiah 'in Context': Some Comments on Jacob Neusner's Proposals," *JBL* 112 (1993) 267-89. Cf. the reply of J. Neusner, "The Mishna in Philosophical Context and out of Canonical Bounds," *JBL* 112 (1993) 291-304. Although I tend to agree with Evans that the Mishnah "is not a worldview, a philosophy of history, or an apocalypse" (p. 268) and that Neusner "wants the Mishna to be something that it is not" (p. 278), I find in Evans's use of the targumic messianic passages no evidence whatsoever for the contribution that he claims the targums make to the understanding "of the messianic hope, in the context of the Mishna and in Judaism of this period" (278). Those targumic passages reveal another kind of Judaism, and Neusner is certainly right in speaking of "the Judaism of the Mishna" (p. 297) and keeping it distinct from various other forms of Judaism, such as that involving Rabbi Aqiba and the Messiah, about which one learns only from the much later Jerusalem Talmud.

the earliest instances of them are found among the scrolls used at least by the Essenes of Qumran, if they were not copied or produced by them.

Many have been the attempts to explain the paucity of messianic references in the Mishnah,[12] but that aspect of these problematic references does not concern us here. From the meager Mishnaic evidence, we may pass on to the targumic, where the situation is quite different.

(3) *Pentateuchal Targums.* The targum, as an Aramaic translation of the Hebrew Scriptures, was composed to record a fixed tradition of interpretation, a written record dating in general from the Amoraic period. It was as much a literary production as the Hebrew MT itself, and it cannot be said to have been composed merely in a colloquial or "spoken" form of the language as opposed to a "literary" form, as some have often claimed. The purpose of the targum was to assure an acceptable reading of the Scriptures which left the original intact. That is why the Hebrew was read first and then accompanied by an Aramaic version of it; and then in some copies of the targum each verse translated was preceded by a lemma of the first Hebrew words of the verse. The targum was never used alone, but always along with the Hebrew original that it rendered, even if copies of the targum are found without the Hebrew lemmata. It does not represent a random collection of stories or homilies, even if at times one finds halakhic or haggadic insertions in the translations.[13] In the targums of the Pentateuch, there are two traditions of interpretation, one Palestinian, the other Babylonian. The former is found in *Targum Neofiti 1* (hereafter *Neof*), the *Fragmentary Targum* (sometimes called *Targum Yerushalmi II* [hereafter *Frg*]), and in a later inferior and very expansive form in *Targum Pseudo-Jonathan* (sometimes called *Targum Yerushalmi I* [hereafter *PsJ*]). The Babylonian tradition is preserved in *Targum Onqelos* (hereafter *Onq*) in its extant form; even though it may have originated in a Palestinian tradition, it seems to have undergone redaction in Babylonia in the fourth/fifth century A.D. — again, a debated and controversial matter. In any case, all these classic targums are products of a Jewish tradition as it existed in the Christian period. The most literal and oldest of them is *Targum*

---

12. See, e.g., van der Woude, *TDNT* 9:522; Neusner, *Messiah in Context*, 17-78, esp. 30; *Foundations of Judaism* (Philadelphia: Fortress, 1989) 36-57.

13. See further D. M. Golomb, *A Grammar of Targum Neofiti*. HSM 34 (Chico: Scholars, 1985) 2-8 ("The Nature of Targum"); P. V. M. Flesher, "The Targumim in the Context of Rabbinic Literature," in J. Neusner, *Introduction to Rabbinic Literature*. ABRL (New York: Doubleday, 1994) 611-29.

Onqelos, which may stem originally from the mid-third century,[14] and which is usually regarded as the official or authoritative targum of the Mosaic Law. The other three pentateuchal targums, *Fragmentary Targum, Targum Neofiti 1,* and *Targum Pseudo-Jonathan,* in their final form all date from considerably later times.[15]

There are many passages in the different targums where the Aramaic term משיחא occurs, and they are often simply a literal rendering of Hebrew משיח and differ little from the meaning of the Hebrew form. As such they are not important for this discussion, since they reveal no difference in meaning or development. There are, however, many other instances of משיחא that are important, more than can be cited here.[16] So I shall include mainly those passages that seem important for this discussion. I begin with the pentateuchal targums, even though the Hebrew term משיח never occurs in the MT of the Pentateuch, because its Aramaic counterpart משיחא (*mĕšîḥā'*) has been introduced a number of times into these targums.

Some older targums from pre-Christian times were found among the Qumran scrolls, and one of them is a small fragment of an Aramaic version of Leviticus,[17] which shows that a pentateuchal targum was al-

---

14. See Neusner, *Messiah in Context,* 240: "One Targum, that bearing the name of Onqelos, cites passages from the Mishnah. So Targum Onqelos may be assumed to have been completed after ca. A.D. 200 and to fall within the rabbinic framework." Some scholars try to claim a date for it in the second century or earlier, but now that we have a good body of Palestinian Aramaic from the first centuries B.C. and A.D., it has become clear that the language of *Tg. Onqelos* cannot be so early. So it is good to see Neusner implicitly recognizing that.

15. For a balanced discussion of the targumim, see P. S. Alexander, "Targum, Targumim," *ABD,* 6:320-31; also A. D. York, "The Dating of Targumic Literature," *JSJ* 5 (1974) 49-62. Cf. M. H. Goshen-Gottstein, "The 'Third Targum' on Esther and Ms. Neofiti 1," *Bib* 56 (1975) 301-29.

Cf. M. McNamara, *The New Testament and the Palestinian Targum to the Pentateuch.* AnBib 27 (Rome: Biblical Institute, 1966), but use with caution what he says about the date of "the Palestinian Targum to the Pentateuch," and note his failure to realize that there are multiple Palestinian targums, not just one.

16. Most of them can be found in S. H. Levey, *The Messiah: An Aramaic Interpretation* (Cincinnati: Hebrew Union College, 1974). See, however, my review of this book in *JBL* 94 (1975) 473-77.

17. See J. T. Milik, "Targum du Lévitique," *Qumrân Grotte 4.II ii: Tefillin, Mezuzot et Targums (4Q128-4Q157).* DJD 6 (Oxford: Clarendon, 1977) 86-89 + pl. XXVIII. The fragment contains an Aramaic translation of Lev 16:12-15, 18-21. Besides 4QtgLev (4Q156), there are also two other fragmentary targums among the Qumran texts: (1) 4QtgJob (4Q157), which is pub-

ready in existence among some pre-Christian Palestinian Jews. The passages preserved on the fragment make no mention of a Messiah, even though the Jews who used this targum were those who had a live messianic expectation.

The following passages in pentateuchal targums mentioning משיחא are important:

(a) *Gen 3:15:* In the MT, this verse reads: "I will put enmity between you and the woman, and between your offspring and hers; it shall bruise your head, and you shall snap at its heel."[18] *Onq* renders this verse without mentioning a "Messiah,"[19] but the targums *PsJ, Frg,* and *Neof* give a fuller version, describing how the offspring of the woman, if faithful to the *Tôrāh* (Law of Moses), will smite the head of the serpent (or kill it). They end by telling how the descendants of the woman are "destined to make peace (with one another) at the end, in the days of the King Messiah" (ועתידין הינון למיעבד שפיותא בעיקבא ביומי מלכא משיחא, *PsJ*).[20]

---

lished in Milik, 90; and (2) 11QtgJob (11Q10), which is found in its latest published form in F. García Martínez et al., *Qumran Cave 11.II: 11Q2-18, 11Q20-31.* DJD 23 (Oxford: Clarendon, 1998) 79-180 + pls. IX-XXI. The preliminary edition of the latter was edited by J. P. M. van der Ploeg and A. S. van der Woude, *Le targum de Job de la Grotte XI de Qumrân* (Leiden: Brill, 1971).

18. See pp. 27-29 above for the meaning of this verse in the MT.

19. See A. Sperber, *The Bible in Aramaic Based on Old Manuscripts and Printed Texts,* 1: *The Pentateuch according to Targum Onkelos* (Leiden: Brill, 1959) 5. Cf. B. Grossfeld, *The Targum Onqelos to Genesis.* Aramaic Bible 6 (Wilmington: Michael Glazier, 1988) 46.

20. There are slight differences in wording among the three targums, but they basically agree with the words cited from *PsJ.* For this version, see E. G. Clarke et al., *Targum Pseudo-Jonathan of the Pentateuch: Text and Concordance* (Hoboken: Ktav, 1984) 4; M. Maher, *Targum Pseudo-Jonathan.* Aramaic Bible 1B (Collegeville: Liturgical, 1992) 27.

In Gen 21:21 of this targum, the unnamed "wife" of the MT is named first as עדישא, "Adisha," and then as פטימא, "Fatima," i.e., by the names of the wife and daughter of Mohammed. Moreover, Exod 26:9; 36:16 mention explicitly "the six orders of the Mishnah" (שית סדרי מתניתא), and Num 24:19 mentions Rome and Constantinople. So the Jewish tradition that is preserved in the final form of this targum comes from a relatively late date, the second half of the seventh century, after the rise of Islam, even though some of its tradition may be older (which no one has been able to sort out).

For *Frg,* see M. L. Klein, *The Fragment-Targums of the Pentateuch According to Their Extant Sources.* AnBib 76/1-2 (Rome: Biblical Institute. 1980), 1:46; 2:7; cf. 1:127; 2:91. As to the date of *Frg,* Klein admits that the Fragmentary Targums "are substantially later than the complete" Palestinian targums (1:25), even though they may contain some elements that date from "the 2nd century C.E." The trouble is that no one can discern clearly which elements do so date.

For *Neof,* see A. Díez Macho, *Neophyti 1: Targum palestinense MS de la Biblioteca*

Whereas the MT promised only enduring hostility between the woman's descendants and the offspring of the serpent, these targums now promise "a remedy" (אסו) for the woman's descendants, and then final peace. This is, therefore, a development in messianic expectation beyond the meaning of the Hebrew MT, which was wholly nonmessianic. Note too the new added title, מלכא, "King," which becomes a frequent appellative of the Messiah in the Jewish interpretive tradition of this late period.[21]

(b) *Gen 35:21:* The MT of this passage reads, "Israel [i.e., Jacob] journeyed on and pitched his tent beyond Migdal-Eder" (*or* the Tower of Eder).[22] In the Aramaic translation, this verse becomes: "Jacob moved on and spread his lodging beyond the Tower of Eder, the place from which the King Messiah is destined to reveal himself at the end of days" (ונטל יעקב ופרס משכניה מן להלא למוגדלא דעדר אתרא דהתמן עתיד דאיתגלי מלכא משיחא בסוף יומייא), *PsJ*).[23] This embellishment of the MT preserves a late Jewish tradition about the place whence the Messiah would appear.

(c) *Gen 49:1:* The MT of this verse reads: "Then Jacob summoned his sons and said, 'Gather together, and I shall tell what may befall you at the end of days.'" Whereas *Onq* renders the verse literally in Aramaic, the invi-

---

Vaticana, Tomo I Génesis . . . Textos y estudios 7 (Madrid: Consejo Superior de Investigaciones Científicas, 1968). Although Díez Macho maintained that this targum "pertenece ya a la época neotestamentaria" (p. 95*), that judgment is certainly wrong. The kind of Aramaic in which it is written is of a date much later than the Aramaic texts found among the Dead Sea Scrolls, which can be said to be of the New Testament period. That of Neofiti comes from ca. 400-500 years later. Moreover, the targumic style is much later than that of *Onq*; being quite paraphrastic, it resembles rather the style of *Frg* and *PsJ*, even if it does not have all the additional embellishments of the latter.

21. See Levey, *The Messiah*, 3. He says about this verse that "the Targum's influence on Christian Messianic thought on this passage is unmistakable." That may be true of patristic messianic interpretation of a certain date, but there is no evidence of such influence on the New Testament itself, where the only allusions to Gen 3:15 are generic in Luke 10:19 and Rev 12:14-17. Cf. M. Pérez Fernández, *Tradiciones mesiánicas en el Targum palestinense: Estudios exegéticos.* Institución San Jerónimo 12 (Valencia: Institución san Jerónimo, 1981) 31-94.

22. "Tower of Eder" is a place between Hebron and Bethlehem, in which Jacob camped after the death of Rachel. It means lit., "tower of the flock," a sense that is used as a name for Mount Zion in Mic 4:8; see 4(q) below.

23. Clarke, *Targum Pseudo-Jonathan of the Pentateuch*, 43; Maher, *Targum Pseudo-Jonathan: Genesis*, 121. *Onq, Frg*, and *Neof* have nothing similar, translating the Hebrew simply into Aramaic. Levey (*The Messiah*, 4) interprets "beyond" in a temporal sense, "a reflection of the history of the Jew," who will wander "until the coming of the Messiah."

tation itself to gather is expanded considerably in *Neof, Frg,* and *PsJ,* but
only in the latter two is the Messiah mentioned:

> Then Jacob summoned his sons and said to them, "Purify yourselves
> from uncleanness, and I shall make known to you hidden secrets, con-
> cealed ends, the giving of a reward to the righteous, and the punish-
> ment of the wicked, and what is the comfort of Eden." The twelve
> tribes of Israel were gathering themselves together, surrounding the
> golden bed on which he lay. As soon as the glory of the Shekinah of the
> LORD was revealed, the end-time, when the King Messiah was destined
> to come, was concealed from him (ומן דאיתגלי איקר שכינתא דייי
> קיצא דעתיד מלכא משיחא למיתי איתכסי מיניה), and therefore he
> said, "Come, and I shall declare to you what may befall you at the end
> of days." *(PsJ)*[24]

The passage is a good example of the still awaited Jewish Messiah, the date
of whose coming is not made known, and of the way eschatological teaching in Judaism gradually became "messianic."

(c) *Gen 49:10:* The MT reads, "A scepter shall not depart from Judah,
nor a mace from between his feet, until tribute comes to him, and his is the
obedience of peoples" (with the problematic clauses, עד כי־יבא שילה
ולו יקהת עמים).[25] Because שילה (*šîlōh*) was not understood correctly for
a long time, it is not surprising that a messianic interpretation was given to
that term in the targums:

(i) *Onq:* "The passing on of dominion shall not depart from the house
of Judah, nor a scribe ever from his children's children, until the Messiah
comes, to whom kingship belongs, and to him peoples will subject themselves (עד דייתי משיחא דדיליה היא מלכותא וליה ישתמעון עממיא).[26]

---

24. Clarke, *Targum Pseudo-Jonathan of the Pentateuch,* 61; Maher, *Targum Pseudo-Jonathan: Genesis,* 157. *Frg* has a slightly different form of the statement about the Messiah: "thinking that he would reveal to them all that is destined to come (about) at the end of the footsteps of the Messiah. As soon as it was revealed to him, it was concealed from him" (להון כל מא דעתיד למיתי בסוף עקבי משיחא מן דאיתגלי ליה איתכסי מיניה ‹סברין› דהוה מגלי). See Klein, *The Fragment-Targums of the Pentateuch,* 1:65; 2:30 (this variant is found in the Paris MS, but not in the Vatican MS).

25. On which, see pp. 70-71 above.

26. Sperber, *Bible in Aramaic,* 1:85; Grossfeld, *The Targum Onqelos to Genesis,* 158, 163. Cf. M. Aberbach and B. Grossfeld, *Targum Onqelos on Genesis 49.* SBL Aramaic Studies 1 (Missoula: Scholars, 1976) 12-15.

(ii) *Neof:* "Kings shall not cease (to be) from among those of the house of Judah, nor shall scribes who teach the law from the children of his children, until the time that the King Messiah shall come, to whom kingship belongs (עד זמן דייתי מלכא משיחא דדידיה היא מלכותא); to him all kingdoms shall subject themselves."[27]

(iii) *Frg:* "Kings and rulers shall not cease (to be) from among those of the house of Judah, nor scribes and teachers of the law from his children's children, until the time that the King who is the Messiah shall come, who is destined to arise from the house of Judah" (עד זמן דייתי מלכא דמשיחא דעתיד למיקום מדבית יהודה).[28]

(iv) *PsJ:* (As in *Frg,* then) ". . . from his offspring, until the time that the King Messiah will come, the young(est) of his sons, and because of him peoples shall be amalgamated" (עממיא עד זמן די ייתי מלכא משיחא זעיר בנוי ובדיליה יתימסון).[29] In each of these targums, then, *šîlōh* has become "the Messiah," to whom different roles are attributed. These roles are described further in targumic verses of the same chapter of Genesis, but the political sense of messianism is noteworthy in some of the targumic versions of this verse: the kingly role of the Messiah and the subjugation of peoples.

(d) *Gen 49:11-12:* In the MT, these verses describe the richness and fertility of the land belonging to Judah: "He ties his donkey to the vine, the foal of his ass to the vine-tendril; in wine he washes his garments, and his robes in the blood of grapes./His eyes are darker than wine, and his teeth whiter than milk." What was said there of Judah is now ascribed to the Messiah of v. 10, as he is said in the targums to enclose Israel in his city and teach its people the Law, while his garments shall be made of fine purple and crimson, and his land shall be rich. The Messiah himself, however, is not mentioned in vv. 11-12 of *Onq* or *Frg,*[30] but he appears in *Neof* thus:

How handsome is the King, the Messiah, who is destined to rise from among those of the house of Judah (מה יאי הוא מלכא משיחא

---

27. Díez Macho, *Neophyti 1: Génesis,* 331; M. McNamara, *Targum Neofiti 1: Genesis.* Aramaic Bible 1A (Collegeville: Liturgical, 1992) 219-20.

28. Klein, *The Fragment-Targums of the Pentateuch,* 1:66; 2:31 (only in the Paris MS).

29. Clarke, *Targum Pseudo-Jonathan of the Pentateuch,* 62; Maher, *Targum Pseudo-Jonathan: Genesis,* 158-59.

30. In *Frg,* however, v. 11 gives a symbolic warlike interpretation of the words as in the coming *Neof,* without mentioning the Messiah. Cf., however, A. Somekh, "Apologia messianica nel Targum Onqelos a *Genesi* 49," *Augustinianum* 28 (1988) 249-57.

דעתיד למיקם מן מדבית יהודה). He has girded his loins and has gone
forth to war against his enemies, to kill kings along with rulers; to
make mountains red with the blood of those slain, and valleys white
with the fat of their heroes . . . ./How much more handsome are the
eyes of the King, the Messiah, than pure wine (עיינוי דמלכא משיחא
מן חמרא זכוכא מה ייאיין); with them he does not look at exposed
nudity[31] or the shedding of innocent blood. His teeth are whiter than
milk; with them he does not eat what is stolen or robbed . . . .[32]

In *PsJ*, these verses are rendered in Aramaic very much in the same way,
with the clauses about the Messiah's handsomeness and eyes virtually
identical.[33] Such embellishments of the Hebrew text are characteristic of
these late targums. Noteworthy, however, is not only the military or political character of the Messiah, but also his being presented as a spiritual
model for the conduct of the faithful Jew who is expected to be chaste, not
a murderer, thief, or violent person.[34]

(e) *Exod 12:42:* The MT describes the Passover as a night of vigil: "It
was a night of watching for the LORD, to bring them out of the land of
Egypt; so on this same night it is a night of watching for the LORD, for all
the Israelites throughout their generations." This verse is translated literally into Aramaic in *Onq*, but the other three targums have an expanded
version that mentions four nights of watching that the Israelites must
keep. Of these, the form in *PsJ* is the shortest and does not mention the
Messiah, whereas both *Neof* and *Frg* (Vatican MS) have a fuller version,
mentioning the Messiah.

The four nights of watching: The first night was "when the *memra* of
the LORD was revealed to create the world."[35] The second was "when the

---

31. The text reads גילוי עריין, lit., "manifestation of what is uncovered." Levey (*The
Messiah,* 9) translates it "incestuous practice." The targum itself echoes Hab 1:13; Num 23:21,
as J. P. M. Walsh reminds me.

32. Díez Macho, *Neophyti 1: Génesis,* 331; McNamara, *Targum Neofiti 1: Genesis,* 220.

33. Clarke, *Targum Pseudo-Jonathan of the Pentateuch,* 82; Maher, *Targum Pseudo-
Jonathan: Genesis,* 159.

34. See Pérez Fernández, *Tradiciones mesiánicas en el Targum palestinense,* 95-169.

35. The Aramaic word מימרא, *mêmrāʾ,* "word, saying," is used in these late targums in
the sense of "the Word of God," i.e., the divine performative activity, an attempt to eliminate
an anthropomorphism in speaking of such activity of God. See further M. L. Klein, "The
Translation of Anthropomorphisms and Anthropopathisms in the Targumim," *Congress
Volume, Vienna 1980,* ed. J. A. Emerton. VTSup 32 (Leiden: Brill, 1981) 162-77, esp. 172-76.

memra of the LORD was revealed to Abram." The third was "when the *memra* of the LORD was revealed upon the Egyptians in the middle of the night." The fourth night will be:

> when the world will reach its time to be redeemed. Evildoers shall be destroyed, and yokes of iron shall be broken; and Moses shall go forth from the midst of the wilderness, and the King Messiah from the midst of Rome (ומשה יפוק מן גו מדברא ומלכא משיחא מן גו רומ'). This one shall lead at the head of the flock, and that one shall lead at the head of the flock, but the *memra* of the LORD shall be between both of them, and I and they shall proceed together. This is the night of Passover before the LORD: preserved and prepared for all the Israelites throughout their generations. *(Frg)*[36]

The translation in *Neof* is very similar, even if the wording is not always identical with that of *Frg*. The crucial clauses run thus in *Neof:* ומשה יסוק מן גו מדברא [ומלכא משיחא מן גו רומא], "and Moses shall go up from the midst of the desert, [and the King, the Messiah, from the midst of Rome]."[37]

This explanation of the fourth night of watching is unique in associating the King Messiah with a coming Moses, and casting them both as leaders of the Israelites. Since it is "the night of Passover before the LORD," one understands the association. It thus gives the Messiah a salvific role similar to that of the historical Moses, who delivered the Hebrews from Egyptian bondage. "The final drama of Israel's history [is] to be a re-enactment of the deliverance which marked the beginning of Israel's career as a nation."[38] In *Frg*, the Messiah shall come מן גו רומ', which is usually understood as "from Rome," i.e., from the homeland of Israel's quondam enemy.[39] "From Rome" may also be the meaning of מן גו רומא of *Neof*, but there רומא could mean "from the height," i.e., from on high (possibly an allusion to Dan 7:13). Puzzling in both targums is the first per-

---

36. See Klein, *The Fragment-Targums of the Pentateuch*, 1:167; 2:126.

37. See A. Díez-Macho, *Neophyti 1: Tomo II, Exodo* (Madrid: Consejo Superior de Investigaciones Científicas, 1970), 79; M. McNamara, *Targum Neofiti 1: Exodus*. Aramaic Bible 2 (Collegeville: Liturgical, 1994) 52. The bracketed words are missing in the body of the text of *Neof*, but added in a marginal gloss.

38. Levey, *The Messiah*, 13.

39. See Mowinckel, *He That Cometh*, 306.

sonal pronoun, ואנא והינון *(Frg)* or ואנה ואינון *(Neof)*, "and I and they." Who is the "I"? M. L. Klein takes it as "the LORD — a shift from the *memra* to the LORD Himself," but the translators of *Neof* consider it as "superfluous," saying that the text should read, "and they [Moses and the Messiah] shall proceed."[40]

(f) *Exod 40:9-11:* The MT reads, "You are to take the oil of anointing, anoint the tabernacle and all that is in it, and consecrate it and its furniture, and it will become holy. You are to anoint the altar of burnt offering and all its utensils and consecrate the altar, and the altar will become most holy. You are to anoint the laver and its base and consecrate it." In *PsJ* these verses are rendered thus:

> You are to take the oil of anointing, anoint the tabernacle and all that is in it, and consecrate it for the crown of the kingship of the house of Judah and the King Messiah who is destined to redeem Israel at the end of days (מטול כליל דמלכותא דבית ישראל ומלכא משיחא דעתיד למיפרק ית ישראל בסוף יומיא)./You are to anoint the altar of burnt offering and all its utensils and consecrate the altar, and the altar will become most holy for the crown of the priesthood of Aaron and his sons, and of Elijah the High Priest who is destined to be sent at the end of the exile (מטול כלילא דכהונתא דאהרן ובנוי ואליהו כהנא רבא דעתיד למשתלחא בסוף גלוובא)./You are to anoint the laver and its base and consecrate it for Joshua, your servant, chief of the Sanhedrin of his people, through whose hand the land of Israel is destined to be divided and from whom the Messiah, son of Ephraim, is to go forth, through whose hand the house of Israel is destined to conquer Gog and his aides at the end of days (דעל ידוי עתידה ארעא דישראל למיתפלגא ומשיחא בר אפרים דנפיק מיניה דעל ידוי עתידין בית ישראל למנצחא לגוג ולסיעתיה בסוף יומיא).[41]

In this late targumic passage, the tabernacle is interpreted as the Davidic dynasty, from which comes the royal Messiah destined to redeem Israel, whereas the altar is interpreted as the Aaronitic priesthood, and Elijah be-

40. See further R. Le Déaut, *La nuit pascale: Essai sur la signification de la Pâque juive à partir du Targum d'Exode XII 42.* AnBib 22 (Rome: Biblical Institute, 1963) 64-65, 279-307; Pérez Fernández, *Tradiciones mesiánicas en el Targum palestinense,* 171-209.

41. See Clarke, *Targum Pseudo-Jonathan of the Pentateuch,* 117-18; M. Maher, *Targum Pseudo-Jonathan: Exodus.* Aramaic Bible 2 (Collegeville: Liturgical, 1994) 273.

comes the High Priest, who takes over the role of the priestly Messiah of earlier times.[42] A new element appears as the laver is interpreted as Joshua of the northern tribe of Ephraim (Num 13:8), from whom is to come a Messiah, son of Ephraim.

This Messiah, son of Ephraim, has not been met before. He is sometimes said to be the same as the "Messiah, son of Joseph," mentioned in the later tradition of *b. Sukkah* 52a-b. Before the discovery of the Qumran texts, he and the Messiah, son of David, were those who made up "the doctrine of the two Messiahs" (to use C. C. Torrey's term, who also considered them as "two eternally appointed Messiahs, divine beings, destined to appear on earth at the end of the present age").[43] As such, they are not the same as the kingly Messiah and the priestly Messiah, known from the *Damascus Document* of the Cairo Genizah or Qumran texts. The Messiah, son of Ephraim, was regarded as the precursor of the Messiah, son of David, and a warrior who would conquer Gog (of Magog, the classic enemy of Israel [Ezekiel 38-39]), whereas the King Messiah, son of David, was the one to redeem Israel.[44]

(g) *Num 24:17:* The MT has this important verse of the fourth Oracle of Balaam, as he blesses the Israelites, "I see him, though not now; I behold him, though not close at hand: a star shall stride forth from Jacob, and a scepter shall arise from Israel; it shall smite the brows of Moab and the skulls of all the sons of Sheth."[45] An explicit messianic interpretation of this verse is given in *Onq* and *PsJ*, but not in *Frg* or *Neof*.

(i) In *Onq*, the verse reads, "I have seen him, but not now; I have perceived him, but he is not near; when a king shall arise out of Jacob and a Messiah shall be anointed out of Israel (כד יקום מלכא מיעקב ויתרבא משיחא מישראל), he shall slay the nobles of Moab and reign over all man-

---

42. According to *PsJ* of Exod 6:18, "Kohath lived to see Phinehas, who is Elijah the High Priest, who is destined to be sent to the exiles of Israel at the end of days." Phinehas was considered a descendant of Aaron.

43. See further Mowinckel, *He That Cometh*, 289-91; Levey, *The Messiah*, 16; Klausner, *The Messianic Idea in Israel*, 483-501; C. C. Torrey, "The Messiah Son of Ephraim," *JBL* 66 (1947) 253-77, esp. 253.

44. For the King Messiah involved with Gog and Magog, see *Frg* of Num 11:26 Vatican MS (Klein, *The Fragment-Targums of the Pentateuch*, 1:193-94; 2:152); *Neof* of Num 11:26 (Díez Macho, *Neophyti 1: Tomo IV, Números* [Madrid: Consejo Superior de Investigaciones Científicas, 1974] 109). Cf. Klausner, *The Messianic Idea in Israel*, 483-501.

45. See p. 71 above for problems in understanding the verse in the MT.

kind."[46] The star and the scepter are now given a personal identification, which would mean "the King Messiah," known from other targumic passages, and the verb in the last two clauses is singular (יקטיל and ישלוט), meaning that he is one person.[47]

(ii) In *PsJ*, the same idea is expressed more fully in different wording: "I see him, but not now; I gaze on him, but he is not near. When a mighty king from among those of the house of Jacob shall rule, and the Messiah and mighty scepter shall be anointed from Israel (כד ימלוך מליך תקיף מדבית יעקב ויתרבי משיחא ושיבט תקיף מישראל), he shall slay the nobles of Moab and bring to nought all the children of Sheth, the armies of Gog, which are destined to draw up battle ranks against Israel; and all their corpses shall fall before him."[48]

(iii) In *Frg*, the Aramaic version is more literal, and no Messiah is mentioned: "I see him, but he is not now; and now I gaze on him, but he is not near. A king from among those of the house of Jacob is destined to arise, a redeemer and ruler from the house of Israel; he shall slay the mighty of the Moabites and bring to nought all children of the East."[49] The text of *Neof* is almost identical with that of *Frg*.[50]

(h) *Deut 30:4:* The MT speaks of God gathering in the dispersed people of Israel: "If your banished ones will be at the end of the heavens, the LORD your God will gather you from there, and from there he will fetch you." In *PsJ*, this becomes: "If your dispersed ones be at the ends of the

46. Sperber, *The Bible in Aramaic*, 1:266; B. Grossfeld, *The Targum Onqelos to Leviticus and the Targum Onqelos to Numbers*. Aramaic Bible 8 (Wilmington: Michael Glazier, 1988) 138.

47. Whereas שת, "Sheth," in the MT reflects an old name for Moab, the targumist here has understood it as "Seth," the son of Adam (see Gen 4:25), and so the King Messiah shall reign over "all the sons of man" (כל בני אנשא).

48. Clarke, *Targum Pseudo-Jonathan of the Pentateuch*, 190; E. G. Clarke and S. Magder, *Targum Pseudo-Jonathan: Numbers*. Aramaic Bible 4 (Collegeville: Liturgical, 1995) 261.

49. Klein, *The Fragment-Targums of the Pentateuch*, 1:105 (Paris), 203 (Vatican); 2:77, 162.

50. Díez Macho, *Neophyti 1: Tomo IV, Números*, 239 (it adds at the end, "he shall bring to nought the lords of possessions"); M. McNamara, *Targum Neofiti 1: Numbers*. Aramaic Bible 4 (Collegeville: Liturgical, 1995) 140. Cf. G. Vermes, *Scripture and Tradition in Judaism: Haggadic Studies*, 2nd ed. StPB 4 (Leiden: Brill, 1973) 127-77; Pérez Fernández, *Tradiciones mesiánicas en el Targum palestinense*, 211-86; J. A. Lund, "Balaam's Third and Fourth Oracles in the Peshitta and Targums," in *Targum Studies*, 2: *Targum and Peshitta*, ed. P. V. M. Flesher. South Florida Studies in the History of Judaism 165 (Atlanta: Scholars, 1998) 75-92.

heavens, the *memra* of the LORD will gather you from there by the hand of Elijah the High Priest, and from there he will bring you near (to Himself) by the hand of the King Messiah."[51] This deliverance from exile and dispersion is to be accomplished by the two figures met above in the targum of Exod 40:9-10, by Elijah, again called "the High Priest," and the King Messiah, i.e., by a kingly and a priestly figure. Implied is the reunion of Israel and Judah.

These are the eight most important passages in the pentateuchal targums.[52] They show how the expectation of a Messiah was developing in the early Christian period well beyond that which was found in the pre-Christian Jewish literature. There is no longer a conviction of two Messiahs, one from Israel and one from Aaron. Rather there is the expectation of a King Messiah and of Elijah, now thought of as the High Priest. In the Old Testament, the latter was "the prophet" who would "come before the day of the LORD, the great and terrible day, to turn the hearts of fathers to their children and the hearts of children to their fathers" (Mal 3:23-24[Eng. 4:5-6]; cf. Sir 48:10).[53] Now, however, in these targums Elijah becomes a High Priest, who is awaited along with the King Messiah. So the idea of a kingly Messiah and a priestly Messiah has developed.

(4) *Targum Jonathan of the Prophets.* This targum covers both the Former and Latter Prophets of the Hebrew Scriptures.[54] It is attributed to Jonathan ben Uzziel, said to be a disciple of Hillel (see *b. Meg.* 3a) in the first century. The targum in its final form cannot be that early. Some date it about the same time as the *Tg. Onqelos* (mid-3d cent. A.D.), but it may be later than the Arab Conquest of Babylonia;[55] some speak of its formation

---

51. Clarke, *Targum Pseudo-Jonathan of the Pentateuch*, 246; E. G. Clarke and S. Magder, *Targum Pseudo-Jonathan: Deuteronomy.* Aramaic Bible 5B (Collegeville: Liturgical, 1998) 83.

52. See Levey, *The Messiah*, 14-28 for less important passages where משיחא occurs: Exod 17:16 *(PsJ)*; Num 11:26 *(Neof* and *Frg* [Vatican]); 23:21 *(PsJ)*; 24:7 *(Frg)*; 24:20, 24 *(PsJ)*; Deut 25:19 *(PsJ)*.

53. See pp. 53-54 above.

54. The "Former Prophets" are Joshua, Judges, 1-2 Samuel, and 1-2 Kings in the Hebrew Canon, whereas "Latter Prophets" are Isaiah, Jeremiah, Ezekiel, and the Twelve Minor Prophets. All the rest of the books of the Hebrew Canon, apart from the Torah (Pentateuch), belong to הכתובים, "the Writings" (*or* Hagiographa).

55. See S. H. Levey, "The Date of Targum Jonathan to the Prophets," *VT* 21 (1971) 186-96. Cf. P. Churgin, *Targum Jonathan to the Prophets.* YOSR 14 (New Haven: Yale University Press, 1927); repr. with L. Smolar and M. Aberbach, *Studies in Targum Jonathan to the*

in two stages. On occasion it too introduces the Messiah into passages that in the MT do not use מָשִׁיחַ and are nonmessianic.[56]

(a) *1 Sam 2:10:* In the MT, Hannah, who has given birth to Samuel, ends her prayer in Shiloh, saying, "Against them [the enemies of Israel] may He thunder from heaven, may the LORD judge the ends of the earth. May He give strength to His king and lift up the horn of His Anointed One." So Hannah prayed in the days when there was as yet no king in Israel. This verse of her prayer becomes in the targum, "May the LORD blast down from heaven upon them with a loud voice; may He exact avenging justice from Gog and the army of the violent nations that come with him from the ends of the earth. May He grant power to His king and magnify the kingdom of His Messiah" (וְיִתֵּן תּוּקְפָא לְמַלְכֵּיהּ וְיַרְבֵּי מַלְכוּת מְשִׁיחֵיהּ).[57] Whereas מְשִׁיחוֹ in the MT had to be translated "His Anointed One," meaning the historical king who was soon to be ruling over the people of Israel, מְשִׁיחֵיהּ in the targum takes on the nuance of "His Messiah," because of the historical context in which this targum has been composed, namely, in a period when the expectation of such a future anointed agent of God was quite vivid. Moreover, the mention of Gog, the classic enemy of Israel, and of his allies makes the military nuance important, as we have already seen in the targumic rendering of Exod 40:11; Num 24:17.[58]

(b) *2 Sam 22:32:* The MT depicts David uttering a hymn of praise when the LORD delivered him from the hand of his enemies, part of which says, "For who is God apart from the LORD, and who is a rock apart from our God?" This verse is rendered in Aramaic thus:

Prophets. Library of Biblical Studies (New York: Ktav, 1983) 229-380, esp. 263; B. Chilton, "Two in One: Renderings of the Book of Isaiah in Targum Jonathan," in *Writing and Reading the Scroll of Isaiah: Studies of an Interpretive Tradition,* ed. C. C. Broyles and C. A. Evans. VTSup 70/2 (Leiden: Brill, 1997) 547-62, esp. 547-49.

56. See P. Humbert, "Le Messie dans le targum des Prophètes," *RTP* 43 (1910) 420-27; 44 (1911) 5-46 [*non vidi*].

57. Sperber, *The Bible in Aramaic, 2: The Former Prophets according to Targum Jonathan* (Leiden: Brill, 1959) 97-98; cf. D. J. Harrington and A. J. Saldarini, *Targum Jonathan of the Former Prophets.* Aramaic Bible 10 (Wilmington: Michael Glazier, 1987) 1-6.

58. By contrast, one should look at the rather literal Aramaic rendering of 1 Sam 2:35, where מְשִׁיחִי occurs, but where it still means "my Anointed One," as in the MT. Even Levey (*The Messiah,* 36) admits, "It is uncertain whether this passage is Messianic, the Targumic text being vague." Nothing in it suggests the messianic nuance found in 1 Sam 2:10. Cf. the targumic rendering of 1 Sam 12:3-5 (מְשִׁיחֵיהּ means "His Anointed"); 16:6; 24:7, 11; 26:9, 11, 16, 23; 2 Sam 1:14, 16; 19:22.

Therefore because of the sign and the deliverance that You wrought for Your Messiah (בכין על נסא ופרקנא דתעביד למשיחך) and for the remnant of Your people who are left, all nations, peoples, and tongues shall confess and say, "There is no God except the LORD (לית אלה אלא יוי), for there is none apart from You." And Your people will say, 'There is no one who is mighty, save our God.'"[59]

The acknowledgement in this targumic verse, לית אלה אלא יוי, "There is no God except the LORD," which changes the questions of the MT into statements, sounds so much like the Muslim profession of monotheistic faith (*lā 'ilāha 'illa 'al-Lāh*, "No god except The God" [*or* "Allah"]) that the targumist seems to see "in the political and theological framework of the Moslems a pattern which might be acceptable in the Messianic age."[60]

(c) *2 Sam 23:1*: The MT records, "These are the last words of David: 'The utterance of David, son of Jesse, the utterance of the man God raised up, the Anointed of the God of Jacob, favorite of the sons of Israel.'" This summary becomes in the targum:

These are the words of the prophecy of David, which he prophesied about the end of the world, about the days of consolation that are destined to come. David son of Jesse said, "The utterance of the man anointed to messianic kingship by the *memra* of the God of Jacob (אימר גברא דמרבא למלכו משיח במימר אלהיה דיעקב), and the one appointed to recite in your lifetime the sweetness of the Psalms of Israel."[61]

Although משיח occurs here, it does not mean "Messiah," because it is describing David's own anointed status, and it has no bearing on "the days of consolation" destined to come.

(d) *2 Sam 23:3*: The MT continues David's words, "The God of Israel has spoken, the Rock of Israel has said to me, 'A ruler of mankind shall be righteous, ruling with the fear of God.'" This becomes in the targum, "David said, 'The God of Israel, the Mighty One of Israel, who has dominion

---

59. Sperber, *The Bible in Aramaic*, 2:204; cf. Harrington and Saldarini, *Targum Jonathan of the Former Prophets*, 202.

60. Levey, *The Messiah*, 39. This verse is the reason why Levey dates the targum after the Arab Conquest of Babylonia; see n. 55 above.

61. Sperber, *The Bible in Aramaic*, 2:206; Harrington and Saldarini, *Targum Jonathan of the Former Prophets*, 203.

over the sons of man, who judges the truth, spoke to me and promised to appoint for me the King, that is the Messiah, destined to arise and rule with the fear of the LORD'" (אמר למנאה לי מלכא הוא משיחא עתיד דיקום וישלוט בדחלתא דיוי). Here a new characteristic of the rule of the expected Messiah is proposed, that he will rule with the fear of God.[62]

(e) *1 Kgs 5:13a(Eng. 4:33a):* The MT cites examples of Solomon's wisdom: "He spoke of the trees, from the cedar that is in Lebanon to the hyssop that goes forth from the wall." This half-verse is given a completely messianic interpretation in the targum: "He prophesied about the kings of the house of David who were destined to rule in this world and in the world of the Messiah" (ואתנבי על מלכי בית דויד דעתידין למשלט בעלמא הדין ובעלמא דמשיחא).[63] Now we learn that "world of the Messiah" is different from "this world," but unfortunately it is not further explained. Likewise, the "kings of the house of David" seems to be distinguished from "the Messiah" in this passage, and there is little to explain the distinction.

It should be recalled that משיח occurs only once in the MT of the book of Isaiah, in 45:1, where it is used of the Persian king, Cyrus. The targum of Isaiah, however, has introduced משיחא in a number of places; the most important of them are the following:

(f) *Isa 9:5-6(Eng. 6-7):* The MT hails God's activity in the birth of a Davidic king:

> For a child has been born to us, a son has been given to us; upon his shoulder dominion has settled; one has named him Wonderful Counselor, Warrior God, Everlasting Father, Prince of Peace. Of the vastness of (his) dominion and of peace there shall be no end, upon David's throne and over his kingdom, to establish it and to sustain it in justice and righteousness from now and for ever. The zeal of the LORD of hosts shall do this.

This becomes in the *Targum Jonathan:*

62. Sperber, *The Bible in Aramaic,* 2:206; Harrington and Saldarini, *Targum Jonathan of the Former Prophets,* 203. Cf. Mowinckel, *He That Cometh,* 174, where there is a discussion of the MT, but strangely enough, Mowinckel does not discuss any of the targumic passages of 1 or 2 Samuel.

63. Sperber, *The Bible in Aramaic,* 2:222-23; Harrington and Saldarini, *Targum Jonathan of the Former Prophets,* 220.

A prophet said to the house of David, "For a boy has been born to us, a son has been given to us; he has received the Law upon himself to keep it. His name has been called in the presence of the One who gives wonderful counsel 'the Warrior God, existing forever, the Messiah,' in whose days peace shall abound for us (ואתקרי שמיה מן קדם מפלי /עיצא אלהא גיברא קיים עלמא משיחא דשלמא יסגי עלנא ביומוהי). Great dignity (shall be) for those who do the Law, and for those who keep peace there is no end: on the throne of David and on his kingdom, to establish it and to build it with justice and righteousness from now and for ever. By the *memra* of the LORD of Hosts shall this be done.[64]

Thus an explicit messianic meaning is given to the child born in the royal house of David, in a passage of the prophet Isaiah, which was in itself nonmessianic.[65] The four names of the MT are differently interpreted.

(g) *Isa 11:1:* In the MT of this verse a promise is made about the continuation of the Davidic dynasty: "But a shoot shall come forth from the stump of Jesse, and a sprout shall blossom from his roots." This becomes in the targum, "A king shall come forth from the sons of Jesse, and the Messiah shall be anointed from among his children's children (ויפוק מלכא מבנוהי דישי ומשיחא מבני בנוהי יתרבי)."[66] What was expressed in the MT by symbols (a shoot and a sprout) is now interpreted explicitly of a person, a king and the Messiah; as in the MT they are undoubtedly meant as two names for the same individual, stressing the Davidic descent of the Messiah. As in the MT, vv. 3b-9 give an idyllic description of the reign of this Davidic descendant.[67] In v. 6, where it is said that "the wolf shall dwell with the lamb, and the leopard shall lie down with the kid," the targum translates these statements literally, but it introduces them with a clause, "In the days of the Messiah of Israel peace shall abound in the land (ביומוהי דמשיחא דישראל יסגי שלמא בארעא), and the wolf . . . ."[68]

---

64. Sperber, *The Bible in Aramaic, 3: The Latter Prophets according to Targum Jonathan* (Leiden: Brill, 1962) 19; cf. B. D. Chilton, *The Isaiah Targum.* Aramaic Bible 11 (Wilmington: Michael Glazier, 1987) 21.

65. For an attempt to interpret the text of King Hezekiah, see Levey, *The Messiah,* 45-46. Strangely enough, although Mowinckel discusses at length the MT of Isa 9:1-6 (*He That Cometh,* 102-10), there is no mention of this passage in the *Tg. Jonathan.*

66. Sperber, *The Bible in Aramaic,* 3:25; Chilton, *The Isaiah Targum,* 28.

67. See Levey, *The Messiah,* 52-54 for further discussion of the context in which this verse occurs.

68. Sperber, *The Bible in Aramaic,* 3:26; Chilton, *The Isaiah Targum,* 28.

(h) *Isa 16:1, 5:* As part of an elegy over Moab, the MT says, "They have sent lambs to the ruler of the land, from Sela to Midbar, to the mountain of the daughter of Zion" (16:1). The verse seems to speak of gifts sent from various towns in Moab to Jerusalem. In *Tg. Jonathan* this becomes, "They will offer tribute to the Messiah of Israel (יהון מסקי מסין למשיחא דישראל), who is mighty over that which was like a desert, the mountain of the congregation of Zion."[69] What were gifts freely offered in the MT has become a tribute of submission to Israel's Messiah and "the mountain of the congregation of Zion." The idea is continued in the MT of 16:5, which reads, "Then a throne will be set up in mercy, and on it will sit with fidelity in the tent of David one who judges, seeks justice, and is quick to act with righteousness." This becomes in the targum, "Then the Messiah of Israel will set up his throne in goodness, and he will sit upon it in truth in the city of David, judging, demanding justice, and doing righteousness" (בכין משיחא דישראל יתקן בטוב כורסוהי ויתיב עלוהי בקשוט בקרתא דדויד דיין ותבע דין ועביד קשוט).[70]

(i) *Isa 52:13:* The Fourth Servant Song begins thus in the MT: "Look, my servant shall prosper; he shall be exalted, lifted up, and be very high."[71] This verse becomes in the targum: "Look, my servant, the Messiah, shall prosper; he shall be exalted, increase, and be very strong (הא יצלח עבדי משיחא יראם ויסגי ויתקף לחדא)."[72] It is not surprising that the Servant is explicitly identified now with the Messiah in this late targum, which thus gives to the Servant a specific individual meaning. This identification, however, has made many interpreters of the MT of Isa 52:13 itself to label it "messianic," which is a misuse of the term for a text that may have been composed in postexilic times, but centuries before the concept of "Messiah" entered the history of ideas. The identification of the Servant as Messiah occurs in this targum again in 43:10-14.[73]

(j) *Isa 53:10:* Toward the end of the Fourth Servant Song, the prophet describes the vicarious suffering of the Servant for others and states: "But

---

69. Sperber, *The Bible in Aramaic,* 3:33; Chilton, *The Isaiah Targum,* 35.

70. Sperber, *The Bible in Aramaic,* 3:33; Chilton, *The Isaiah Targum,* 35.

71. See pp. 41-43 above for comments on the context of this verse.

72. Sperber, *The Bible in Aramaic,* 3:107; Chilton, *The Isaiah Targum,* 103. Cf. Chilton, "Two in One," 555-59; H. Hegermann, *Jesaja 53 in Hexapla, Targum und Peschitta.* BFCT 2/56 (Gütersloh: Bertelsmann, 1954) 66-67.

73. Also in 42:1 in the edition of the targum by P. A. de Lagarde, *Prophetae chaldaice* (Leipzig: Teubner, 1872; repr. Osnabrück: Zeller, 1967) 267.

the LORD was pleased to crush him with infirmity, that if he made himself an offering for sin, he might see offspring and prolong his days, and that the will of the LORD might be implemented through him." This becomes in the translation of the targum, "Yet it was the good pleasure of the LORD to purify and cleanse the remnant of His people in order that, in the cleansing of their souls of sins, they might gaze upon the kingdom of their Messiah (יחזון במלכות משיחהון), abound in sons and daughters, prolong (their) days, be observers of the Law of the LORD, and prosper according to His will."[74] One notes here a shift in meaning, because what was said in the MT about the Servant is now transferred to "the remnant" of God's people, who are said to be implementing God's will.[75] The targumist thus gives a collective interpretation to the Servant, meaning the righteous remnant of Israel. This shift makes it impossible to think that the targumist was writing about a dying Messiah, as is sometimes held.

Other less important passages in the targum of Isaiah that introduce the Messiah are 4:2; 10:27; 14:29; 28:5.[76]

(k) *Jer 23:5:* After reproving the rulers of Judah as evil shepherds for neglecting their people, the prophet Jeremiah quotes God, who promises to raise up a wise and righteous king. The MT runs: "'Look! Days are coming,' says the LORD, 'when I will raise up for David a righteous scion (צמח צדיק), and he shall rule as king and deal wisely, executing justice and righteousness in the land.'" This becomes in the targum: "'Look! Days are coming,' says the LORD, 'when I will raise up for David a righteous Messiah, and he shall rule as a king and prosper and execute true justice and righteousness in the land'" (ואקים לדויד משיח דצדקא וימלוך מלכא ויצלח ויעביד דין דקשוט וזכו בארעא).[77]

---

74. Sperber, *The Bible in Aramaic,* 3:108; Chilton, *The Isaiah Targum,* 104.

75. See further J. Ådna, "The Servant of Isaiah 53 as Triumphant and Interceding Messiah: The Reception of Isaiah 52:13–53:12 in the Targum of Isaiah with Special Attention to the Concept of the Messiah," in B. Janowski and P. Stuhlmacher, *The Suffering Servant* (Grand Rapids: Wm. B. Eerdmans, 2004) 189-224; R. A. Aytoun, "The Servant of the Lord in the Targum," *JTS* 23 (1921-22) 172-80; Hegermann, *Jesaja 53 in Hexapla, Targum und Peschitta,* 87-89; K. Koch, "Messias und Sündenvergebung in Jesaja 53 — Targum: Ein Beitrag zur Praxis der aramäischen Bibelübersetzung," *JSJ* 3 (1972) 117-48; R. Syrén, "Targum Isaiah 52:13–53:12 and Christian Interpretation," *JJS* 40 (1989) 201-12; Mowinckel, *He That Cometh,* 330-32.

76. See Levey, *The Messiah,* 43, 47-48, 55, 58; Chilton, "Two in One," 550-54; Mowinckel, *He That Cometh,* 292.

77. Sperber, *The Bible in Aramaic,* 3:188; cf. R. Hayward, *The Targum of Jeremiah.* Aramaic Bible 12 (Wilmington: Michael Glazier, 1987) 111.

Again, the Davidic descent of the Messiah is stressed, and also his qualities of righteousness, wisdom, and justice in activity and conduct.[78]

(l) *Jer 30:8-9:* Jeremiah writes to Jewish elders of the Babylonian Captivity and passes on God's promise to raise up a future David and bring them back to Jerusalem. The MT reads thus: "'On that day it will come to pass,' says the LORD, 'that I will break the yoke off their necks and burst their bonds; and strangers shall no more make slaves of them. Instead they shall serve the LORD, their God, and David, their king, whom I will raise up for them.'" This, however, becomes in the targum: "'It will come to pass at that time,' says the LORD of Hosts, 'that I will break the yoke of the nations from your necks, and your chains I will cut off, and nations shall no longer enslave Israel. But they shall worship the LORD, their God, and submit themselves to the Messiah, son of David, their king, whom I will raise up for them" (ויפלחון קדם יוי אלההון וישתמעון למשיחא בר דויד מלכהון דאקים להון).[79]

Whereas in the MT God's promise was to raise up as king a future David, now he is said to be explicitly the Messiah, son of David, their future king.

(m) *Jer 30:21:* Jeremiah's consolation sent to Israel and Judah in exile continues, and the MT reads: "'Its prince shall be from among them, and its ruler shall come forth from its midst. I will make it [Israel] draw near, and it shall approach me, for who is the one that would pledge his heart to approach me?' says the LORD." This becomes in the targum: "'Their king shall be anointed from among them, and their Messiah shall be revealed from among them (ויתרבא מלכהון מנהון ומשיחהון מביניהון יתגלי), I will draw them near, and he shall give them over to the worship of Me, for who is the one whose heart desires to be drawn near to the worship of Me?' says the LORD."[80]

(n) *Jer 33:13, 15:* In the MT, these verses are part of the so-called appendix to Jeremiah's Book of Consolation (30:1–31:40). Verse 13 tells where shepherds will once again be able to pasture their flocks: "'In the cities of the hills, in the cities of the Shephelah, in the cities of the Negeb, in the land of Benjamin, in the environs of Jerusalem, and in the lands of Judah, a flock shall again pass under the hand of the one who counts them,' says the

---

78. See Mowinckel, *He That Cometh*, 308.
79. Sperber, *The Bible in Aramaic*, 3:203; Hayward, *The Targum of Jeremiah*, 128.
80. Sperber, *The Bible in Aramaic*, 3:204-5; Hayward, *The Targum of Jeremiah*, 129.

LORD." This becomes in the targum: "'In the cities of the hills, in the cities of the Shephelah, in the cities of the south, in the land of the tribe of Benjamin, in the surroundings of Jerusalem, and in the cities of the house of Judah, the people shall again repeat the sayings of the Messiah,' says the LORD" (עוד יתנהון עמא לפתגמי משיחא אמר יוי). Verse 15 repeats, in effect, God's promise expressed in 23:5, as the MT states: "In those days and at that time I will cause a scion of righteousness to sprout for David, and he shall execute justice and righteousness in the land." In the targum one reads: "In those days and at that time I will raise up for David a Messiah of righteousness (משיח דצדקא), and he will execute true justice and righteousness in the land."[81] These verses of Jeremiah merely repeat the continued expectation of the coming Messiah and the good that he will achieve for the land of Judah, especially in terms of restoring the habitation of Judah and the reunion of Israel and Judah.[82]

(o) Although several places in the book of Ezekiel speak of the coming of a future David and call him עבדי (*'abdî*, "my slave, servant") and נשיא (*nāśî*, "prince, leader"), e.g., Ezek 17:22-24; 34:23-24; 37:24-25, in none of these passages is the term משיח introduced. This is striking, because the prophet Ezekiel otherwise shared the expectation of such a future David with Jeremiah.[83] Similarly striking is the absence of the term משיחא in the targum of Hosea, in such passages as 2:2(Eng. 1:11); 3:4-5, which could have been given readily a messianic interpretation. There is, however, a single occurrence.

(p) *Hos 14:8(Eng. 7):* The prophet Hosea uttered his words to the Northern Kingdom just about the time of the fall of Samaria in 721 B.C. and the subsequent Assyrian deportation of Jews under Tiglath-pileser III. He ends his prophecy with an exhortation to Israel to return to its merciful God. In the MT, v. 8 runs: "They shall return and dwell in His shadow; they shall grow grain and blossom as a vine, and its fragrance shall be like the wine of Lebanon." This verse becomes in the targum: "They shall be gathered in from their exile; they will dwell in the shadow of their Messiah (יתבון בטלל משיחהון). The dead shall come to life, and goodness shall

---

81. Sperber, *The Bible in Aramaic*, 3:215; Hayward, *The Targum of Jeremiah*, 141.

82. See Mowinckel, *He That Cometh*, 269-70.

83. See further S. H. Levey, *The Targum of Ezekiel*. Aramaic Bible 13 (Wilmington: Michael Glazier, 1987) 6, 87 n. 10, 99 n. 12, 105 n. 12. Cf. B. W. R. Pearson, "Dry Bones in the Judean Desert: The Messiah of Ephraim, Ezekiel 37, and the Post-Revolutionary Followers of Bar Kokhba," *JSJ* 29 (1998) 192-201.

abound in the land. The remembrance of their goodness shall enter and not come to an end, as (is) the remembrance of the trumpet sounds over the old wine poured in libation in the Temple."[84] In this interpretive translation, God's shadow has become the shadow of the people's Messiah.

(q) *Mic 4:8:* Although Micah was a contemporary of Isaiah, his words about the future restoration of the Davidic dynasty come from a postexilic date. In the MT, v. 8 states: "As for you, O tower of the flock, hill of the daughter of Zion, unto you shall it come: the dominion of old shall come, kingship to the daughter of Jerusalem." In the targum this is messianically interpreted: "And you, O Messiah of Israel, who have been hidden because of the sins of the congregation of Zion (ואת משיחא דישראל דטמיר מן קדם חובי כנשתא דציון), to you kingship is destined to come; and the former dominion shall come to the kingdom of the congregation of Jerusalem."[85] The former dominion is probably a reference to the reign of David, which is expected to be restored, as will be evident in the following passage, but the restoration is delayed because of the sins of the people of Jerusalem.[86]

(r) *Mic 5:1(Eng. 2):* In the MT this verse reads: "But you, Bethlehem-Ephrathah, too small to be among the clans of Judah, from you shall come forth for me one who is to be ruler in Israel, whose origin is from of old, from ancient times."[87] This verse too is interpreted messianically in the targum's Aramaic rendition: "But you, Bethlehem-Ephrath, were like one too small to be numbered among the thousands of the house of Judah; from you shall come forth in My presence the Messiah to exercise dominion over Israel, he whose name was mentioned from of old, from everlasting days" (מנך קדמי יפוק משיחא למהוי עביד שולטן על ישראל ודי שמיה אמיר מלקדמין מיומי עלמא).[88]

The last clause of this verse formulates a conviction about the premundane existence of the Messiah, i.e., on the eve of the Sabbath or before the creation of the world, as it is also taught in *b. Pesaḥ.* 54a.[89]

---

84. Sperber, *The Bible in Aramaic,* 3:408; K. J. Cathcart and R. P. Gordon, *The Targum of the Minor Prophets.* Aramaic Bible 14 (Wilmington: Michael Glazier, 1989) 61.

85. Sperber, *The Bible in Aramaic,* 3:445; Cathcart and Gordon, *The Targum of the Minor Prophets,* 120.

86. See Mowinckel, *He That Cometh,* 306.

87. See p. 53 above for the context of this verse.

88. Sperber, *The Bible in Aramaic,* 3:446; Cathcart and Gordon, *The Targum of the Minor Prophets,* 122.

89. Several things are said there to have been brought into being before the creation

(s) *Zech 3:8:* In the fourth of the eight visions that make up the first part of the prophecy of Zechariah, the prophet sees Joshua, the postexilic High Priest, standing before the Angel of the Lord and his accuser, Satan. The vision is, in effect, a defense of the High Priest, and Satan symbolizes the critics and opponents of Joshua in the Jewish community. The interpreting angel addresses Joshua thus in the MT: "Listen, O Joshua, High Priest, you and your friends, who sit before you, for they are men of significance: Look! I am bringing forth my servant, a scion" (עבדי צמח, *'abdî ṣemaḥ*). In *Tg. Jonathan* this verse reads: "Now listen, O Joshua, High Priest, you and your companions that are sitting before you, for they are men suited for having a sign given to them: 'Look! I am causing my servant, the Messiah, to come, and he shall be revealed'" (ארי האנא מיתי ית עבדי משיחא ויתגלי).[90] The servant who was identified as "scion" in the MT is now given the title Messiah. Zechariah may well be echoing Jer 23:5; 33:15 in using such a title as "scion" (צמח). Thus in addition to the anointed High Priest, the Messiah "shall be revealed," and they will be further associated together in the next chapter as "two sons of oil" (Zech 4:14).[91]

(t) *Zech 4:7:* In the fifth vision the prophet is shown two olive trees that symbolize Zerubbabel and Joshua and their importance in the restored postexilic community. Of the former the interpreting angel says as he describes Zerubbabel's task in building the new Temple, in the MT: "Who are you, O great mountain? Before Zerubbabel you shall be a plain; and he shall bring forward the headstone amid shouts of 'Grace, grace to it.'" The phrase "O great mountain" seems to denote a nation that has been hostile to the people of Judah and that meets its nemesis in Zerubbabel. This verse becomes in the targum: "What are you reckoned as before Zerubbabel, O foolish kingdom? Are you not like a plain? For He shall re-

---

of the world: garden of Eden, God's Throne of glory, Gehenna, the Temple, the name of the Messiah, and the Torah.

90. Sperber, *The Bible in Aramaic,* 3:481; Cathcart and Gordon, *The Targum of the Minor Prophets,* 192.

91. Cf. *Abot R. Nat.* 1 (J. Goldin, *The Fathers According to Rabbi Nathan* [New York: Schocken, 1974] 137-38), where reference is made to Aaron and the Messiah: "'These are the two sons of oil, who stand by the Lord of the whole earth' [Zech 4:14]. This is a reference to Aaron and the Messiah, but I cannot tell which is the more beloved. However, from the verse, 'The Lord has sworn and will not repent, "Thou art a priest forever after the manner of Melchizedek"' [Ps 110:4], one can tell that the Messianic King is more beloved than the righteous priest." Cf. G. J. Blidstein, "A Rabbinic Reaction to the Messianic Doctrine of the Scrolls," *JBL* 90 (1971) 330-32.

veal his Messiah whose name was mentioned of old, and he shall have do-minion over all the kingdoms (מלכוותא ויגלי ית משיחיה דאמיר שמיה מלקדמין וישלוט בכל)."[92] The "name" probably means "Messiah" itself, which elsewhere in Jewish tradition of this late period was said to have been created before the world.[93] Here it may be implied that Zerubbabel is that Messiah.

(u) *Zech 6:12-13:* After the eighth vision, the prophet tells of the crowning of the leader of the restored postexilic community. In the MT, v. 12 states: "Here is a man whose name is scion; he shall sprout from his place, and he shall build the temple of the LORD." This is recognized nor-mally as a reference to Zerubbabel. The targum of this verse reads: "You shall tell him, saying, 'Thus speaks the LORD of Hosts, saying, "Look! The man whose name is Messiah is destined to be revealed and to be anointed; he shall build the temple of the LORD" (הא גברא משיחא שמיה עתיד דיתגלי ויתרבי ויבני ית היכלא דיוי)."[94] Again the "scion" (צמח) is iden-tified as the Messiah and now regarded as the one to build the Second Temple. In the following v. 13, the MT continues: "He indeed shall build the temple of the LORD and bear majesty. He shall sit and rule upon his throne; there shall be a priest by his throne, and peaceful counsel shall exist between the two of them." This is translated literally into Aramaic; the only differences being זיו, "radiance," instead of Hebrew הוד, "majesty," and כהין רב, "a High Priest," instead of merely "priest" of the MT. The High Priest is not identified, but it is noteworthy that the kingly Messiah is ac-companied again by a priestly figure, as we have already seen even in the pre-Christian Jewish tradition of the Qumran texts.

Whereas the three foregoing messianic passages of the targum of Zechariah were interpretive translations of verses coming from the late sixth-century part of the Prophecy of Zechariah, a famous passage in the fourth/third-century Deutero-Zechariah, 9:9-10, is given no such messi-anic interpretation in the targum. In the MT, it reads:

> Look! Your king comes to you [Jerusalem]; righteous and victorious is he, meek and riding on an ass, even on a colt, the foal of an ass. He

92. Sperber, *The Bible in Aramaic*, 3:482; Cathcart and Gordon, *The Targum of the Mi-nor Prophets*, 194.

93. See Mowinckel, *He That Cometh*, 334.

94. Sperber, *The Bible in Aramaic*, 3:485; Cathcart and Gordon, *The Targum of the Mi-nor Prophets*, 198.

shall eliminate the chariot from Ephraim, the horse from Jerusalem; the warrior's bow shall be eliminated, and he shall announce peace to nations. His dominion shall be from sea to sea, and from the River to the ends of the earth.

About this passage, S. H. Levey writes: "These verses are rendered literally by the Targum, with no specific Messianic reference whatsoever, bearing out the contention that the humble, suffering, and dying Messiah was not acceptable to the Jewish mind."[95] There is, however, one passage in the targum of Deutero-Zechariah where משיחא is introduced.

(v) *Zech 10:4:* In ch. 10, the prophet speaks of God as the one who gives rain and punishes the shepherds of the people. He will eventually care for His flock, the house of Judah. In the MT, v. 4 declares: "Out of it shall come the cornerstone, out of it the tent-peg; out of it the warrior's bow, out of it every ruler." The targum individualizes and personalizes the subjects: "From it (comes) its king; from it its Messiah; from it his might in war; from it all its leaders together shall be anointed" (מניה מלכיה מניה משיחיה מניה תקוף קרביה מניה יתרבון כל פרנסוהי כחדא).[96]

This brings us to the end of the passages in the *Tg. Jonathan* where משיחא has been introduced.[97]

(5) *Targum of the Psalms.* This targum forms part of that which developed for some of the books of the Writings or Hagiographa, the third part of the Hebrew Scriptures. It dates from a time hardly earlier than *Tg. Jonathan* of the Prophets, and it may be considerably later than it.

(a) There are several psalms in this targum where משיחא occurs, which is simply an Aramaic form of the Hebrew משיח in Psalms of the MT. In these cases, משיחא means merely "Anointed One," referring to David or some historical king on his throne, and so it has no more of a "messianic" connotation than the Hebrew text: Ps 2:2; 18:51(Eng. 50) (= 2 Sam 22:51); 20:7(6); 28:8; 84:10(9); 89:39(38); 105:15 (= 1 Chr 16:22); 132:10 (= 2 Chr 6:42), 17.[98]

---

95. Levey, *The Messiah,* 100.

96. Sperber, *The Bible in Aramaic,* 3:491; Cathcart and Gordon, *The Targum of the Minor Prophets,* 209.

97. Perhaps one should mention also Hab 3:13 (a nonmessianic occurrence) and 3:18 (where משיחך has been freely introduced; see Sperber, *The Bible in Aramaic,* 3:466; cf. Levey, *The Messiah,* 95).

98. *Pace* Levey (*The Messiah,* 124), who thinks v. 17 "is probably Messianic."

(b) There are other Psalms in this targum where מֹשִׁיחָא is found, but without a Hebrew counterpart in the MT. In these cases, מֹשִׁיחָא has been introduced to translate or interpret some other word.

(i) *Ps 45:3 (Eng. 2):* This verse is part of an ode for a royal wedding, in which a court poet addresses an unnamed king. It reads in the MT: "You have become more handsome than the children of men; grace has been poured from your lips. So God has blessed you forever." This becomes in the targum: "Your beauty, O King Messiah, is more remarkable than that of the children of men (שׁוּפְרָך מַלְכָּא מְשִׁיחָא עָדִיף מִבְּנֵי נְשָׁא); a spirit of prophecy has been granted to your lips. So the LORD has blessed you forever."[99] The unnamed king of the MT has now become the "King Messiah," probably because v. 8b(Eng. 7b) of the MT speaks of God anointing the king with the oil of gladness (מְשָׁחָך אֱלֹהִים אֱלֹהֶיך שֶׁמֶן שָׁשׂוֹן).[100]

(ii) *Ps 61:7-9 (Eng. 6-8):* These verses are part of a prayer for an unnamed king inserted in a "Psalm of David," usually regarded as a lament for protection. In the MT the verses run thus: "May You add days to the days of the king; may his days be as generation upon generation./May he sit enthroned forever before God; bid steadfast love and fidelity guard him./So will I ever sing praise to Your name!" This becomes in the targum:

> May You add the days of the King Messiah (to) days for the world to come (יוֹמִין עַל עָלְמָא דְאָתֵי יוֹמֵי מַלְכָּא מְשִׁיחָא תּוֹסִיף); may his years be like the generations of this world and generations of the world to come./May he sit enthroned forever before the LORD; may goodness and truth from the LORD of the world guard him./Therefore will I praise Your name forever, as I fulfill my vows on the day of Israel's deliverance and on the day when the King Messiah is anointed to be king (וּבְיוֹם דִּיתְרַבֵּי מַלְכָּא מְשִׁיחָא לְמֶהֱוֵי מְלִיך).[101]

(iii) *Ps 72:1:* This is a "Psalm of Solomon," a prayer uttered as a blessing of the king. In the MT it begins: "Bestow, O God, your judgment on the king, and your righteousness on the son of the king." In the targum, this

---

99. See P. A. de Lagarde, *Hagiographa chaldaice* (Leipzig: Teubner, 1873; repr. Osnabrück: Zeller, 1967) 25; D. M. Stec, *The Targum of Psalms.* Aramaic Bible 16 (Collegeville: Liturgical, 2004) 95-96.

100. For an explanation of the context in which this verse occurs, see Levey, *The Messiah,* 111-13.

101. De Lagarde, *Hagiographa chaldaice,* 34; Stec, *The Targum of Psalms,* 121.

becomes: "Bestow, O God, the rules of Your justice on the King Messiah, and Your righteousness on the son of King David" (אלהא הילכות דינך **למלכא משיחא הב וצדקתך לבריה דדוד מלכא**).[102] Since in the targum v. 1 begins with the attribution of the psalm to Solomon as author ("It is uttered by Solomon in prophecy" [על ידוי דשלמה אתאמר בנבואה]), the "son of King David" is undoubtedly to be understood as another way of referring to King Messiah in the preceding clause.

(iv) *Ps 80:16(Eng. 15)*: This verse, which is poorly transmitted in Hebrew, is part of a plea for deliverance from national enemies. After asking God to look with concern on the vine symbolizing Israel, v. 16 continues: "And on the stock(?) that Your right hand has planted, and on a son (that) You have strengthened for Yourself." This becomes in the targum: "On the stock, the planting of Your right hand, and on the King Messiah whom You have strengthened for Yourself" (ועוברא די נציבת ימינך ועל מלכא **משיחא דחיילתא לך**).[103] The plea is repeated in v. 18, where both in the MT and the targum "the man" and "the son of man" take the place of the "stock" and the "son." Levey notes that this is the only place in the targum where "son" is rendered as "King Messiah."[104] Moreover, the earlier association of the Messiah with the "son of man" in Dan 7:13 is probably part of the reason for the messianic interpretation of this verse of Psalm 80.[105]

(v) *Ps 89:52(Eng. 51)*: In this psalm, in which a Davidic king prays for deliverance from his enemies and the targum renders Hebrew משיחך of v. 39(38) with the same word, meaning simply, "Your Anointed," the targum of v. 52 introduces a clear messianic nuance of the same word. In the MT, the psalmist asks God to be mindful of the insults "with which Your enemies have taunted, O LORD, with which they have taunted the footsteps of Your Anointed One" (משיחך). This becomes in the targum: "With which Your enemies have scoffed, O LORD, with which they have scoffed at the delay of the footprints of Your Messiah, O LORD" (די חסידו **איחור רושמת ריגלי משיחך יהוה**).[106] The object of their insults is not merely משיחך, but the delay in his coming, which is a new detail.

(6) *Other Targumic Passages of the Hagiographa*. Beyond the Psalter,

---

102. De Lagarde, *Hagiographa chaldaice*, 41; Stec, *The Targum of the Psalms,* 139.
103. De Lagarde, *Hagiographa chaldaice*, 48; Stec, *The Targum of Psalms,* 157.
104. Levey, *The Messiah,* 119.
105. See Mowinckel, *He That Cometh,* 335.
106. De Lagarde, *Hagiographa chaldaice*, 54; Stec, *The Targum of Psalms,* 170.

the term משיחא is found in other books of the Writings, the most important of which are the following:[107]

(a) *Lam 4:20:* In a passage that tells of the sack of Jerusalem by the Babylonians in 586 B.C., v. 20 speaks of the abduction of the king, and the MT of it reads as follows: "The breath of our nostrils, the Anointed One of the LORD, was taken captive in their pits, he of whom we used to say, 'In his shadow we shall live among the nations.'" This becomes in the targum: "King Josiah, who was beloved of us, like the breath of the spirit of life that is in our nostrils, and was anointed with the oil of the majesty of the LORD (והוה מתרבי במשח רבותא דיהוה), was handled roughly in the net of the crimes of the Egyptians, he of whom we used to say, 'In the shadow of his righteousness we shall live among the nations.'"[108] The king who is meant in the MT is usually said to be King Zedekiah (because of 2 Kgs 25:4-6), but the targum interprets it as referring to Josiah, king of Judah (640-609 B.C.), who was killed by Pharaoh Neco at Megiddo as he sought in vain to preserve his newly won independence by preventing the pharaoh from joining forces with the Assyrians against the Babylonians. As a result, Judah became a vassalage of Egypt.

(b) *Lam 4:22:* The passage continues with a promise of the end of the exile and the punishment of Edom for its treachery, and the MT reads: "Finished is your chastisement, O daughter of Zion; one shall not add to your exile. One punishes your iniquity, O daughter of Edom; one lays bare your sins." This is rendered in Aramaic in the targum:

> Afterwards your iniquity shall be complete, O congregation of Zion; you shall be rescued by the hands of the King Messiah and Elijah, the High Priest (ותתפרקין על ידוי דמלכא משיחא ואליהו כהנא רבא), and the LORD shall no longer turn to your exile. At that time one punishes your iniquity, O wicked Rome, built up in Italy, full of armies from the Edomites; Persians shall come, oppress you, and take you captive, for you are exposed before the LORD because of your sins.[109]

---

107. Of less importance are the following passages: Song 1:8, 17; 7:4, 14(Eng. 3, 13); 8:1, 2, 4; Ruth 1:1; 3:15; Lam 2:2; Qoh 1:11; 7:24; Add Esth 1:1. On these passages, see Levey, *The Messiah*, 125-41.

108 De Lagarde, *Hagiographa chaldaice*, 178.

109. De Lagarde, *Hagiographa chaldaice*, 178. Cf. R. Kasher, "On the Portrayal of Messiahs in Light of an Unknown Targum to Lam 4:21-22," *JSQ* 7 (2000) 22-41. Kasher publishes the text of MS Moscow-Guenzburg 333, fol. 149b and translates vv. 21-22, which have a signifi-

Once again the King Messiah is joined with Elijah, as the High Priest, in the role of joint deliverers of Jerusalem from all its diverse enemies.

(c) *1 Chr 3:24:* The Chronicler records the descendants of David down to his own time (*ca.* 350-300 B.C.), and the last verse (3:24) reads in the MT: "The sons of Elioenai: Hodaviah, Eliashib, Pelaiah, Akkub, Johanan, Delaiah, and Anani, seven." This becomes in the targum: "The sons of Elioenai: Hodaviahu, Eliashib, Pelaiah, Akkub, Johanan, Delaiah, and Anani, who is the King Messiah, who is destined to be revealed (וענני הוא מלכא משיחא דעתיד לאתגלאה). All of them seven."[110] The novelty now is the name of the King Messiah, "Anani," which is a proper noun developed from the word for "clouds" in Dan 7:13. There the prophet recounts how in a vision of the night he has seen "one like a son of man" coming "with the clouds of heaven" (עם־ענני שמיא, *'im-'ănānê šĕmayyā'*) to "the Ancient of Days." Whereas in Daniel *'ănānê* is a plural common noun, its consonants are interpreted in this targum as a singular proper noun, *'ănānî*, "Anani," i.e., the Cloud-Man, which thus becomes the name of the Messiah.[111]

(d) *Song 4:5:* In the bridegroom's description of his lover, he says in the MT: "Your breasts are like two fawns, twins of a gazelle, which feed among the lilies." This becomes in the targum:

> Your two deliverers who are destined to deliver you, the Messiah, son of David, and the Messiah, son of Ephraim, resemble Moses and Aaron (תרין פריקיך דעתידין למיפרקיך משיח בר דוד ומשיח בר אפרים דמין למשה ואהרן), the sons of Jochebed, whom one compares to two fawns, twins of a gazelle. By their meritorious deeds they have been shepherding the people of the house of Israel for forty years in the desert, with manna, fatted fowl, and water of Miriam's well.[112]

---

cant variant. Instead of redemption by "the King Messiah and Elijah, the High Priest," this copy reads "the King Messiah of the House of David and the King Messiah of the House of Joseph from the House of Ephraim, who are destined to come from their noble families" (מלכא משיחא דבית דוד ומלכא משיחא דבית יוסף מדבית אפרים דעתידין למיפק מן אוגיותיהון). Here the Messiah son of Joseph/Ephraim takes the place of Elijah, the High Priest, in the other targum of Lamentations.

110. De Lagarde, *Hagiographa chaldaice*, 275; J. S. McIvor, *The Targum of Chronicles.* Aramaic Bible 19 (Collegeville: Liturgical, 1993) 57; cf. R. Le Déaut, *Targum des Chroniques (Cod. Vat. Urb. Ebr. 1).* AnBib 51/1-2 (Rome: Biblical Institute, 1971) 1:47; 2:18.

111. See Mowinckel, *He That Cometh*, 389-90.

112. De Lagarde, *Hagiographa chaldaice*, 154; P. S. Alexander, *The Targum of Canticles.*

Once again the targum mentions two Messiahs, one the son of David and the other the son of Ephraim, who are said to be like Moses and Aaron, a civil leader and a priestly figure who assists him. The same pair is found again in the targum of 7:4. The Messiah, son of Ephraim, sometimes called the Messiah, son of Joseph, has been met already in the targum on Exod 40:12, where he is said to be the one to defeat Gog in the end time,[113] but he has not appeared before in a priestly role, as he does here.

This brings the discussion of the messianic passages in the various targums to an end. With one of the conclusions that Levey draws from his study of the targums one can readily agree in general:

> While a main current of Messianic thought in general outline is discernible throughout the Targum, individual Messianic interpretations vary in detail, depending upon the nature of the Hebrew text and upon the Targumic mind which fashioned the interpretation in question. There is no absolute consistency or unanimity of viewpoint.[114]

The lack of consistency or unanimity, however, does not come from "the Targum," because there is no one targum for all the different books of the Hebrew Scriptures, and not even for the Pentateuch, where in addition to the official targum (Onqelos) there are several Palestinian targums. Consequently, there is no one "Targumic mind" that fashioned the foregoing diverse interpretations, but the diversity of interpretations is indeed noteworthy.

(7) *Jerusalem Talmud.* Above we considered the few passages in the Mishnah and Tosephtah where "Messiah" is found. The rabbinic Judaism of the Mishnah continued to develop until the fifth and sixth centuries when another stage of interpretation, גמרא, *gĕmārā'*, "completion," was added to the Mishnah in two forms, to produce תלמוד ירושלמי, *Talmûd Yĕrûšalmî*, "Jerusalem Talmud," dated roughly A.D. 450; and תלמוד בבלי, *Talmûd Babli*, "Babylonian Talmud," dated roughly A.D. 550. *Talmûd* literally means

---

Aramaic Bible 17A (Collegeville: Liturgical, 2003) 135; cf. Torrey, *JBL* 66 (1947) 254-55. Torrey even claimed that the doctrine of the Messiah son of Ephraim "antedated the Christian era by several centuries" (255). Although he rightly rejected the derivation of this doctrine from Obadiah 18 (as G. F. Moore had argued) and from Deut 33:17 (as G. Dalman, E. Schürer, et al. had proposed), Torrey appealed to the Servant Songs of Deutero-Isaiah (esp. 42:1-4; 52:13; and 53:9) for evidence, but interprets these passages in light of *4 Ezra* 7:28-31; *2 Bar.* 29, 30, 40, as if such an interpretation really "antedated the Christian era."

113. See p. 159 above; cf. Mowinckel, *He That Cometh,* 290, 292.

114. Levey, *The Messiah,* 142.

"learning," and the writing so called has gathered the discussions (legal decisions, wise sayings, and stories) of the Jewish Sages called the Amora'im, who commented on the Tractates of the Mishnah of the Tanna'im.[115]

The Mishnah quoted in the two Talmuds is not always verbatim the same, which reveals that the Mishnah itself was still in a state of development. Whereas the Mishnah was written in a form of postbiblical and post-Qumran Hebrew, the Gemara was composed mainly in a form of Late Aramaic, related to Syriac, but sometimes uses Hebrew. In its Babylonian form, the Talmud is the most important writing of rabbinic Judaism.

The Jerusalem Talmud, which is also called "the Palestinian Talmud" or "the Talmud of the Land of Israel," has a Gemara for only the first four Orders of the Mishnah; it lacks the Order *Qodashim* and has only one tractate *(Niddah)* from the Order *Tohoroth*. It treats thus only thirty-nine of the sixty-three tractates of the Mishnah, and much of its text, when not commenting on Mishnaic problems, supplies an interpretation of Scripture passages or historical and biographical stories about holy or wise people. In such passages, where the Gemara is not commenting on Mishnaic problems, it discusses the coming of the Messiah, and the passages where it does mention the Messiah are not many. Thus:

(a) *y. Ber. 2:3 [VI. A]:* "If the King Messiah comes from among the living, his name will be David; if from among the dead, it will be King David himself."[116]

(b) *y. Šeqal. 3:3 [VI. A]:* It quotes from *m. Soṭah* 9:15 (ad finem) a saying of Rabbi Pinhas ben Yair about "Heedfulness . . . ," but passes over in silence the mention of "the footprints of the Messiah (בעקבות המשיח)," which is found in the same part of *m. Soṭah*.[117] Instead it concentrates on "the resurrection of the dead" that "comes through Elijah, blessed be his memory. Amen!"[118]

(c) *y. Sukkah 5:1 [VII. L]:* There is no use of the word "Messiah" here,

---

115. See further Neusner, *Introduction to Rabbinic Literature,* 153-81 (The Talmud of the Land of Israel), and 182-220 (The Talmud of Babylonia); H. L. Strack and G. Stemberger, *Introduction to the Talmud and Midrash* (Minneapolis: Fortress, 1992) 182-207, 208-44.

116. Cf. T. Zahavy, *Berakhot.* The Talmud of the Land of Israel 1 (Chicago: University of Chicago Press, 1989) 87.

117. See §2b above (p. 148).

118. J. Neusner, *The Talmud of the Land of Israel,* 15: *Sheqalim,* Chicago Studies in the History of Judaism, ed. W. S. Green and C. Goldscheider (Chicago: University of Chicago Press, 1991) 68.

but it does mention that the horn of Israel, having been cut off, "is not destined to return to its place, until the son of David comes," an implicit reference to an expected Messiah.[119]

(d) *y. Ta'an. 1:1 [X. V]:* "If Israel repents for one day, the son of David shall come immediately." Again [X. X]: "If Israel keeps only one Sabbath in the proper way, immediately shall the son of David come."[120] Here the coming of the future David is dependent on the religious observance of the people of Israel.

(e) *y. Ta'an. 4:5 [X. G]:* "Rabbi Simeon ben Yoḥai taught, 'Aqiba, my master, would interpret the verse, "A star *(kôkāb)* comes forth from Jacob" [Num 24:17]: A liar *(kôzĕbā')* shall come forth from Jacob.'" [X. H]: "Rabbi Aqiba, when he saw Bar Kozeba', said, 'This is the King Messiah'" (הוא דין מלכא משיחא). [X. I]: "Rabbi Yoḥanan ben Torta answered him, 'Aqiba! Grass will grow out of your jaw-bone before the Messiah comes!'"[121]

Simon bar Kosiba was the leader of the Jews in Judea during the Second Revolt against Rome (A.D. 132-135); he was not of Davidic descent, but he was known on coins as שמעון נשיא ישראל, *Šimĕ'ôn nĕśî' Yiśrā'ēl,* "Simon, prince of Israel." The correct form of his name, שמעון בן כוסבא, *Šimĕ'ôn ben Kôsibā',* is known from a Hebrew document (Mur 24B 3), dated A.D. 133.[122] Hence Aqiba was playing on the similar sounds of his patronymic and of the word for "star" in Num 24:17, making *Kôsibā'* mean *Kôkĕbā'* (the Aramaic form of Hebrew *kôkāb,* "star"), but Simeon ben Yoḥai rather made of *Kôsibā'* a derogatory name, "liar" *(kôzĕbā').* Simon was so regarded by subsequent rabbis because he had been defeated by the Romans. Hence Aqiba's hailing Bar Kokhba as a Messiah was regarded as erroneous.[123]

(f) *y. Ketub. 12:3 [III. E]:* Rabbi Jeremiah gives instructions for his burial and ends with: "If the Messiah comes, I shall be ready." [XIII. A]:

---

119. J. Neusner, *The Talmud of the Land of Israel,* 17: *Sukkah,* Chicago Studies in the History of Judaism, ed. W. S. Green and C. Goldscheider (Chicago: University of Chicago Press, 1988) 119.

120. J. Neusner, *The Talmud of the Land of Israel,* 18: *Besah and Taanit,* Chicago Studies in the History of Judaism, ed. W. S. Green and C. Goldscheider (Chicago: University of Chicago Press, 1987) 149; cf. Mowinckel, *He That Cometh,* 297.

121. Neusner, *The Talmud of the Land of Israel,* 18:275.

122. See J. T. Milik, "24. Contrats de fermage, en hébreu (an 133)," *Les grottes de Murabba'ât,* ed. P. Benoit, Milik, and R. de Vaux. DJD 2 (Oxford: Clarendon, 1961) 122-34, esp. 124.

123. Cf. van der Woude, *TDNT* 9:523; J. A. Fitzmyer, "The Bar Cochba Period," *ESBNT,* 305-54; or *SBNT,* 305-54.

"When Rabbi Meir lay dying in Asya, he said, 'Tell the children of Israel that your Messiah is coming home for burial.'"[124] Apparently the dying Rabbi Meir casts himself here as "anointed," but he scarcely means that he is "the Messiah."

These, then, are passages of the Jerusalem Talmud where the Gemara goes beyond the Mishnah and teaches about the coming of the Messiah. Other rabbinic writings of roughly the same time or later continue to speak of the coming of the Messiah and use the expectation as a means of exhorting the people of Israel to greater fidelity in the observance of the Torah, the keeping of the Sabbath, and a righteous way of life. For instance, among the midrashim the *Mekilta de-Rabbi Ishmael* 5:74-76, which, as it interprets Exod 16:25a ("Eat it today"), declares: "If you succeed in observing the Sabbath, you shall rescue yourselves from three visitations: the day of Gog, the pangs of the (coming) Messiah (ומחבלו של משיח), and the great Day of Judgment."[125] There are also several passages in the *Babylonian Talmud*, which continue the developing tradition of messianic expectation among the Jewish people of the sixth century.[126] What has been presented so far in this chapter serves to show how that tradition developed in the early centuries of the Christian period. It makes clear that the Jewish messianic interpretation of the Hebrew Scriptures continued in its own fashion as it paralleled the Christian development. Sometimes its own development was influenced by that of Christianity and at times has even been an attempt to offset the Christian application of Scripture passages to Jesus of Nazareth as the Christian Messiah.[127] For instance, when the Suffering Servant of Isaiah 53 is called "My servant, the Messiah" in *Targum Jonathan*, the Jewish tradition showed that it too had a suffering Messiah. The most important trait of this Jewish development, however, was the expectation of the "King Messiah," and the troubles and signs that would precede his coming, which is found in various texts listed above.[128]

---

124. J. Neusner, *The Talmud of the Land of Israel,* 22: *Ketubot,* Chicago Studies in the History of Judaism, ed. W. S. Green and C. Goldscheider (Chicago: University of Chicago Press, 1985) 345, 350.

125. See J. Z. Lauterbach, *Mekilta de-Rabbi Ishmael* (3 vols.; Philadelphia: Jewish Publication Society of America, 1976) 2:120. Cf. J. Neusner, *Messiah in Context,* 131-65.

126. See Neusner, *Messiah in Context,* 167-231.

127. See Klausner, *The Messianic Idea in Israel,* 405, 519-31; cf. Castelli, *Il Messia secondo gli Ebrei,* 220-24.

128. See Klausner, *The Messianic Idea in Israel,* 427-50, 502-17.

Conclusion

The foregoing chapters have tried to trace the emergence of messianic hopes in human history by showing the roots of such an idea in the Old Testament record of Judaism and its developments in later extrabiblical Jewish writings. Because messianism was a notion that surfaced when it did in world history, its record has been important not only for Judaism, but for Christianity too, which grew out of it and developed its own form of messianism. Being a specific phenomenon that appeared at a given time and place, it was not merely a passing or ephemeral fad, but rather a phenomenon that shaped human history in different ways.

As did Joseph Klausner before me, I end this discussion with a contrast of the Jewish and Christian Messiah. To sum up, first, the Jewish belief, one must stress that the expectation of a Jewish Messiah was not of one form, for we have seen that the expectation envisaged at times a kingly and a priestly figure, a Messiah of Aaron and a Messiah of Israel, a Messiah of David and a Messiah of Joseph (or Ephraim). Moreover, it even cast the prophet Elijah, who was thought to return, as an awaited High Priest. The dominant expectation, however, was one that awaited a human kingly figure who was (and is) to bring deliverance, at once political, economic, and spiritual, to the Jewish people, and through them peace, prosperity, and righteousness to all humanity. Moreover, in the *Babylonian Talmud* such a figure was also said to be among the seven things created before the world came to be.[1] That means that at times the Messiah was thought of as a

---

1. See *b. Pesaḥ.* 54a; *b. Ned.* 39b, where mention is made of "the name of the Messiah."

preexistent being. He was also considered eventually as the King Messiah, destined to fulfill the role of the child of whom Isaiah spoke and described as "Everlasting Father, Prince of Peace" (Isa 9:5). For in his day all peoples would be gathered to worship the God of Israel, who was regarded as the sole deliverer and redeemer of humanity. This aspect of redemption varied at times when some Jewish sages understood the Messiah as a corporate personality or believed that redemption would take place without a personal Messiah — a form of messianism without a Messiah. In all of this Jewish belief the expectation was (and is) still focused on the future: a Messiah still to come.

How different that Jewish Messiah is from the Christian Messiah, who has already come. He has not only been identified with Jesus of Nazareth, who was crucified as a criminal and rebel, but he bears in human history the name Jesus Christ (= Jesus the Messiah), both among those who are his followers and among those who are not. His mission differed too, because it was no longer deliverance in a political or economic sense, but solely in a spiritual sense; and because it was aimed directly at all human beings, it no longer was considered as coming through a chosen people. Moreover, his death by crucifixion was understood in a vicarious sense, intended to deliver all who would accept him from evil, sin, and suffering. The Christian Messiah, then, is known as the one who fulfills the role of Deutero-Isaiah's Suffering Servant of God (Isaiah 53), who has not only suffered and died for humanity, but was also raised by God to give it hope of sharing a blissful afterlife with Him in the Father's glorious presence. The Christian Messiah is also known to be the Son of God in a transcendent sense, the Word *(Logos)* of God, and Second Person of the Triune God. In this, he is the God-Man. In these respects, the Christian Messiah differs radically from the awaited Jewish Messiah, without whom, however, he would not be known in human history as "Jesus Christ, the Son of God" (Mark 1:1).

Index of Ancient Writings

Index of Authors

Index of Subjects

CPSIA information can be obtained
at www.ICGtesting.com
Printed in the USA
FSHW012317291221
87283FS

9 780802 840134